GREEN CROSS INTERNATIONAL (GCI) is an independent non-profit and non-governmental organisation that works to address the interconnected global challenges of security, poverty eradication and environmental degradation through a combination of high level advocacy and local projects. GCI is headquartered in Geneva and has a growing network of national offices in over 30 countries.

The call for setting up a 'Red Cross' for the environment was made during the 1992 Earth Summit in Rio. Having stated that 'after the fall of the Berlin Wall the most pressing challenge for humanity relates to the relationship between man and nature', former Soviet President Mikhail Gorbachev was asked to lead this effort and became the founder of Green Cross International.

MIKHAIL GORBACHEV, born in 1931, was General Secretary of the Communist Party of the USSR from 1985 to 1991. As head of state he introduced the radical turnaround of his country's foreign and internal policies which led to a complete transformation of the Eastern Bloc and Europe. He was awarded the Nobel Peace Prize in 1990, and in 1991 resigned as Head of State. He became President of the Gorbachev Foundation in 1992, and since 1993 he has been President of Green Cross International. He is the recipient of numerous awards and the author of many publications including *Memoirs* and *Manifesto for the Earth*.

D0569973

MIKHAIL GORBACHEV: PROPHET OF CHANGE

FROM THE COLD WAR
TO A SUSTAINABLE WORLD

Compiled and edited by Green Cross International

CLAIRVIEW

Clairview Books
Hillside House, The Square
Forest Row, East Sussex RH18 5ES

www.clairviewbooks.com

Published by Clairview 2011

*Clairview Books would like to thank the staff of Green Cross International for
their cooperation in compiling and editing the text of this book:
Alexander Likhotal (idea/concept); Fiona Curtin (editorial); Adam Koniuszewski
(organisation); Michelle Laug (communication & compilation); and Tim McCann
(compilation of material)*

A catalogue record for this book is available from the British Library

ISBN 978 1 905570 30 0 (hardback)
ISBN 978 1 905570 31 7 (paperback)

Cover by Andrew Morgan Design featuring a photograph of Mikhail Gorbachev
by Audrey Trukhachev
Typeset by DP Photosetting, Neath, West Glamorgan
Printed and bound by Gutenberg Press Ltd., Malta

Contents

Foreword   1

Part One: THE WORDS OF GORBACHEV

The World in Transition — End of the Cold War   5
  Issyk-Kul Forum (*Speech, 20 October 1986*)   5
  Murmansk Initiative (*Speech, 1 October 1987*)   9
  Freedom of Choice (*Speech to 43rd UN General Assembly
    Session, 7 December 1988*)   16
  Europe as a Common Home (*Council of Europe, 6 July 1989*)   25
  Environment and Development for Survival (*Address to the
    Global Forum of Spiritual and Parliamentary Leaders,
    Moscow, 19 January 1990*)   39
  The Grim Legacy of Old (*Speech at 28th Communist Party
    Congress, 2 July 1990*)   46
  Nobel Peace Prize Acceptance Speech (*10 December 1990*)   51
  The Nobel Lecture (*Speech, 5 June 1991*)   53
  Final Televised Address as President of the USSR
    (*25 December 1991*)   67
  Speech at the Opening of the Fourth International Global
    Forum of Spiritual and Parliamentary Leaders
    (*20 April 1993*)   71
  What Made Me a Crusader (Time *special issue,
    November 1997*)   79
  Nature Will Not Wait (World Watch *magazine,
    March/April 2001*)   82

A World Free of Weapons of Mass Destruction   85
  The Importance of Chemical Weapons Abolition
    (*Speech, Geneva Forum on the Worldwide Destruction of
    Chemical Weapons, 26 June 2003*)   86
  Message Sent to the Second Rally for International
    Disarmament: Nuclear, Biological and Chemical
    (*6–8 May 2006*)   93
  The Nuclear Threat (Wall Street Journal, *31 January 2007*)   95

Overcoming Nuclear Dangers (*Speech at Conference in Rome,*
16 April 2009)   99

Disarmament Lessons from the Chemical Weapons
Convention (Bulletin of the Atomic Scientists,
16 June 2009)   104

Two First Steps on Nuclear Weapons (New York Times,
25 September 2009)   107

Resetting the Nuclear Disarmament Agenda (*Speech at the*
United Nations in Geneva, 5 October 2009)   110

The Ice Has Broken (New York Times, *22 April 2010*)   116

Address sent to the Nobel Peace Laureates Forum
(*12–14 November 2010*)   119

The Senate's Next Task: Ratifying the Nuclear Test Ban Treaty
(New York Times, *28 December 2010*)   123

The Green Agenda   126

The New Path to Peace and Sustainability (*El Pais,*
30 January 2004)   126

A New Glasnost for Global Sustainability (The Optimist,
April 2004)   130

Energy Shift, NOW! (*Forum in Barcelona, 2 June 2004*)   138

The Third Pillar of Sustainable Development (*Foreword to*
Toward a Sustainable World: The Earth Charter in
Action, *2005*)   143

The Lessons of Chernobyl (*Interview,* The Optimist, *April 2006*)   146

Interview with *The House Magazine* (2006)   154

Antarctica: The Global Warning (*Foreword to book,*
October 2007)   160

The World Food Crisis (Rossiskaya Gazeta *daily,*
13 May 2008)   162

Keynote Address to the Club of Rome (*26 October 2009*)   165

Tear Down This Wall! And Save the Planet (The Times,
9 November 2009)   171

Failure in Copenhagen would be 'catastrophic risk':
Gorbachev (*Interview, Agence France-Presse,*
3 December 2009)   174

Playing Russian Roulette with Climate Change
(*Project Syndicate, 3 December 2009*)   176

We Have a Real Emergency (New York Times,
9 December 2009)   179

After Copenhagen: A New Leadership Challenge (*GCI website,*
  22 December 2009)   182
Let's Get Serious About Climate Talks (New York Times,
  3 November 2010)   186

Water for Peace   189
A New Glasnost for Our Future: The Right to Water and
  Dignified Life (*Speech, World Urban Forum,*
  13 September 2004)   189
Our Common Future (*Speech, La Plata Basin Dialogues,*
  12 September 2005)   198
Access to Water is Not a Privilege, It's a Right!
  (The Optimist, *2005*)   204
All of Us Should Be Ashamed (Financial Times,
  21 March 2007)   208
Climate Change and Water Security: Solving the Equation
  (*Project Syndicate, 6 June 2007*)   211
Call for Global Law on Access to Water. Gorbachev leads
  campaign for UN convention (*By Fiona Harvey,*
  Financial Times, *12 June 2007*)   214
Water for Peace — Peace for Water (*Foreword to publication,*
  2008)   216
Tomorrow May Be Too Late to Address Water Crisis
  (*Speech, 'Peace with Water' conference, 12 February 2009*)   221
The Right to Water (New York Times, *16 July 2010*)   224
Interview with Mikhail Gorbachev (CSA-World, *Autumn 2010*)   227

Part Two: TRIBUTES TO GORBACHEV

Contributors —
  Ruud Lubbers   233
  Mario Soares   236
  George H.W. Bush   239
  Margaret Thatcher   240
  Frederik Willem de Klerk   243
  Shimon Peres   245
  Ricardo Lagos   247
  Achim Steiner   250
  Federico Mayor Zaragoza   254
  Maurice Strong   260

Ismail Serageldin   262
Sergei Kapitsa   265
Professor Sir David King   270
Jean-Michel Cousteau   274
Steven Rockefeller   276
Martin Lees   282
Ted Turner   290
Jan Kulczyk   292
Pat Mitchell and Scott Seydel   295
Diane and Charlie Gallagher   304
Rabbi Awraham Soetendorp   305
Diane Meyer Simon   309
Shoo Iwasaki   312
Guido Pollice   314
Giorgio Armani   316
Sam Cheow   317
Jean-Christophe Babin   318
Alexander Likhotal   319

Picture Credits   325

Foreword

Mikhail Gorbachev is living proof that the word is mightier than the sword and that ideas, not armies, change the world. In the beginning there were the words, two words that have since come to represent change and freedom in the universal consciousness of humankind: perestroika and glasnost. The words of Mikhail Gorbachev resonated with people everywhere, igniting sweeping reforms in the Soviet Union, inspiring liberation movements across Eastern Europe, and thawing decades of cold war enmity.

As a politician and as a person, Mikhail Gorbachev's decisions when he became leader of the USSR were guided by his unwavering belief in human values that seemed completely idealistic in a world that lived under the shadow of humiliating dependence on deadly superpower rivalry, the nuclear arms race and the ruthless and unaccounted destruction of nature. It became his life's work to secure liberty for people the world over, and thus to build a peaceful, sustainable world, backing up his words and his values with decisive action and courageous leadership.

To celebrate the 80th birthday of its remarkable Founding President, Green Cross International has compiled this select volume of his speeches and writings. They reveal a man who has always been ahead of his time, a true pioneer with the foresight to predict what the challenges of the future would be and pave the way towards meeting them. Mikhail Gorbachev was an environmentalist long before it became fashionable. He was dedicated to ridding the world of weapons of mass destruction when many leaders were intent only on accumulating them. He called for multilateral action to forge a common future at a time when the world had never been more divided. The ideas behind the 'new political thinking' of perestroika and glasnost are as relevant today for the world as they were a quarter of a century ago in the Soviet Union.

The pieces in this volume were chosen to trace the evolution of Mikhail Gorbachev's revolutionary thoughts, particularly the origins and outcomes of his environmental agenda, which belongs to the important legacy of the changes he enacted in the Soviet Union and the world. Without these transformations the global environmental movement we see today, including Green Cross International itself, would not have been possible.

Abraham Lincoln said that in the end it is not the years in your life that count, but the life in your years. Mikhail Gorbachev makes every year, every day, in his life count. This collection, which contains only a small selection of his works, illustrates the fact that he does not indulge in empty rhetoric; his words are always backed up by his deeds. He continues to speak out and take action for what he believes — his life's work is far from over.

No birthday would be complete without the well-wishes of friends and colleagues. To mark this milestone year, messages of admiration and affection have been sent from all over the world, many of which, from political contemporaries and partners in the environmental and peace movements, are included in this book. They reflect the esteem in which Mikhail Gorbachev is held, and the special place he occupies in the history of our times — a history that is very much alive and continuing.

The entire Green Cross International family joins in this celebration of Mikhail Gorbachev's 80th year. Happy Birthday, Mr President!

Part One

THE WORDS OF GORBACHEV

The World in Transition — End of the Cold War

Dialogue with Participants of the Issyk-Kul Forum

Moscow, 20 October 1986

Politics needs scientific arguments. Politics can provide necessary answers to problems if it is based on scientific analysis and is free from swinging from one side to another, from arbitrariness and improvisation.

I can say today with great conviction that politics must be nurtured by everything contained within the intellectual wealth of all nations and of human civilisation. Our intelligentsia has always considered man above all as the object of its constant study, concern and thoughts. A policy that is not fortified by considerations of human destinies is a bad, an immoral policy unworthy of respect.

That is why I share the idea of the need for a natural tie, I would say a reciprocal need experienced by politicians and representatives of contemporary culture to be in touch, to meet, to maintain a constant exchange of views. I believe that both sides can only be richer as a result. [...]

Let me express a polemic view. I ask you to recall the way things were in the past, even in the recent past. Mankind has always had the intelligence, courage and conscience to seek the reasons for one upheaval or another. Unfortunately, as a rule this occurred after the difficulty. What kind of world could there be today if people would eliminate difficulties at the proper time?

What will happen if we are unable to save our human hope from the nuclear threat? Should this happen there would be no possibility of correcting the error. We are truly facing a critical moment in history, when it is obvious that a fatal menace can be eliminated only through joint efforts.

In his time, V.I. Lenin expressed an idea of tremendous depth: the idea of the priority of the interest of social development and of all human values over the interests of a given class. Today, in the nuclear missile age, the significance of this thought is felt particularly sharply. It would please us very much if the other side of the world would also understand and accept the thesis of the priority of the universal value of peace over any other which one person or another may support.

We must most strongly voice the concerns of our time and jointly seek the right solutions for the sake of a peaceful present and future and awaken the conscience and responsibility of every person for the fate of the world. Despite difficulties and contradictions we must preserve civilisation for the sake of life and mankind. If it survives it will some-how resolve its contradictions. [. . .]

I share your view that we live in a world which is quite imperfect. In any case no one can say that we live in a perfect world. However, I am confident that it could be made better. I believe that the intellectual potential and, as you said, scientific discoveries and technology could be put at the service of attaining this goal. But first we must safeguard the world from the threat of nuclear annihilation.

What is uniting all of us today, regardless of where we live, our ideology or faith is the shared concern of the people throughout the world related to the nuclear threat. [. . .] At the Issyk-Kul Forum these concerns were the centre of attention and were reflected in the declaration you adopted. This, in my view, is a major undertaking. Every politician has his own possibilities, just as much as artists have their own possibilities.

What can leaders of culture do to oppose the forces leading mankind to catastrophe? On the eve of the First World War, such problems greatly concerned Leo Tolstoy, as they do us today. The 80-year-old patriarch of world literature sensed the approaching war. He said that those that find war profitable have money in the millions and millions of soldiers. The writer has only one weapon but a powerful one: the truth. This is sufficient for us to say that the struggle is not hopeless.

The Issyk-Kul Forum declaration is a tremendous document con-firming the results of the new way of thinking. We see new shoots growing on the political field. We see them on the cultural front, which is a most encouraging feature.

Here virtually everyone spoke of the fact that a new way of thinking is needed in order to adequately comprehend today's realities. It is on this basis that in Reykjavik we formulated suggestions from which the Soviet Union has never retreated. Nevertheless, this type of new thinking was not enough. The way I formulated the question there was as follows. We came not with demands or ultimatums but brought proposals, far-reaching proposals, hoping that the US President would respond. A great deal has been already said about Reykjavik. It is not a failure or hopeless. We have made substantial progress. This meeting indicated that one could reach agreements that would mark the beginning of the elimination of nuclear weapons. The programme of new proposals formulated by the USSR does not close but opens the doors to a search for mutually acceptable solutions. It provides the real opportunity to come out of the dead-end street. However, this meeting also proved that many difficulties must be surmounted on the way to an agreement.

One of the main lessons of Reykjavik is that a new political thinking, consistent with the realities of the nuclear age, is a mandatory pre-requisite for coming out of the critical situation in which mankind finds itself at the end of the twentieth century. Profound changes must take place in the political thinking of mankind. Naturally, the propaganda and the interest of different groups and alliances, elections, and so on, greatly hindered the application of the results of Reykjavik in the United States. Nothing can be done about this. However, the elections will pass but the problems will remain and one must think and seek ways of solving them.

I would be very interested to learn what you saw in our country and the way our society appeared to you. We are going through an interesting state, an interesting period of historical development. We wish to renovate all aspects of our life on a socialist basis. We are not abandoning our values or what we believe in, or what brought Russia to its present level. We simply discovered or, to put it gently, we made insufficient use of that which our system can provide for the development of the economy, the social sphere and culture. Furthermore, we found out that some distortions, totally inconsistent with socialist values, had taken place in our country. The fact that today we have taken the path of reorganisation, using openness and democracy, has triggered a tremendous response in our people. We feel the type of support which had not existed, perhaps, for decades.

We shall follow this path. Throughout the world, some are welcoming it and share with us our plans, supporting our intentions and wishes. For some reason, others are afraid of this. We believe that what we are doing is not only consistent with the expectations of the Soviet people but that it also opens opportunities for finding new ways of cooperation with other nations and states. There are those who would like to hinder us. You know, however, that the Russian character is such that if it is obstructed it becomes even stronger! Those who have suggested such a policy of opposition are even inspiring us: the fact that some of its aspects have worried them is proof that we are on the right track.

We realise that this requires great efforts. Here and there the processes are painful. But just think: we are 280 million people, more than 100 nations and nationalities! All of us today must rethink a great deal of things. We must see the prospects that the present policy offers to our society from a new angle, a new point of view. This is no simple matter.

We are relying on the tremendous help of our intelligentsia. The Soviet intelligentsia – this is a very important point – has actively joined the reconstruction process. It has not only joined but has become its warm supporter. This opens extensive opportunities for solving not only domestic but also global problems. Our possibilities will increase and so will our material, political, intellectual and moral contribution.

I wish you sincerely the greatest possible happiness so that perhaps even part of what you agreed upon at the Issyk-Kul Forum may happen.

© Izdatel'stvo TsK KPSS 'Pravda', *Kommunist*, 1986

By stating clearly that universal human values, in particular peace, must prevail over the interests of any state or class, Gorbachev opened a 'Pandora's box' of possibilities at this discussion with international cultural figures invited to the USSR by the writer Chingiz Aimatov. This overturned the traditional Soviet policy of the primacy of 'class' interest, and created an ideological window in the Soviet Union for both expanding individual freedoms and becoming an active partner for peace and cooperation in international affairs.

Speech at the Presentation of the Order of Lenin and the Gold Star to the City of Murmansk

Murmansk, USSR, 1 October 1987

Indeed, the international situation is still complicated. The dangers to which we have no right to turn a blind eye remain. There has been some change, however, or at least change is starting. Certainly, judging the situation only from the speeches made by top Western leaders, including their 'programme' statements, everything would seem to be as it was before: the same anti-Soviet attacks, the same demands that we show our commitment to peace by renouncing our order and principles, the same confrontational language: 'totalitarianism', 'communist expansion', and so on.

Within a few days, however, these speeches are often forgotten, and at any rate the theses contained in them do not figure during businesslike political negotiations and contacts. This is a very interesting point, an interesting phenomenon. It confirms that we are dealing with yesterday's rhetoric, while real life processes have been set into motion. This means that something is indeed changing. One of the elements of the change is that it is now difficult to convince people that our foreign policy, our initiatives, our nuclear-free world programme are mere 'propaganda'.

A new, democratic philosophy of international relations, of world politics, is breaking through. The new mode of thinking with its humane, universal criteria and values is penetrating diverse strata. Its strength lies in the fact that it accords with people's common sense. Considering that world public opinion and the peoples of the world are very concerned about the situation in the world, our policy is an invitation to dialogue, to a search, to a better world, to normalisation of international relations. This is why, despite all attempts to besmirch and belittle our foreign policy initiatives, they are making their way in the world, because they are consonant with the moods of the broad masses of working people and realistically minded political circles in the West.

Favourable tendencies are also gaining ground in international relations. The substantive and frank East-West dialogue, far from proving fruitless for both sides, has become a distinguishing feature of contemporary world politics. Just recently the entire world welcomed the accord reached at the talks in Washington to promptly complete drafting an agreement on medium- and shorter-range missiles to be signed at the top level. Thus, we are close to a major breakthrough in the field of actual nuclear disarmament. If it happens, it will be the first such breakthrough to be achieved in the post-war years.

So far, the arms race has proceeded either unimpeded or with some small limitations, but no concrete move has as yet been made towards disarmament, towards eliminating nuclear weapons.

The road to the mutual Soviet-American decision was hard. Reykjavik was a crucial event along that road. Life has confirmed the correctness of our assessment of the meeting in the Icelandic capital. Contrary to panic wavering of all sorts, sceptical declarations and the propaganda talk about the 'failure', developments have started moving along the path paved by Reykjavik. They have borne out the correctness of the assessment we made, as you remember, just 40 minutes after the dramatic end of the meeting.

Reykjavik indeed became a turning point in world history; it demonstrated the possibility of improving the international situation. A different situation has developed, and no one could act after Reykjavik as if nothing had happened. It was for us an event that confirmed the correctness of our course, the need for and constructiveness of new political thinking.

Militarist and anti-Soviet forces are clearly concerned lest the interest among the people and political quarters of the West in what is happening in the Soviet Union today and the growing understanding of its foreign policy erase the artificially created 'image of the enemy', an image which they have been exploiting unashamedly for years. Well, it's their business after all. But we shall firmly follow the road of restructuring and new thinking.

Comrades, speaking in Murmansk, the capital of the Soviet polar region, it is appropriate to examine the idea of cooperation between all people also from the standpoint of the situation in the northern part of this planet. In our opinion, there are several weighty reasons for this.

The Arctic is not only the Arctic Ocean, but also the northern tips of three continents: Europe, Asia and America. It is the place where the Eurasian, North American and Asian Pacific regions meet, where the frontiers come close to one another and the interests of states belonging to mutually opposed military blocs and nonaligned ones cross.

The north also has the problem of security of the Soviet Union's northern frontiers. We have had some historical experience, which cost us dearly. The people of Murmansk remember well the years 1918–19 and 1941–45.

The wars fought during this century were severe trials for the countries of northern Europe. It seems to us they have drawn some serious conclusions for themselves. And this is probably why the public climate in those countries is more receptive to the new political thinking.

It is significant that the historic Conference on Security and Cooperation in Europe was held in one of the northern capitals – Helsinki. It is significant that another major step in the development of that process – the first ever accord on confidence-building measures – was achieved in another northern capital, Stockholm. Reykjavik has become a symbol of hope that nuclear weapons are not an eternal evil and that mankind is not doomed to live under that sword of Damocles.

Major initiatives in the sphere of international security and disarmament are associated with the names of famous political figures of northern Europe. One is Urho Kekkonen. Another is Olof Palme, whose death at the hand of a vile assassin shocked Soviet people. Then there is Kalevi Sorsa, who has headed the Socialist International Advisory Council for many years now. And we applaud the activities of the authoritative World Commission on Environment and Development headed by Prime Minister Gro Harlem Brundtland of Norway.

The Soviet Union duly appreciates the fact that Denmark and Norway, while being members of NATO, unilaterally refused to station foreign military bases and deploy nuclear weapons on their territory in peacetime. This stance, if consistently adhered to, is important for lessening tensions in Europe.

However, this is only part of the picture. The community and interrelationship of the interests of our entire world is felt in the northern part of the globe, in the Arctic, perhaps more than anywhere else. For the Arctic and the North Atlantic are not just the 'weather kitchen', the point where cyclones and anticyclones are born to influence the climate in Europe, the USA and Canada, and even in South Asia and Africa. One can feel here the freezing breath of the 'Arctic strategy' of the Pentagon. An immense potential of nuclear destruction concentrated aboard submarines and surface ships affects the political climate of the entire world and can be detonated by an accidental political-military conflict in any other region of the world.

The militarisation of this part of the world is assuming threatening dimensions. One cannot but feel concern over the fact that NATO, anticipating an agreement on medium- and shorter-range missiles being reached, is preparing to train military personnel in the use of sea- and air-based cruise missiles from the North Atlantic. This would mean an additional threat to us and to all the countries of northern Europe.

A new radar station, one of the Star Wars elements, has been made operational in Greenland in violation of the ABM Treaty. US cruise missiles are being tested in the north of Canada. The Canadian Government has recently developed a vast programme for the build-up of forces in the Arctic. The US and NATO military activity in areas adjoining the Soviet polar region is being stepped up. The level of NATO's military presence in Norway and Denmark is being built up.

Therefore, while in Murmansk, and standing on the threshold of the Arctic and the North Atlantic, I would like to invite, first of all, the countries of the region to a discussion on the burning security issues.

How do we visualise this? It is possible to take simultaneously the roads of bilateral and multilateral cooperation. I have had the opportunity to speak on the subject of 'our common European home' on more than one occasion. The potential of contemporary civilisation could permit us to make the Arctic habitable for the benefit of the national economics and other human interests of the near-Arctic states, for Europe and the entire international community. To achieve this, security problems that have accumulated in the area should be resolved above all.

The Soviet Union is in favour of a radical lowering of the level of military confrontation in the region. Let the north of the globe, the Arctic, become a zone of peace. Let the North Pole be a Pole of peace. We suggest that all interested states start talks on the limitation and scaling down of military activity in the north as a whole, in both the eastern and western hemispheres.

What, specifically, do we mean?

Firstly, a nuclear-free zone in northern Europe. If such a decision were adopted, the Soviet Union, as has already been declared, would be prepared to act as a guarantor. It would depend on the participating countries how to formalise this guarantee: by multilateral or bilateral agreements, governmental statements or in some other way.

The Soviet Union simultaneously reaffirms its readiness to discuss with each of the interested states, or with a group of states, all the problems related to the creation of a nuclear-free zone, including possible measures applicable to the Soviet territory. We could go so far as to remove submarines equipped with ballistic missiles from the Soviet Baltic Fleet.

As it is known, the Soviet Union earlier unilaterally dismantled launchers of medium-range missiles in the Kola Peninsula and the greater part of the launchers of such missiles on the remaining territory of the Leningrad and Baltic military areas. A considerable number of shorter-range missiles were removed from those districts. The holding of military exercises was restricted in areas close to the borders of Scandinavian countries. Additional opportunities for military detente in the region will open up after the conclusion of the agreement on 'global double zero'.

Secondly, we welcome the initiative of Finland's President Mauno Koivisto on restricting naval activity in the seas washing the shores of northern Europe. For its part, the Soviet Union proposes consultations between the Warsaw Treaty Organisation and NATO on restricting military activity and scaling down naval and air force activities in the Baltic, North, Norwegian and Greenland Seas, and on the extension of confidence-building measures to these areas.

These measures could include arrangements on the limitation of rivalry in anti-submarine weapons, on the notification of large naval and air force exercises, and on inviting observers from all countries participating in the European process to large naval and air force exercises. This could be an initial step in the extension of confidence-building measures to the entire Arctic and to the northern areas of both hemispheres.

At the same time we propose considering the question of banning naval activity in mutually agreed upon zones of international straits and in intensive shipping lanes in general. A meeting of representatives of interested states could be held for this purpose, for instance, in Leningrad.

The following thought suggests itself in connection with the idea of a nuclear-free zone. At present the northern countries, that is Iceland, Denmark, Norway, Sweden and Finland, have no nuclear weapons. We are aware of their concern over the fact that we have a testing range for nuclear explosions on Novaya Zemlya.

We are thinking how to solve this problem, which is a difficult one for us because so much money has been invested in the testing range. But, frankly speaking, the problem could be solved once and for all if the

United States agreed to stop nuclear tests or, as a beginning, to reduce their number and yield to the minimum.

Thirdly, the Soviet Union attaches much importance to peaceful cooperation in developing the resources of the north, the Arctic. Here an exchange of experience and knowledge is extremely important. Through joint efforts it could be possible to work out an overall concept of rational development of northern areas. We propose, for instance, reaching agreement on drafting an integral energy programme for the north of Europe. According to existing data, the reserves there of such energy sources as oil and gas are truly boundless. But their extraction entails immense difficulties and the need to create unique technical installations capable of withstanding the polar elements. It would be more reasonable to pool efforts in this endeavour, which would cut both material and other outlays. We have an interest in inviting, for instance, Canada and Norway to form mixed firms and enterprises for developing oil and gas deposits of the shelf of our northern seas. We are prepared for relevant talks with other states as well.

We are also prepared for cooperation in utilising the resources of the Kola Peninsula, and in implementing other major projects in various forms, including joint enterprises.

Fourthly, the scientific exploration of the Arctic is of immense importance for the whole of mankind. We have a wealth of experience here and are prepared to share it. In turn, we are interested in the studies conducted in other sub-Arctic and northern countries. We already have a programme of scientific exchanges with Canada. [...]

Questions bearing on the interests of the indigenous population of the north, the study of its ethnic distinctions and the development of cultural ties between northern peoples require special attention.

Fifthly, we attach special importance to the cooperation of the northern countries in environmental protection. The urgency of this is obvious. It would be well to extend the joint measures for protecting the marine environment of the Baltic, now being carried out by a commission of seven maritime states, to the entire oceanic and sea surface of the globe's north.

The Soviet Union proposes jointly drawing up an integrated comprehensive plan for protecting the natural environment of the north. The northern European countries could set an example to others by reaching an agreement on establishing a system to monitor the state of the natural environment and radiation safety in the region. We must hurry to protect the nature of the tundra, forest tundra and the northern forest areas.

Sixthly, the shortest sea route from Europe to the Far East and the Pacific Ocean passes through the Arctic. I think that depending on progress in the normalisation of international relations we could open the northern sea route to foreign ships, with ourselves providing the services of ice-breakers.

Such are our proposals. Such is the concrete meaning of Soviet foreign policy with regard to the north. Such are our intentions and plans for the future. Of course, safeguarding security and developing cooperation in the north is an international matter and by no means depends on us alone. We are ready to discuss any counter-proposals and ideas. The main thing is to conduct affairs so that the climate here is determined by the warm Gulf Stream of the European process and not by the polar chill of accumulated suspicions and prejudices.

What everybody can be absolutely certain of is the Soviet Union's profound and certain interest in preventing the north of the planet, its polar and sub-polar regions and all northern countries, from ever again becoming an arena of war, and in forming there a genuine zone of peace and fruitful cooperation.

Gorbachev was the first head of state to use the concept of 'ecological security' and made the review of mankind's relationship with nature a key element in his promotion of a new political model. In Murmansk, he introduced the synergy between security, development and the environment for the first time – five years before the 1992 Earth Summit. By highlighting environmental concerns, Gorbachev was instrumental in raising sustainable development and the recommendations of the 1987 Brundtland Report to the level of inter-state politics.

Freedom of Choice

Speech delivered at the 43rd General Assembly Session, United Nations, New York, 7 December 1988

Two great revolutions, the French Revolution of 1789 and the Russian Revolution of 1917, have exerted a powerful influence on the actual nature of the historical process and radically changed the course of world events.

Both of them, each in its own way, have given a gigantic impetus to man's progress. They have also formed in many respects the way of thinking which is still prevailing in the public consciousness.

That is a very great spiritual wealth, but there emerges before us today a different world, for which it is necessary to seek different roads towards the future – relying, of course, on accumulated experience – while also seeing the radical differences between that which was yesterday and that which is taking place today.

The newness of the tasks and at the same time their difficulty are not limited to this. Today we have entered an era when progress will be based on the interests of all mankind. Consciousness of this requires that world policy, too, should be determined by the priority of the values of all mankind.

The history of the past centuries and millennia has been a history of almost ubiquitous wars, and sometimes desperate battles, leading to mutual destruction. They occurred in the clash of social and political interests and national hostility, be it from ideological or religious incompatibility. Even now many still claim that this past – which has not been overcome – is an immutable pattern. However, parallel with the process of wars, hostility and alienation of peoples and countries, another process, just as objectively conditioned, was in motion and gaining force: the process of the emergence of a mutually connected and integral world.

Further world progress is now possible only through the search for a consensus of all mankind in movement towards a new world order. We have arrived at a frontier at which controlled spontaneity leads to a dead end. The world community must learn to shape and direct the process in such a way as to preserve civilisation, to make it safe for all and more pleasant for normal life. It is a question of cooperation that could be more accurately called co-creation and co-development. The formula of development 'at another's expense' is becoming outdated. In light of present realities, genuine progress by infringing upon the rights and liberties of man and peoples or at the expense of nature is impossible.

The very tackling of global problems requires a new 'volume' and 'quality' of cooperation by states and socio-political currents regardless of ideological and other differences.

Of course, radical and revolutionary changes are taking place and will continue to take place within individual countries and social structures. This has been and will continue to be the case, but our times are making corrections here, too. Internal transformational processes cannot achieve their national objectives merely by taking a parallel course with others without using the achievements of the surrounding world and the possibilities of equitable cooperation. In these conditions, interference in those internal processes with the aim of altering them according to someone else's prescription would be all the more destructive for the emergence of a peaceful order.

In the past, differences often served as a factor in pulling away from one another. Now they are being given the opportunity to be a factor in mutual enrichment and attraction. Behind differences in social structure, in the way of life and in the preference for certain values stand interests. There is no getting away from that, but neither is there any getting away from the need to find a balance of interests within an international framework, which has become a condition for survival and progress. As you ponder all this, you come to the conclusion that if we wish to take account of the lessons of the past and the realities of the present, if we must reckon with the objective logic of world development, it is necessary to seek – and to seek jointly – an approach towards improving the international situation and building a new world. If that is so, then it is also worth agreeing on the fundamental and truly universal prerequisites and principles of such activities. It is evident, for example, that force and the threat of force can no longer be and should not be instruments of foreign policy. [...]

The compelling necessity of the principle of freedom of choice is also clear to us.

The failure to recognise this is fraught with very dire consequences, consequences for world peace. Denying that right to the peoples, no matter what the pretext, no matter what the words used to conceal it, means infringing upon even the unstable balance that is, has been possible to achieve.

Freedom of choice is a universal principle to which there should be no exceptions. We have not come to the conclusion of the immutability of this principle simply through good intentions. We have been led to it through impartial analysis of the objective processes of our time. The increasing varieties of social development in different countries are becoming an ever more perceptible feature of these processes. This relates to both the capitalist and socialist systems. The variety of socio-political structures which has grown over the last decades from national liberation movements also demonstrates this. This objective fact pre-supposes respect for other people's views and stands, tolerance, a pre-paredness to see phenomena that are different as not necessarily bad or hostile, and an ability to learn to live side by side while remaining dif-ferent and not agreeing with one another on every issue.

The de-ideologisation of interstate relations has become a demand of the new stage. We are not giving up our convictions, philosophy or traditions. Neither are we calling on anyone else to give up theirs. Yet we are not going to shut ourselves up within the range of our values. That would lead to spiritual impoverishment, for it would mean renouncing so powerful a source of development as sharing all the original things created independently by each nation. In the course of such sharing, each should prove the advantages of his own system, his own way of life and values, but not through words or propaganda alone, but through real deeds as well. That is, indeed, an honest struggle of ideology, but it must not be carried over into mutual relations between states. Otherwise we simply will not be able to solve a single world problem; arrange broad, mutually advantageous and equitable cooperation between peoples; manage rationally the achievements of the scientific and tech-nical revolution; transform world economic relations; protect the environment; overcome underdevelopment; or put an end to hunger, disease, illiteracy and other mass ills. Finally, in that case, we will not manage to eliminate the nuclear threat and militarism.

Such are our reflections on the natural order of things in the world on the threshold of the twenty-first century. We are, of course, far from claiming to have infallible truth but, having subjected the previous realities – realities that have arisen again – to strict analysis, we have come to the conclusion that it is by precisely such approaches that we must search jointly for a way to achieve the supremacy of the common human idea over the countless multiplicity of centrifugal forces, to preserve the vitality of a civilisation that is possibly the only one in the universe. [...]

Our country is undergoing a truly revolutionary upsurge. The process of restructuring is gaining pace. We started by elaborating the theoretical concepts of restructuring; we had to assess the nature and scope of the problems, to interpret the lessons of the past, and to express this in the form of political conclusions and programmes. This was done. The theoretical work, the re-interpretation of what had happened, the final elaboration, enrichment and correction of political stances have not ended. They continue. However, it was fundamentally important to start from an overall concept, which is already now being confirmed by the experience of past years, which has turned out to be generally correct and to which there is no alternative.

In order to involve society in implementing the plans for restructuring it had to be made more truly democratic. Under the badge of democratisation, restructuring has now encompassed politics, the economy, spiritual life and ideology. We have unfolded a radical economic reform, we have accumulated experience, and from the New Year we are transferring the entire national economy to new forms and work methods. Moreover, this means a profound reorganisation of production relations and the realisation of the immense potential of socialist property. In moving towards such bold revolutionary transformations, we understood that there would be errors, that there would be resistance, that the novelty would bring new problems. We foresaw the possibility of breaks in individual sections. However, the profound democratic reform of the entire system of power and government is the guarantee that the overall process of restructuring will move steadily forward and gather strength.

We completed the first stage of the process of political reform with the recent decisions by the USSR Supreme Soviet on amendments to the Constitution and the adoption of the Law on Elections. Without stopping, we embarked upon the second stage of this. At which the most important task will be working on the interaction between the central government and the republics, settling relations between nationalities on the principles of Leninist internationalism bequeathed to us by the great revolution and, at the same time, reorganising the power of the Soviets locally. We are faced with immense work. At the same time we must resolve major problems.

We are more than fully confident. We have both the theory, the policy and the vanguard force of restructuring a party which is also restructuring itself in accordance with the new tasks and the radical changes throughout society. And the most important thing: all peoples and all generations of citizens in our great country are in favour of restructuring.

We have gone substantially and deeply into the business of constructing a socialist state based on the rule of law. A whole series of new laws has been prepared or reached a completion stage. Many of them come into force as early as 1989, and we trust that they will correspond to the highest standards from the point of view of ensuring the rights of the individual. Soviet democracy is to acquire a firm, normative base. This means such acts as the Law on Freedom of Conscience, on glasnost, on public associations and organisations, and on much else. There are now no people in places of imprisonment in the country who have been sentenced for their political or religious convictions. It is proposed to include in the drafts of the new laws additional guarantees ruling out any form of persecution on these bases. Of course, this does not apply to those who have committed real criminal or state offences: espionage, sabotage, terrorism, and so on, whatever political or philosophical views they may hold.

The draft amendments to the criminal code are ready and waiting their turn. In particular, those articles relating to the use of the supreme measure of punishment are being reviewed. The problem of exit and entry is also being resolved in a humane spirit, including the case of leaving the country in order to be reunited with relatives. As you know, one of the reasons for the refusal of visas is citizens' possession of secrets. Strictly substantiated terms for the length of time for possessing secrets are being introduced in advance. On starting work at a relevant institution or enterprise, everyone will be made aware of this regulation. Disputes that arise can be appealed under the law. Thus the problem of the so-called refuseniks is being resolved.

We intend to expand the Soviet Union's participation in the monitoring mechanism on human rights in the United Nations and within the framework of the pan-European process. We consider that the jurisdiction of the International Court in The Hague with respect to interpreting and applying agreements in the field of human rights should be obligatory for all states.

Within the Helsinki process, we are also examining an end to the jamming of all the foreign radio broadcasts to the Soviet Union. On the whole, our credo is as follows. Political problems should be solved only by political means, and human problems only in a humane way. [...]

Now about the most important topic, without which no problem of the coming century can be resolved: disarmament. [...] Today I can inform you of the following. The Soviet Union has made a decision on reducing its armed forces. In the next two years, their numerical strength will be reduced by 500,000 persons, and the volume of conventional arms will also be cut considerably. These reductions will be made on a unilateral basis, unconnected with negotiations on the mandate for the Vienna meeting. By agreement with our allies in the Warsaw Pact, we have made the decision to withdraw six tank divisions from the GDR, Czechoslovakia and Hungary, and to disband them by 1991. Assault landing formations and units, and a number of others, including assault river-crossing forces, with their armaments and combat equipment, will also be withdrawn from the groups of Soviet forces situated in those countries. The Soviet forces situated in those countries will be cut by 50,000 persons, and their arms by 5000 tanks. All remaining Soviet divisions on the territory of our allies will be reorganised. They will be given a different structure from today's and will become unambiguously defensive, after the removal of a large number of their tanks. [...]

By this act, just as by all our actions aimed at the demilitarisation of international relations, we would also like to draw the attention of the world community to another topical problem, the problem of changing over from an economy of armament to an economy of disarmament. Is the conversion of military production realistic? I have already had occasion to speak about this. We believe that it is, indeed, realistic. For its part, the Soviet Union is ready to do the following. Within the framework of the economic reform we are ready to draw up and submit our internal plan for conversion, to prepare in the course of 1989, as an experiment, the plans for the conversion of two or three defence enterprises. We will publish our experience of job relocation of specialists from the military industry, and also of using its equipment, buildings and works in civilian industry. It is desirable that all states, primarily the major military powers, submit their national plans on this issue to the United Nations. [...]

Finally, being on US soil, but also for other, understandable reasons, I cannot but turn to the subject of our relations with this great country. Relations between the Soviet Union and the United States of America span five and a half decades. The world has changed, and so have the nature, role and place of these relations in world politics. For too long they were built under the banner of confrontation, and sometimes of hostility, either open or concealed. But in the last few years, throughout the world people were able to heave a sigh of relief, thanks to the changes for the better in the substance and atmosphere of the relations between Moscow and Washington.

No one intends to underestimate the serious nature of the disagreements, and the difficulties of the problems which have not been settled. However, we have already graduated from the primary school of instruction in mutual understanding and in searching for solutions in our and in the common interests. The USSR and the United States created the biggest nuclear missile arsenals, but after objectively recognising their responsibility they were able to be the first to conclude an agreement on the reduction and physical destruction of a proportion of these weapons, which threatened both themselves and everyone else.

Both sides possess the biggest and the most refined military secrets. But it is they who have laid the basis for and are developing a system of mutual verification with regard to both the destruction and the limiting and banning of armaments production. It is they who are amassing experience for future bilateral and multilateral agreements. We value this.

We acknowledge and value the contribution of President Ronald Reagan and the members of his administration, above all Mr George Shultz. All this is capital that has been invested in a joint undertaking of historic importance. It must not be wasted or left out of circulation. The future US administration, headed by newly elected President George Bush, will find in us a partner, ready – without long pauses and backward movements – to continue the dialogue in a spirit of realism, openness and goodwill, and with a striving for concrete results, over an agenda encompassing the key issues of Soviet-US relations and international politics.

We are talking first and foremost about consistent progress towards concluding a treaty on a 50 per cent reduction in strategic offensive weapons, while retaining the ABM Treaty; about elaborating a convention on the elimination of chemical weapons (here, it seems to us, we have the preconditions for making 1989 the decisive year); and about talks on reducing conventional weapons and armed forces in Europe. We are also talking about economic, ecological and humanitarian problems in the widest possible sense. [...]

We are not inclined to oversimplify the situation in the world. Yes, the tendency towards disarmament has received a strong impetus, and this process is gaining its own momentum, but it has not become irreversible. Yes, the striving to give up confrontation in favour of dialogue and cooperation has made itself strongly felt, but it has by no means secured its position for ever in the practice of international relations. Yes, the movement towards a nuclear-free and nonviolent world is capable of fundamentally transforming the political and spiritual face of the planet,

Presidents Bush and Gorbachev share a laugh while they pause during a walk around the grounds of the George Bush Presidential Library and Museum

but only the very first steps have been taken. Moreover, in certain influential circles, they have been greeted with mistrust, and they are meeting resistance. The inheritance of inertia of the past is continuing to operate.

Profound contradictions and the roots of many conflicts have not disappeared. The fundamental fact remains that the formation of the peaceful period will take place in conditions of the existence and rivalry of various socio-economic and political systems. However, the meaning of our international efforts, and one of the key tenets of the new thinking, is precisely to impart to this rivalry the quality of sensible competition in conditions of respect for freedom of choice and a balance of interests. In this case it will even become useful and productive from the viewpoint of general world development. Otherwise, if the main component remains the arms race, as it has been until now, rivalry will be fatal. Indeed, an ever greater number of people throughout the world, from the man in the street to leaders, are beginning to understand this.

Esteemed Mr Chairman, esteemed delegates, I finish my first speech at the United Nations with the same feeling with which I began it: a feeling of responsibility to my own people and to the world community. We have met at the end of a year that has been so significant for the United Nations, and on the threshold of a year from which all of us expect so much. One would like to believe that our joint efforts to put an end to the era of wars, confrontation and regional conflicts, aggression against nature, the terror of hunger and poverty, as well as political terrorism, will be comparable with our hopes.

This is our common goal, and it is only by acting together that we may attain it.

Perestroika had already ushered in significant changes in the Soviet Union by 1988, and it was clear that the people of Eastern Europe were watching the situation closely while growing increasingly angered by their own situation. By proclaiming at the UN, before the eyes of the world, that he believed in freedom of choice – without exception – Gorbachev tacitly abandoned the 'Brezhnev Doctrine', which had considered any threat to the socialist system in any 'socialist camp' state to be justification for the use of force.

This statement sent a clear political signal to the opposition movements in Warsaw Pact countries to start testing their governments, to see how far they would be permitted to probe. Gorbachev made it clear that he would be reluctant to use force to crush any demonstrations, or stand in the way of 'internal processes'. Less than a year after this address the Berlin Wall had fallen and the old regimes in Poland, Hungary, East Germany, Czechoslovakia and elsewhere had been peacefully overturned.

Europe as a Common Home

Address to the Council of Europe, Strasbourg, France, 6 July 1989

Mr President, ladies and gentlemen, I thank you for the invitation to make an address here – in one of the epicentres of European politics and of the European Idea.

This meeting could, perhaps, be viewed both as evidence of the fact that the pan-European process is a reality and of the fact that it continues to evolve.

Now that the twentieth century is entering a concluding phase and both the post-war period and the cold war are becoming a thing of the past, Europeans have a truly unique chance – to play a role in building a new world, one that would be worthy of their past, of their economic and spiritual potential.

Now more than ever before the world community is experiencing profound changes. Many of its components are currently at the turning point of destiny.

The material foundation of life is changing drastically as are its spiritual parameters. There are new and increasingly more powerful factors of progress emerging.

But alongside these factors and in their wake, there continue to persist and even escalate the threats emanating from this very progress.

There is an inevitable need to do everything within the power of modern intellect to allow man to continue the role assigned to him on this Earth, perhaps in the universe at large, so that he will be able to adapt himself to the stress-inducing newness of modern existence and win the fight for survival for present and succeeding generations.

This applies to all mankind. But it applies three times as much to Europe – in the sense of its historic responsibility, in the sense of the urgency and immediacy of the problems and tasks at hand, and in the sense of opportunities.

It is also the specific feature of the situation in Europe that it can cope with all this, live up to the expectations of its peoples and do its international duty at the new stage of world history only by recognising its wholeness and by making the right conclusions.

The 1920s saw the theory of 'a declining Europe' gain wide currency. But that theme seems to be in vogue with some people even today. As far as we are concerned, we do not share the pessimism regarding the future of Europe.

Europe experienced, before everyone else, the consequences of internationalisation, first and foremost of economics and subsequently of the whole public life.

The interdependence of countries, as a higher stage of the process of internationalisation, made itself felt here before it did in other parts of the world.

Europe experienced more than once the attempts at unification by force. But it also experienced lofty dreams of a voluntary democratic community of European peoples.

Victor Hugo said that the day would come when you, France, you, Russia, you, Italy, you, England, you Germany – all of you, all the nations of the continent – will, without losing your distinguishing features and your splendid distinctiveness, merge inseparably into some high society and form a European brotherhood (...). The day would come when the only battlefield would be markets open for trade and minds open to ideas.

Nowadays it is no longer enough merely to ascertain the commonality of destiny and interdependence of European states.

The idea of European unification should be collectively thought over once again in the process of the co-creation of all nations – large, medium and small.

Is it realistic to raise the question in these terms? I know that many people in the West perceive that the main difficulty lies in the existence of two social systems.

Yet the difficulty lies elsewhere – it lies in the rather widespread belief (or even in the political objective) that what is meant by overcoming the division of Europe is actually overcoming socialism.

But this is a course for confrontation, if not something worse. There will be no European unity along these lines.

The fact that the states of Europe belong to different social systems is a reality. The recognition of this historical fact and respect for the sovereign right of each people to choose their social system at their own discretion are the most important prerequisites for a normal European process.

The social and political order in some particular countries did change in the past, and it can change in the future as well. But this is exclusively a matter for the peoples themselves and of their choice.

Any interference in internal affairs, any attempts to limit the sovereignty of states — whether of friends and allies or anybody else — are inadmissible.

Differences between states cannot be eliminated. In fact, they are even salutary, as we have said on more than one occasion — provided, of course, that the competition between different types of society is aimed at creating better material and spiritual conditions of life for people.

Thanks to perestroika, the Soviet Union will be in a position to take full part in such honest, equal and constructive competition. For all our present shortcomings and lagging behind, we know full well the strong points of our social system which follow from its essential character-istics.

And we are confident that we shall be able to make use of them both to the benefit of ourselves and of Europe.

It is time to consign to oblivion the cold war postulates when Europe was viewed as an arena of confrontation divided into 'spheres of influ-ence' and someone else's 'forward-based defences', as an object of military confrontation — namely a theatre of war.

In today's interdependent world these geopolitical notions, brought forth by a different epoch, turn out to be just as helpless in real politics as the laws of classical mechanics in the quantum theory.

In the meantime, it is precisely on the basis of outmoded stereotypes that the Soviet Union continues — although less than in the past — to be suspected of hegemonistic designs and of the intention to decouple the United States from Europe.

There are even some people who are not unwilling to put the USSR outside of Europe from the Atlantic to the Urals by confining it to the space 'from Brest to Brest'. To them, the Soviet Union is ostensibly too big for joint living; the others will not feel very comfortable next to it, or so they say.

The realities of today and the prospects for the foreseeable future are obvious: the Soviet Union and the United States are a natural part of the European international and political structure.

Their involvement in its evolution is not only justified, but also his-torically conditioned. No other approach is acceptable. In fact, it will even be counterproductive.

For centuries Europe has been making an indispensable contribution to world politics, economy, culture and to the development of the entire civilisation.

Its world historic role is recognised and respected everywhere.

Let us not forget, however, that the metastases of colonial slavery

can well be achieved, naturally, given the elimination of all asymmetries and imbalances.

I emphasise, all asymmetries and imbalances. No double standards are admissible there.

We are convinced that it is high time talks on tactical nuclear systems were initiated among all interested countries. The ultimate objective is to completely eliminate those weapons. Only Europeans who have no intention of waging war against one another are threatened by those weapons. What are they for then and who needs them?

Are nuclear arsenals to be eliminated or retained at all costs? Does the strategy of nuclear deterrence enhance or undermine stability?

On all these questions the positions of NATO and the Warsaw Pact appear to be diametrically opposed.

We, however, are not dramatising our differences. We are looking for solutions and invite our partners to join us in this quest.

After all, we see the elimination of nuclear weapons as a stage-by-stage process. Europeans can travel part of the distance separating us from complete destruction of nuclear weapons together, without backing away from their positions – with the USSR remaining faithful to its non-nuclear ideals, and the West to the concept of 'minimum deterrence'.

However, there is merit in figuring out what lies behind the concept of 'minimum' deterrence and where the limit is, beyond which nuclear retaliation capability is transformed into an attack capability. Here much remains unclear, and ambiguity breeds mistrust.

Why shouldn't experts from the USSR, the United States, the United Kingdom and France, as well as the states who have nuclear weapons located on their territories, hold an in-depth discussion on those questions?

If they arrive at some common views, the problem would become simpler at the political level, too.

If it becomes clear that NATO countries are ready to join us in negotiations on tactical nuclear weapons, we could, naturally after consulting our allies, carry out without delay further unilateral reductions in our tactical nuclear missiles in Europe.

The Soviet Union and other Warsaw Pact countries, notwithstanding the Vienna talks, are already unilaterally reducing their armed forces and armaments in Europe.

Their posture and operational structure are changing in line with the defensive doctrine of reasonable sufficiency.

That doctrine – both in terms of quantities of armaments and troops and in terms of their deployment, training and all military activities – makes it physically impossible to launch an attack or to conduct large-scale offensive operations.

In any case, as was declared at the USSR Supreme Soviet, we intend, if the situation permits, to cut sharply – by one and a half to two times – the share of our defence expenditure in national income by 1995.

We have seriously addressed conversion of the military industry. All CSCE participating countries will come to face this problem one way or another. We are ready to exchange views and share experience.

We think that the opportunities offered by the United Nations can also be used and, say, a joint working group can be set up within the Economic Commission for Europe to look into conversion problems.

Facing the European parliamentarians, and consequently the whole of Europe, I should like to say once again a few words about our straightforward and clear-cut positions on disarmament. These positions are the result of the new thinking and they were laid down on behalf of our entire people in the Resolution of the Congress of People's Deputies of the USSR, according to which: we are in favour of a nuclear-free world and in favour of eliminating all nuclear weapons by the turn of the century; we are in favour of complete elimination of chemical arms at the earliest possible date, and we favour the destruction, once and for all, of the production base for the development of such arms; we are in favour of a radical reduction in conventional arms and armed forces down to a level of reasonable defence sufficiency that would rule out the use of military force against other countries for the purposes of attack; we are in favour of complete withdrawal of all foreign troops from the territories of other countries; we are absolutely opposed to the development of any space weapons; we are in favour of dismantling military blocs and launching immediately a political dialogue between them to that end; we are in favour of creating an atmosphere of trust that would rule out any surprises; we are in favour of a deep, consistent and effective verification of all treaties and agreements that may be concluded with respect to disarmament issues.

I am convinced that it is high time the Europeans brought their policies and their conduct into line with a new common sense – not to prepare for war, not to intimidate one another, not to compete with one another either in improving weapons or, especially, in attempts to offset the initiated reductions, but rather to learn to make peace together and to lay jointly a solid basis for it.

If security is the foundation of a common European home, then all-round cooperation is its bearing frame.

What is symbolic about the new situation in Europe and throughout the world in recent years is an intensive interstate dialogue, both bilateral and multilateral. The network of agreements, treaties and other accords has become considerably more extensive. Official consultations on various issues have become a rule.

For the first time contacts have been established between NATO and the Warsaw Pact, between the European Community and the Council for Mutual Economic Assistance (CMEA), not to mention many political and public organisations in both parts of Europe.

We are pleased with the decision of the Parliamentary Assembly of the Council of Europe to grant the Soviet Union the status of a special guest state. We are prepared to cooperate. But we think that we can go further than that.

We could accede to some of the international conventions of the Council of Europe that are open to other states – on the environment, culture, education, television broadcasting. We are prepared to cooperate with the specialised agencies of the Council of Europe.

The Parliamentary Assembly, the Council of Europe and the European Parliament are situated in Strasbourg. Should our ties be expanded in the future and be put on a regular basis, we would open here, with the French Government's consent, of course, a Consulate General.

Interparliamentary ties have major significance for making the European process more dynamic. An important step has already been made: late last year a first meeting of the parliamentary leaders of 35 countries was held in Warsaw.

We have duly appreciated the visit to the USSR of the delegation of the Parliamentary Assembly of the Council of Europe headed by its President, Mr Björck.

The delegation could, I hope, feel directly the potent and energetic pulse of the Soviet perestroika.

We regard as particularly important the recently initiated contacts with the European Parliament.

Inter alia, we took note of its resolutions on military-political issues which are seen by the Parliament as the core of the Western European consensus in the area of security.

In this connection I cannot but mention the plans for 'the Western European defence'. Of course, any state or any group of states have the right to take care of their security in the forms they consider most appropriate.

It is important, though, that these forms are not in contradiction with the prevailing positive trends, that is, the trend towards a military détente, that they do not lead to the reappearance of confrontational tendencies in European politics and hence to a renewed arms race. [. . .]

As far as the economic content of the common European home is concerned, we regard as a realistic prospect — though not a close one — the emergence of a vast economic space from the Atlantic to the Urals where Eastern and Western parts would be strongly interlocked.

In this sense the Soviet Union's transition to a more open economy is essential, and not only for ourselves, for a higher economic effectiveness and for meeting consumer demands.

Such a transition will increase East-West economic interdependence and thus will tell favourably on the entire spectrum of European relations.

Similarities in the functioning of economic mechanisms, strengthening of ties and economic interest, mutual adaptation, training of experts — these are all long-term factors of cooperation, a guarantee of stability of the European and the international process as a whole.

My contacts with prominent representatives of the business communities of the United Kingdom, the Federal Republic of Germany, France, Italy and the United States during my trips abroad and on numerous occasions in Moscow testify to an increased interest in doing business with us in the conditions of perestroika.

Many of them do not overdramatise our difficulties, but take into account the specificity of the moment, when the reform is more successful in destroying obsolete mechanisms than in introducing new ones.

I have also noted the resolve of experienced businessmen with a broad political outlook to take justified risks, demonstrate audacity and act with long-term prospects in mind.

And incidentally, not only in the interests of business but also in the interests of progress and peace and in universal human interests.

We also feel aware that focusing on the immediate commercial profit may mean missing out on the chance for broad-scale and much more beneficial long-term economic cooperation with us as an integral part of the European process.

I think that the distinguished audience will agree that in our age segregating economic ties from scientific and technological ties is something less than normal. Yet East-West relations have of late been bled white by COCOM (Coordinating Committee for Multilateral Export Controls).

If one could justify such practices at the peak of the cold war, today many restrictions seem utterly ridiculous.

Of course, we too are often excessively closed. However, we have begun to straighten this out. We have started to take down our 'domestic COCOM' – the wall separating military and civilian production – in particular in connection with conversion.

So maybe experts and representatives of the respective governments could get together and break all these cold war log-jams, bring secrecy down to reasonable limits which are indeed required for security, and give the green light to the normal two-way flow of scientific knowledge and technical art?

The following projects, for example, are equally urgent for both East and West Europe: a trans-European high-speed railway; a common European programme on new solar-energy technologies and equipment; processing and storing nuclear waste and enhancing the safety of nuclear power stations; additional fibre optic channels for transmitting information; an all-European satellite television system. [...]

In 1985 in Paris, President Mitterrand and I put forward the idea of developing an international experimental thermo-nuclear reactor. It is an inexhaustible source of environmentally clean energy.

Under the aegis of the International Atomic Energy Agency (IAEA), this project – the result of pooling the scientific capabilities of the Soviet Union, West European countries, the United States, Japan and other countries – is moving to the stage of practical research.

Scientists believe that such a reactor could be built by the end of the century. It is a great achievement of academic thought and technological art, which will serve the future of Europe and the entire world.

The model of economic rapprochement between Eastern and Western Europe will to a large extent be determined by the relations between Western regional organisations – the European Community, EFTA, and the CMEA. Each of them has its own dynamics of development and its own problems.

We do not doubt that the integration processes in Western Europe are acquiring a new quality. We are far from underestimating the emergence in the next few years of a single European market.

The Council for Mutual Economic Assistance is also working towards establishing an integrated market, though we are lagging far behind in this respect.

The rate of internal change in the CMEA will to a considerable degree determine what will have a priority development in the near future: ties between the CMEA and the European Community as groups or ties between individual socialist countries and the European Community.

It is quite possible that now and then one or the other form will come to the forefront. What is important is that both forms fit into the logic of establishing a common European economic dimension.

As for the Soviet Union, we shall shortly see a trade and economic agreement between our country and the European Community. We attach substantial significance to this act from the standpoint of all-European interests too.

We are, naturally, far from seeing our ties with the EC as opposed to ties with other associations or states. The EFTA countries are our good and old partners.

It might be reasonable to talk also about developing ties between the CMEA and EFTA and use this channel of multilateral cooperation, too, in the construction of a new Europe.

The common European home will have to be environmentally clean as well. Life has taught us bitter lessons. Major ecological problems have long ago transcended national confines. Setting up a regional ecological security system is therefore an urgent task.

It is quite possible that it is in this direction, which is indeed a priority direction, that the all-European process will advance most rapidly.

Elaborating a long-term continental ecological programme could be a first step.

We have proposed setting up a United Nations centre for emergency ecological assistance.

Such a centre or agency with a warning and monitoring system is urgently needed in Europe.

We might also give thought to establishing an all-European institute for ecological research and assessment, and ultimately to the creation of an organ with binding authority.

The Vienna meeting decided that an environmental forum of the 35 would be held this autumn in Sofia, Bulgaria. It could also discuss the problems in practical terms.

Humanity is suffering increasingly grave losses as a result of natural and technological disasters. Scores and even thousands of lives are lost each year. Huge sums are spent to control the consequences. Scientists are alarmed because the largest cities are increasingly vulnerable in the face of natural disasters.

We are aware of the major projects designed to cope with this growing global threat.

The USSR Academy of Sciences has established an International Institute for the Theory of Earthquake Prediction, and it invites scientists from around the world to take part in developing a scientific basis for the problems of security and safety of larger cities, forecasting of droughts and possible climatic catastrophes.

The Soviet Union is ready to provide for these purposes satellites, oceanic vessels and new technology. It would probably be useful to involve also the military services of various countries, above all medical and engineering units, in the international rescue and restoration efforts.

The humanitarian content of the pan-European process is one of the crucial aspects.

A world where military arsenals would be reduced but where human rights would be violated would not be a safe place.

We have come to this conclusion ourselves once and for all.

The decisions made by the Vienna meeting represent a real breakthrough in this respect. It laid down a programme of joint actions by European countries, made up of all kinds of activities. Understanding was reached on many issues which until very recently had been stumbling blocks in East–West relations.

We are convinced that the all-European process should rest on a solid legal ground. We are thinking of an all-European home as a community rooted in law. And for our part we have begun to move in that direction.

The resolution adopted by the Congress of People's Deputies of the USSR says, *inter alia*: 'Guided by international rules and principles, including those in the Universal Declaration of Human Rights, the Helsinki accords and agreements, and bringing its domestic legislation in line with the above, the USSR will seek to contribute to the establishment of a world community of states rooted in law.'

Europe could set an example in that respect. Naturally, its international legal integrity includes national and social specific features of states. Each European country, the United States and Canada have their own laws and traditions in the humanitarian sphere, even though there exist some universally recognised rules and principles.

It would, perhaps, be useful to make a comparison of the existing

legislation on human rights by setting up to that end an ad hoc working group or a kind of European institute for comparative humanitarian law.

In view of the different social systems we are not likely to achieve a complete identity of views. However, the Vienna meeting and the recent London and Paris conferences have demonstrated that common views and common approaches do exist and can be multiplied.

This makes it possible to speak of the possibility of creating a European legal space.

At the Paris Humanitarian Forum, the Soviet Union and France co-sponsored an initiative to that effect. They were joined by the Federal Republic of Germany, Austria, Hungary, Poland and Czechoslovakia. [...]

Ladies and gentlemen, Europeans can meet the challenges of the coming century only by pooling their efforts.

We are convinced that what they need is one Europe – peaceful and democratic, a Europe that maintains all its diversity and common humanistic ideas, a prosperous Europe that extends its hand to the rest of the world. A Europe that confidently advances into the future.

It is in such a Europe that we visualise our own future.

Perestroika, which seeks to radically renew Soviet society, determines our policy aimed at the development of Europe precisely in that direction.

Perestroika is changing our country, advancing it to new horizons. That process will continue, extend and transform Soviet society in all dimensions, economic, social, political and spiritual, in all domestic affairs and in human relations.

We have firmly and irreversibly embarked on that road. This was confirmed by the resolution passed by the Congress of People's Deputies on the 'Basic guidelines of domestic and foreign policies of the USSR'. That document confirmed in the name of the people our choice, our path of perestroika.

I commend this resolution to your attention. It has a fundamental and revolutionary significance for the destinies of the country to which you yourselves refer as a superpower.

As a result of its implementation, you and your governments, your parliaments and peoples will soon be dealing with a socialist nation totally different from what it has been up to now.

And this will have and cannot but have a favourable impact on the entire world process.

The summer of 1989 was a feverish time in Europe, with huge changes stirring in the East. In the spring, Hungary had begun dismantling its border fence with Austria, leading to the 'escape' of thousands of East Germans to the West. In June, the Polish Solidarity Party had been permitted to stand in parliamentary elections and won 99 per cent of the seats it contested. The Iron Curtain was being replaced by a Velvet Revolution, and in this historic speech Gorbachev welcomed this, calling for a united European continent embracing all countries regardless of political systems. He reconfirmed that he would not prevent changes in the social or political order of other states, thus issuing the final invitation to citizens of Eastern Europe to use their right to freedom, and warning the current leaders not to expect to be propped up.

By the end of 1989, change had truly swept through Eastern Europe, replacing totalitarian regimes with fledgling democracies, and the Warsaw Pact was officially dissolved in 1991. Gorbachev wanted his country to be part of a new, peaceful Europe, free from divisions. Russia became a full member of the Council of Europe in 1994.

Environment and Development for Survival

Address to the Global Forum of Spiritual and Parliamentary Leaders, Palace of Congresses, the Kremlin, Moscow, 19 January 1990

The five days that you have spent here in Moscow, in an atmosphere of intense creative communication, your meaningful discussions and the final conference documents you adopted all justify the conclusion: an important step in moulding mankind's ecological self-awareness has been made.

The threat of a military thermonuclear catastrophe has been understood. Scientists also made an irreplaceable contribution to this. International forces at all levels – political, diplomatic and public – have already been mobilised to stave off this threat. We are witnessing the first results. But a second threat the assessment of which was until recently clearly inadequate to its gravity – the threat to life on Earth as a result of damage to the environment – has emerged.

The great minds of the past foresaw the consequences of the thoughtless 'conquering' of nature by man. They warned that humankind could kill itself by destroying the vegetable and animal kingdoms and poisoning the earth, water and air. Yet, at the end of the twentieth century, we have a very acute crisis in relations among man, society and nature. Paraphrasing Immanuel Kant, it is safe to say that the ecological imperative has forcefully entered both the policy of states and people's everyday life. It is becoming unconditional, and not only because perhaps irreparable damage has been done to nature. The new scientific, technical and technological revolution, the full consequences of which we do not yet know, can make this damage irreversible.

As distinct from some absolute pessimists, we are not fatalists. But the hour of decision – the hour of historic choice – has come, and there is no reasonable alternative for man because he is not predisposed to suicide.

Humanity is a part of the single and integral biosphere. The stability of ecosystems and, hence, the quality of the environment depend on the preservation and maintenance of biological diversity and equilibrium of the biosphere. Your Forum has said in no uncertain terms that something should be substantially changed in the factors of further progress in order to ensure man's initial right – the right to life. We agree with this conclusion.

I must admit that in the Soviet Union we only recently came to understand the vital importance of ecological problems to a proper extent at the level of policy. The danger of war stood in our light. Fewer words are needed here. But the gist of the matter lies not only in this. After the revolution, having started industrialising our country, we were not inclined to 'divert our attention' to secondary questions, as they seemed to us at that time, especially not to spend our limited funds on this. The size of our country and its riches encouraged this ecological carelessness.

Even when the pollution of the environment in some regions began to reach a dangerous scale, this was not properly assessed at once. It is our scientists – to their credit – who sounded the ecological alarm, and the public followed them. Having changed the philosophical approach to the development of society, perestroika has also altered our views on ecology. A detailed report on the national ecological situation, the first in the history of the Soviet state, has recently been published in our country. An unbiased analysis of our woes and dangers was made in this 'green book'. The pollution of the atmosphere in some big cities exceeds permissible levels. The state of water resources spells grave consequences for the vegetable and animal kingdoms. Soils degrade, harm is being done to people's health, and even the full possibilities of future generations is being called into question.

In its resolution 'On the Guidelines of the Home and Foreign Policy of the USSR', the first Congress of People's Deputies predetermined a deep revision of our entire development, including our attitude to nature, with a view to ecologising our policy. What do we mean by this?

We mean, above all, a radical change in the character of production activity from the standpoint of its ecological consequences. We must take into account the ecological capacity of territories when siting economic complexes. We must balance the ecosystems of regions with the corresponding national economic plans and take this into account in demographic, regional and ethnic policy. Of course, we mean the consistent and strict implementation of nature-protection measures, technology used in industry and agriculture, conserving energy and resources, and the introduction of waste-free technologies and production units.

The ecologisation of politics means a new look at the problem of consumption and its rationalisation. People's living standards should not be raised by exhausting natural resources. This process should be accompanied by a restoration of the living conditions of the animal and plant world.

The ecologisation of politics affects the methods of handling many social problems, especially damage to people's health as a result of damage to the environment.

The ecologisation of politics implies all possible support for scientific research and fundamental studies of the biosphere and its ecosystems.

The ecologisation of politics requires acknowledgement of the priority of universal human values in making ecology a part of education and instruction from an early age, moulding a new contemporary attitude to nature and, at the same time returning to man a sense of being a part of nature. No moral improvement of society is possible without that.

We have already begun a major overhaul of the entire system of nature conservation in this country. Specific programmes have been adopted or are being drawn up for individual regions and sites. The Supreme Soviet of the USSR has passed a resolution 'On Emergency Measures to Improve the Ecological Situation in the Country'. Work is almost completed on the draft of a national long-term programme for environmental protection and national use of natural resources. [...] We are to exert great efforts to harmonise our relations with nature. There is work for everyone here: legislative and executive bodies, science and education, public organisations and movements and individual initiative.

Environmentalist public movements in our country have greatly expanded their activities. They have landed telling blows against the technocratic ignorance and resistance which exist in this area as well as others. [...]

What is the best solution here? Ecological security based on unbiased scientific analysis on a national and, in some cases, international basis is the key to the rational location of productive forces and power-engineering and other projects of national importance. [...]

There is yet another factor to which I would like to draw your attention. There are ecosystems within the territory of this country that have not yet been affected by human activity. Therefore, we attach great importance to the creation of reserves and other protected territories. By 2000 their area is set to increase by approximately three times. These are unique nature laboratories situated over a vast territory from the Arctic islands to central Asia. They may serve as standards of primeval nature and sites for international ecological cooperation.

The ecological situation in different countries is different. Many countries have accumulated valuable experience in nature conservation and practical use. The ecological crisis we are experiencing today is tragic but convincing proof that the world we all live in is interrelated and interdependent. It appears that all people everywhere realise this now.

This means, however, that we need appropriate international policy in the field of ecology. Only if we formulate such policies will we be able to avert catastrophe. True, the elaboration of international policy poses unconventional and difficult problems which sometimes affect the sovereignty of states. Yet it is a solvable problem, but only through cooperative effort and a search forward at this Forum for ways to formulate a global ecological policy. I assure you that we shall study all options. In principle, the Soviet Union supports working out as soon as possible an international programme to save the biosphere and restore its vitality. Here are our main ideas on this score.

First, the Soviet Union fully supports the nature conservation plans and actions of our global universal organisation, the United Nations and its agencies. We want the UN Conference on the Environment and Development, which is to be held in Brazil in 1992, to be conducted at summit level. It would be right if that conference discussed the question of drafting an international code of ecological ethics. Binding on all states, it should contain common standards of a civilised attitude to nature. Such an action would symbolise the willingness of the international community, represented by its top leaders, to arrange life in the twenty-first century in accordance with new laws.

The 1992 conference could also adopt a global programme of action for environmental protection and rational use of natural resources. Such a programme should embrace the protection of the world climate and the animal and plant life on our planet and preservation of biological diversity, without which it is impossible to preserve the regulating properties of the biosphere and, consequently, of life on Earth.

Second, the Soviet Union finds it necessary to develop an international legal mechanism for protecting unique natural zones of global importance. This primarily refers to the Antarctic. The thick Antarctic ice cap is an invaluable treasury of the Earth's past, of its geological and ecological history. Significantly, the Antarctic has become the world's first nuclear-free zone and the first territory ever fully open for international research programmes. The Soviet Union shares the concern of many scientists and public figures over the exploitation of the Antarctic's natural resources. Our grandchildren will never forgive us if we fail to preserve this phenomenal ecological system. The USSR is ready to join the programme for creating a life-support system for the Antarctic continent which is our common laboratory.

Now about the problems of the Danube and of the Black and Mediterranean Seas: 75 per cent of the pollution is brought to the Black Sea by the Danube. Over the past few decades, the upper line of the hydrogen sulphide layer has risen from the depth of 200 metres to 75 metres. Any day now the polluted waters may escape over the Bosphorus threshold and move to the Sea of Marmara and to the Aegean Sea and Mediterranean. Meanwhile, the Black Sea agreements have been signed only by Bulgaria, Romania, Turkey and the USSR. Can we solve the Black Sea problem by cleaning the Dnieper, the Dniester and the Azov Sea alone, without the Danube and all the countries along its banks? Can the problems of protecting the Mediterranean be solved without the Black Sea states, without the USSR? The time has come to think about this problem together.

Then again, do not tropical forests and coral reefs — the ecological heritage of mankind — need our common care and concern? Or what about such unique natural phenomena as Lake Baikal?

Third, the Soviet Union believes that the world is in urgent need of an international mechanism for technological cooperation in nature conservation. Our civilisation is indivisible and demands united efforts in this area as well. We support developing an international system of exchanging ecologically clean technologies effectively accessible to all nations. Also, we are ready to open our territory for inspection in order to dispel all fears that technologies might not be used according to their purpose. I therefore agree that there should have been more businessmen at the Moscow meeting. At the next meeting this mistake should not repeat itself.

Fourth, the transition to new forms of cooperation worthy of the twenty-first century has highlighted the need to create an international mechanism of ecological monitoring control. Today, measures for building ecological confidence could be based on the methods, procedures and instruments similar to those used in arms control, including opening up of on-site inspections. We could begin with national nature reserves.

Fifth, the right to a healthy environment is one of the basic human rights. However, we should also ensure the right of the individual and groups of people to participate in drafting ecological policies. The Soviet Union supports this conclusion of the Sofia Ecological Conference of the states involved in the European process. What is meant here is the completeness and authenticity of ecological information. We need a system whereby every state would regularly present its nature-conservation activity and report about the ecological accidents that have been prevented.

At the moment, the member states of the European Community are actively debating the organisation and functions of a European Environmental Protection Agency. The Soviet Union supports the idea of setting up such an agency and is ready to join its work from the very beginning. Many ideas deserve attention. Among them is Austria's initiative to set up international nature-protection units called 'UN Green Helmets'.

Perhaps it would be useful to institute a kind of international Green Cross that offers its assistance to states in ecological trouble. The Soviet idea of setting up a UN centre for urgent ecological aid has the same purpose. The centre's chief mission, as we see it, is to organise international groups of experts to be sent to the sites of ecological disasters. Soon, the UN Secretary General will receive the list of Soviet experts and researchers whom the Soviet Government will be ready to send to such places at its own expense on instructions from the centre.

Sixth, and last but not least, the Soviet Union believes that the time has come when the limitation of military activity is needed not only for lessening the danger of war but for protecting the environment. The best thing to do here would be to ban all nuclear tests. Before this authoritative international forum I reiterate the Soviet Union's readiness to ban

Gorbachev taking the initiative to launch GCI in the fall of 1992

nuclear tests completely, for all time and at any moment, if the USA does the same.

The convention on and the prohibition and complete elimination of chemical weapons which, we hope, will be signed soon, misses the need to ensure an ecologically safe method of accomplishing this task. Here, too, international cooperation would be extremely welcome, for we are going to eliminate tens of thousands of tonnes of these lethal weapons. Generally speaking, military activity on land, in the air, in the seas and oceans, and even in outer space, should always be run with due account taken of its ecological consequences. With this end in view we are planning to introduce certain limitations on the flights of military aviation, and on the movement of the land forces and of warships. We are also prepared to sign international agreements on this score.

Fairly often new terms eventually change their meaning. This is true for the term 'ecology', which was born in the nineteenth century as a purely scientific term and which has acquired a truly fateful meaning for us today. The same has happened to the term 'biosphere', also the product of the nineteenth century. The great Russian scientist Vladimir Vernadsky filled it with a new content. He created a theory of the biosphere and raised the problem of turning the entire medium mankind lives in into a sphere ruled by reason.

In conclusion, I would like to say the following: the problems you have discussed and the documents you have adopted are a call for the triumph of the trinity of scientific knowledge, human reason and universal moral principles. This task is as magnificent as it is difficult. I wish all of you – and all of us – every success.

Green Cross International was conceived by Gorbachev at this Forum. With the cold war over – as declared by Gorbachev and President Bush at the Malta Summit in December 1989 – and the first agreements to curb the nuclear arms race in place, Gorbachev knew that the most serious global challenge was now the environment. He proposed the creation of an organisation that would act as a 'Red Cross for the environment', protecting people and nature during and after conflicts, and preventing conflicts related to natural resources. Launched by Gorbachev in 1993, Green Cross International is today a world leader in the field of ecological security.

The Grim Legacy of Old

Excerpts from President Mikhail S. Gorbachev's speech at the 28th Communist Party Congress in Moscow, 2 July 1990, as translated and distributed by the Soviet press agency Tass

It was an extremely grim legacy that we inherited. Let us jointly recall and consider the facts.

Take the neglect in the countryside, in farming and in the processing industry. Did it arise yesterday, after 1985? Yet it affects the food situation to this day as well as farmers' lives and positions.

Or take the sorry state of our forests and rivers, the millions of hectares of fertile land flooded as a result of the former policy of power generation. Are these deeds of the past few years?

The grim environmental situation: more than 100 cities in a disaster zone, with 1000 industrial establishments brought to a standstill as a result; the drama of Lake Baikal, the Aral Sea, Lake Ladoga and the Sea of Azov; Chernobyl and other accidents; the disasters involving railways and gas pipelines. Are not all these the consequences of a policy pursued for decades?

The costs of militarism
Not to speak of the militarisation of the economy, which swallowed colossal material and intellectual resources, the best that there were. Or the irreparable human losses due to the war in Afghanistan.

Let us be impartial and let us stick to principle. In matters of high politics it is wrong to succumb to petty passions. That is why it is impossible to agree when it is said that the past has been blamed enough and when all problems are attributed to perestroika. Yes, it is our job to set things right, change them for the better, improve the life of Soviet people. Yet it is wrong to assert that all these are consequences of perestroika.

By blundering in our assessments, we might also blunder in our actions, in our practical work.

In speaking of all this, comrades, I certainly do not want to mitigate assessments or conclusions concerning the activities of the Central Committee, the Politburo or the Communists working in party, government and economic organisations in the republics or locally.

There are many things we could have foreseen and there are negative processes, above all, in the economic and social spheres, in inter-ethnic relations, and in the sphere of culture and ideology, whose development we could have prevented.

The Politburo does not deny its responsibility for these errors.

No hasty judgements

But as I see it the Congress has gathered not to pass hasty judgement. We need to continue analysing the reasons and correctly evaluate the situation in which the country found itself when the need for revolutionary changes arose before us.

Moreover, the changes were pressing because the country was gathering speed in lapsing into a second-rate state. By the early 1980s it had become clear that our apparent well-being rested on a savage, wasteful use of natural and human resources. Indeed, it may be said candidly that we would very soon have been in dire straits with unpredictable consequences.

We must also look thoroughly into the work we have done in the five years after the 27th Congress of the Communist Party.

For a correct understanding of the current situation it is above all essential to bear in mind the incompleteness of perestroika itself. We are in a transitional period in which the dismantling of the old system, and still less the building of the new one, has not been completed. We must therefore act more resolutely, because any delay is sure to aggravate the situation in the country.

One of the serious reasons for the difficulties we are encountering in many fields is the resistance to change put up by the bureaucratic stratum in the managerial structures and by the social forces associated with it.

Getting goods to market

At the same time the situation in the consumer market, far from becoming less strained, has in many cases grown more acute and become intolerable. I would say that this is a critical point in the socio-economic situation of the country. This has happened above all because cash incomes have been growing much faster than the production of goods. [...]

Growth of cash incomes was naturally affected by the implementation of decisions for raising the salaries of schoolteachers, medical doctors, and other brackets, and also pensions and stipends.

As a result of all these measures, the cash incomes of the population

just last year rose by 64 billion roubles as against the usual increase of 12 to 15 billion roubles. The same situation persists this year.

People naturally ask: 'Could the mistakes have been avoided, and the negative economic tendencies prevented?'

Blame for the Government

In any case – and this should be admitted – the consequences could have been far less painful if the Government had comprehensively approached the economic reform and had managed to stand up to the pressure of various industries and the old managerial structures that sought to keep their position and maintain the command methods of administration.

That was where the Government should have had the help of the Politburo, where higher demands should have been set for it, and where it should have received support in its work. One should say that such signals came from society and from economic services, specifically from the Central Committee's economic department.

But unfortunately this was not done. Although discussions were held more than once, not all of what should have been done was done. That is why we bear direct responsibility for the aggravation of the situation in the consumer market, which complicated the entire situation in the country.

This is a serious lesson for our work. It is this that dictates the imperative need to accelerate and radicalise the economic reform. We can no longer tolerate the managerial system that rejects scientific and technological progress and new technologies; that is committed to cost-ineffectiveness and generates squandering and waste.

As before, the country is expending 100 to 150 per cent more material resources and 50 per cent more fuel and energy than the developed countries. A tremendous number of enterprises are in the red, and government subsidies add up to 23 billion roubles.

All this has to be resolutely changed, so as to achieve a considerable improvement in people's living standards not in the distant but in the immediate future.

The logic of perestroika

Thus, the very logic of perestroika and the dramatic social and economic situation in the country bring us face to face with the need for fundamental changes in the economic system. What we are talking about is establishing a basically new model of the economy: a multi-sectoral model, with diverse forms of ownership and management, and with a modern market infrastructure.

This will clear the road to people's business activity and initiative, and create new and powerful motivations for fruitful work, for greater economic efficiency.

We had set this objective in the opening stage of perestroika. But it is only now that we can tackle the passage to a market economy, for we now have certain experience in working with new forms of management, have taken major steps as concerns political reform, and have enacted a number of crucial laws, notably on property, land, lease-holding and the like.

Revising the revisions

[…] We should do everything for the people to be confident that during this difficult stage in the transition to new forms of economic management and to new forms of economic life the people will be socially protected and their interests guaranteed.

When going over to a market economy we must single out the measures that come first. Even today nothing prevents us from beginning to turn state enterprises into joint stock companies, from granting real freedom of enterprise, from leasing small enterprises and shops, and putting up housing, stocks, shares and other equities, as well as part of the means of production, for purchase and sale.

Freedom of choice

Deep-rooted change is under way in Eastern Europe. When somebody says this is the 'collapse of socialism' we counter it with the question: What 'socialism'? That which had been, in point of fact, a variation of Stalin's authoritarian bureaucratic system that we have ourselves discarded?

Of course, whether these countries will go in their social and economic development is an open question. But that is up to the peoples concerned. We on the other hand have acted and we will act in strict compliance with the principle of the freedom of choice, which has become an imperative for the progress and a condition for the survival of all modern civilisation.

How are we to build our relations with the East European countries today and tomorrow? As with good neighbours that not only geography but history as well have made us. There has been much that is really good and valuable in it, particularly after the war. [. . .]

We have made a tremendous stride forward in developing democracy and inner-party glasnost and openness. All attempts to suppress different opinions have been denounced.

But there is a threshold to overstep which would mean to cripple the party. And that is to form factions with their own special discipline.

Let me specify this point. When speaking about the inadmissibility of forming such factions, we do not mean that the party members who have their own point of view on certain issues, differing from that of the majority, cannot freely discuss and popularise their views, publicly expressing them up to addressing the party congresses. Let us make it clear that we have reached understanding on that score.

While the rest of the world was still celebrating the fall of the Iron Curtain, the situation inside the USSR was very tense. The end of the 1980s had brought many problems as the painful process of restructuring took hold; food shortages, rising prices and the sovereignty movements in different republics all led to public protests and political confrontations. At the congress conservatives mounted a fierce counter-offensive against some of Mikhail S. Gorbachev's reforms, but he succeeded in this struggle to keep the reforms that were needed to tackle both national and global challenges – including the environment – on track. This was to be the last congress of the Soviet Communist Party.

Nobel Peace Prize Acceptance Speech

Delivered by a representative, Oslo, Norway, 10 December 1990

To the Chair of the Norwegian Nobel Committee, Mrs Gidske Anderson: Esteemed Mrs Anderson,

I am deeply and personally moved by the decision of the Nobel Committee to award me the 1990 Nobel Peace Prize.

The prestige and authority of the Nobel Peace Prize are universally recognised. The prize has been awarded ever since the beginning of this century. The disasters and tragedies of this period, which have not managed to subdue man's optimism and unflagging belief in human reason, have given the Peace Prize the unique aura associated with it today.

Immanuel Kant prophesied that mankind would one day be faced with a dilemma: 'either to be joined in a true union of nations or to perish in a war of annihilation ending in the extinction of the human race'. Now, as we move from the second to the third millennium, the clock has struck the moment of truth.

In this respect, the year 1990 represents a turning point. It marks the end of the unnatural division of Europe. Germany has been reunited. We have begun resolutely to tear down the material foundations of a military, political and ideological confrontation. But there are some very grave threats that have not been eliminated: the potential for conflict and the primitive instincts which allow it, aggressive intentions, and totalitarian traditions.

I would like to assure you that the leadership of the USSR is doing and will continue to do everything in its power to ensure that future developments in Europe and the world as a whole are based on openness, mutual trust, international law and universal values.

The recent meeting in Paris of heads of state and government from the European nations, the United States and Canada, embodying all the best elements in international movements such as the Helsinki Process, has established the framework for a Europe based on the rule of law, stability, good relations between neighbouring countries and humane attitudes. It is my hope that such a Europe will be understood and accepted by nations and governments in other parts of the world as an example of universal security and genuine cooperation.

I do not regard the 1990 Nobel Peace Prize as an award to me personally, but as a recognition of what we call perestroika and innovative political thinking, which is of vital significance for human destinies all over the world.

The Nobel Peace Prize for 1990 confirms that perestroika and innovative political thinking no longer belong only to us, the people of the Soviet Union. They are the property of the whole of mankind and are an inseparable part of its destiny and of a safe, peaceful future. We are deeply grateful to Norway and other members of the international community who have shown such understanding and who, through their conduct in international issues and in their relations with the Soviet Union, have shown their solidarity as we proceed with our perestroika and their sympathy as we struggle to resolve our problems. If we all took this as our point of departure, mankind would have no cause to regret the loss of a unique opportunity for reason and the logic of peace to prevail over that of war and alienation.

Once more, I would like to express my appreciation for this very great honour. I intend to do everything in my power to live up to the expectations and hopes of my countrymen and all those who support the Nobel Committee's choice.

With my sincere wishes for peace and prosperity.

The award of the Nobel Peace Prize was the first, and most important, recognition of Gorbachev's historic role in building a more peaceful world. For Gorbachev, the award bestowed not only great honour but also great responsibility to continue his work for peace and to spread the message of perestroika and universal human values to this day.

The Nobel Lecture

Oslo, Norway, 5 June 1991

This moment is no less emotional for me than the one when I first learned about the decision of the Nobel Committee. For on similar occasions great men addressed humankind – men famous for their courage in working to bring together morality and politics. Among them were my compatriots.

The award of the Nobel Peace Prize makes one think once again about a seemingly simple and clear question: What is peace?

Preparing for my address I found in an old Russian encyclopedia a definition of 'peace' as a 'commune' – the traditional cell of Russian peasant life. I saw in that definition the people's profound understanding of peace as harmony, concord, mutual help and cooperation.

This understanding is embodied in the canons of world religions and in the works of philosophers from antiquity to our time. The names of many of them have been mentioned here before. Let me add another one to them. Peace 'propagates wealth and justice, which constitute the prosperity of nations'; a peace which is 'just a respite from wars ... is not worthy of the name'; peace implies 'general counsel'. This was written almost 200 years ago by Vasily Fyodorovich Malinovsky – the dean of the Tsarskoye Selo Lyceum at which the great Pushkin was educated.

Since then, of course, history has added a great deal to the specific content of the concept of peace. In this nuclear age it also means a condition for the survival of the human race. But the essence, as understood both by the popular wisdom and by intellectual leaders, is the same.

Today, peace means the ascent from simple coexistence to cooperation and common creativity among countries and nations.

Peace is movement towards globality and universality of civilisation. Never before has the idea that peace is indivisible been so true as it is now.

Peace is not unity in similarity but unity in diversity, in the comparison and conciliation of differences.

And, ideally, peace means the absence of violence. It is an ethical value. And here we have to recall Rajiv Gandhi, who died so tragically a few days ago.

I consider the decision of your Committee as a recognition of the great international importance of the changes now under way in the Soviet Union, and as an expression of confidence in our policy of new thinking which is based on the conviction that at the end of the twentieth century force and arms will have to give way as a major instrument in world politics.

I see the decision to award me the Nobel Peace Prize also as an act of solidarity with the monumental undertaking which has already placed enormous demands on the Soviet people in terms of efforts, costs, hardships, will-power and character. And solidarity is a universal value that is becoming indispensable for progress and for the survival of humankind.

But a modern state has to be worthy of solidarity, in other words, it should pursue in both domestic and international affairs policies that bring together the interests of its people and those of the world community. This task, however obvious, is not a simple one. Life is much richer and more complex than even the most perfect plans to make it better. It ultimately takes vengeance for attempts to impose abstract schemes, even with the best of intentions. Perestroika has made us understand this about our past, and the actual experience of recent years has taught us to reckon with the most general laws of civilisation.

This, however, came later. But back in March–April 1985 we found ourselves facing a crucial and, I confess, agonising choice. When I agreed to assume the office of the General Secretary of the Communist Party of the Soviet Union Central Committee, in effect the highest state office at that time, I realised that we could no longer live as before and that I would not want to remain in that office unless I got support in undertaking major reforms. It was clear to me that we had a long way to go. But of course I could not imagine how immense were our problems and difficulties. I believe no one at that time could foresee or predict them.

Those who were then governing the country knew what was really happening to it and what we later called *zastoi*, roughly translated as 'stagnation'. They saw that our society was marking time, that it was running the risk of falling hopelessly behind the technologically advanced part of the world. Total domination of centrally managed state property, the pervasive authoritarian-bureaucratic system, ideology's grip on politics, monopoly in social thought and sciences, militarised industries that siphoned off our best, including the best intellectual resources, the unbearable burden of military expenditures that suffocated civilian industries and undermined the social achievements of the period since the Revolution, which were real and of which we used to be proud – such was the actual situation in the country.

As a result, one of the richest countries in the world, endowed with immense overall potential, was already sliding downwards. Our society was declining, both economically and intellectually.

And yet to a casual observer the country seemed to present a picture of relative well-being, stability and order. The misinformed society under the spell of propaganda was hardly aware of what was going on and what the immediate future had in store for it. The slightest manifestations of protest were suppressed. Most people considered them heretical, slanderous and counter-revolutionary.

Such was the situation in the spring of 1985, and there was a great temptation to leave things as they were, to make only cosmetic changes. This, however, meant continuing to deceive ourselves and the people.

This was the domestic aspect of the dilemma then before us. As for the foreign policy aspect, there was the East-West confrontation, a rigid division into friends and foes, the two hostile camps with a corresponding set of cold war attributes. Both the East and the West were constrained by the logic of military confrontation, wearing themselves down more and more by the arms race.

The mere thought of dismantling the existing structures did not come easily. However, the realisation that we faced inevitable disaster, both domestically and internationally, gave us the strength to make a historic choice, which I have never since regretted.

Perestroika, which once again is returning our people to common sense, has enabled us to open up to the world, and has restored a normal relationship between the country's internal development and its foreign policy. But all this takes a lot of hard work. To a people which believed that its government's policies had always been true to the cause of peace, we proposed what was in many ways a different policy, which would genuinely serve the cause of peace while differing from the prevailing view of what it meant and particularly from the established stereotypes as to how one should protect it. We proposed new thinking in foreign policy.

Thus, we embarked on a path of major changes that may turn out to be the most significant in the twentieth century, for our country and for its peoples. But we also did this for the entire world.

I began my book about perestroika and the new thinking with the following words: 'We want to be understood.' After a while I felt that it was already happening. But now I would like once again to repeat those words here, from this world rostrum. Because to really understand us – to understand so as to believe us – proved to be not at all easy, owing to the immensity of the changes under way in our country. Their magnitude and character are such as to require in-depth analysis. Applying conventional wisdom to perestroika is unproductive. It is also futile and dangerous to set conditions, to say: 'We'll understand and believe you, as soon as you, the Soviet Union, come completely to resemble "us", the West.'

No one is in a position to describe in detail what perestroika will finally produce. But it would certainly be a self-delusion to expect that perestroika will produce 'a copy' of anything.

Of course, learning from the experience of others is something we have been doing and will continue to do. But this does not mean that we will come to be exactly like others. Our state will preserve its own identity within the international community. A country like ours, with its uniquely close-knit ethnic composition, cultural diversity and tragic past, the greatness of its historic endeavours and the exploits of its peoples – such a country will find its own path to the civilisation of the twenty-first century and its own place in it. Perestroika has to be conceived solely in this context, otherwise it will fail and will be rejected. After all, it is impossible to 'shed' the country's thousand-year history – a history which we still have to subject to serious analysis in order to find the truth that we shall take into the future.

We want to be an integral part of modern civilisation, to live in harmony with mankind's universal values, abide by the norms of international law, follow the 'rules of the game' in our economic relations with the outside world. We want to share with all other peoples the burden of responsibility for the future of our common house.

A period of transition to a new quality in all spheres of society's life is accompanied by painful phenomena. When we were initiating perestroika we failed to properly assess and foresee everything. Our society turned out to be hard to move off the ground, not ready for major changes which affect people's vital interests and make them leave behind everything to which they had become accustomed over many years. In the beginning we imprudently generated great expectations, without taking into account the fact that it takes time for people to realise that all have to live and work differently, to stop expecting that new life would be given from above.

Perestroika has now entered its most dramatic phase. Following the transformation of the philosophy of perestroika into real policy, which began literally to explode the old way of life, difficulties began to mount. Many took fright and wanted to return to the past. It was not only those who used to hold the levers of power in the administration, the army and various government agencies and who had to make room, but also many people whose interests and way of life was put to a severe test and who, during the preceding decades, had forgotten how to take the initiative and to be independent, enterprising and self-reliant.

Hence the discontent, the outbursts of protest and the exorbitant, though understandable, demands which, if satisfied right away, would lead to complete chaos. Hence the rising political passions and instead of a constructive opposition, which is only normal in a democratic system, one that is often destructive and unreasonable – not to mention the extremist forces which are especially cruel and inhuman in areas of inter-ethnic conflict.

During the last six years we have discarded and destroyed much that stood in the way of the renewal and transformation of our society. But when society was given freedom it could not recognise itself, for it had lived too long, as it were, 'beyond the looking glass'. Contradictions and vices rose to the surface, and even blood has been shed, although we have been able to avoid a bloodbath. The logic of reform has clashed with the logic of rejection, and with the logic of impatience which breeds intolerance.

In this situation, which is one of great opportunity and of major risks, at a high point of perestroika's crisis, our task is to stay the course while also addressing current everyday problems – which are literally tearing this policy apart – and to do it in such a way as to prevent a social and political explosion.

Now, about my position. As to the fundamental choice, I have long ago made a final and irrevocable decision. Nothing and no one, no pressure, either from the right or from the left, will make me abandon the positions of perestroika and new thinking. I do not intend to change my views or convictions. My choice is a final one.

It is my profound conviction that the problems arising in the course of our transformations can be solved solely by constitutional means. That is why I make every effort to keep this process within the confines of democracy and reforms.

This applies also to the problem of self-determination of nations, which is a challenging one for us. We are looking for mechanisms to solve that problem within the framework of a constitutional process; we recognise the peoples' legitimate choice, with the understanding that if a people really decides, through a fair referendum, to withdraw from the Soviet Union, a certain agreed transition period will then be needed.

Steering a peaceful course is not easy in a country where generation after generation of people were led to believe that those who have power or force could throw those who dissent or disagree out of politics or even in jail. For centuries all the country's problems used to be finally resolved by violent means. All this has left an almost indelible mark on our entire 'political culture', if the term is at all appropriate in this case.

Our democracy is being born in pain. A political culture is emerging – one that presupposes debate and pluralism, but also legal order and, if democracy is to work, strong government authority based on one law for all. This process is gaining strength. Being resolute in the pursuit of perestroika, a subject of much debate these days, must be measured by the commitment to democratic change. Being resolute does not mean a return to repression, diktat or the suppression of rights and freedoms. I will never agree to having our society split once again into Reds and Whites, into those who claim to speak and act 'on behalf of the people' and those who are 'enemies of the people'. Being resolute today means to act within the framework of political and social pluralism and the rule of law to provide conditions for continued reform and prevent a breakdown of the state and economic collapse, prevent the elements of chaos from becoming catastrophic.

All this requires taking certain tactical steps, to search for various ways of addressing both short- and long-term tasks. Such efforts and political and economic steps, agreements based on reasonable compromise, are there for everyone to see. I am convinced that the 'One-Plus-Nine Statement' will go down in history as one such step, as a great opportunity. Not all parts of our decisions are readily accepted or correctly understood. For the most part, our decisions are unpopular; they arouse waves of criticism. But life has many more surprises in store for us, just as we will sometimes surprise it. Jumping to conclusions after every step taken by the Soviet leadership, after every decree by the President, trying to figure out whether he is moving left or right, backward or forward, would be an exercise in futility and would not lead to understanding.

We will seek answers to the questions we face only by moving forward, only by continuing and even radicalising reforms, by consistently democratising our society. But we will proceed prudently, carefully weighing each step.

There is already a consensus in our society that we have to move towards a mixed market economy. There are still differences as to how to do it and how fast we should move. Some are in favour of rushing through a transitional period as fast as possible, no matter what. Although this may smack of adventurism we should not overlook the fact that such views enjoy support. People are tired and are easily swayed by populism. So it would be just as dangerous to move too slowly, to keep people waiting in suspense. For them life today is difficult, a life of considerable hardship.

Work on a new Union Treaty has entered its final stage. Its adoption will open a new chapter in the history of our multinational state.

After a time of rampant separatism and euphoria, when almost every village proclaimed sovereignty, a centripetal force is beginning to gather momentum, based on a more sensible view of existing realities and the risks involved. And this is what counts most now. There is a growing will to achieve consensus, and a growing understanding that we have a state, a country, a common life. This is what must be preserved first of all. Only then can we afford to start figuring out which party or club to join and what God to worship.

The stormy and contradictory process of perestroika, particularly in the past two years, has made us face squarely the problem of criteria to measure the effectiveness of state leadership. In the new environment of a multi-party system, freedom of thought, rediscovered ethnic identity and sovereignty of the republics, the interests of society must absolutely be put above those of various parties or groups, or any other sectoral, parochial or private interests, even though they also have the right to exist and to be represented in the political process and in public life, and, of course, they must be taken into account in the policies of the state.

Ladies and gentlemen, international politics is another area where a great deal depends on the correct interpretation of what is now happening in the Soviet Union. This is true today, and it will remain so in the future.

We are now approaching what might be the crucial point when the world community and, above all, the states with the greatest potential to influence world developments will have to decide on their stance with regard to the Soviet Union and to act on that basis.

The more I reflect on the current world developments, the more I become convinced that the world needs perestroika no less than the Soviet Union needs it. Fortunately, the present generation of policy-makers, for the most part, are becoming increasingly aware of this interrelationship, and also of the fact that now that perestroika has entered its critical phase the Soviet Union is entitled to expect large-scale support to assure its success.

Recently, we have been seriously rethinking the substance and the role of our economic cooperation with other countries, above all major Western nations. We realise, of course, that we have to carry out measures that would enable us really to open up to the world economy and become its organic part. But at the same time we come to the conclusion that there is a need for a kind of synchronisation of our actions towards that end with those of the Group of Seven and of the European Community. In other words, we are thinking of a fundamentally new phase in our international cooperation.

In these months much is being decided and will be decided in our country to create the prerequisites for overcoming the systemic crisis and gradually recovering a normal life.

The multitude of specific tasks to be addressed in this context may be summarised within three main areas:

- Stabilising the democratic process on the basis of a broad social consensus and a new constitutional structure of our Union as a genuine, free and voluntary federation.
- Intensifying economic reform to establish a mixed market economy based on a new system of property relations.
- Taking vigorous steps to open the country up to the world economy through rouble convertibility and acceptance of civilised 'rules of the game' adopted in the world market, and through membership in the World Bank and the International Monetary Fund.

These three areas are closely interrelated. Therefore, there is a need for discussion in the Group of Seven and in the European Community. We need a joint programme of action to be implemented over a number of years.

If we fail to reach an understanding regarding a new phase of cooperation, we will have to look for other ways, for time is of the essence. But if we are to move to that new phase, those who participate in and even shape world politics also must continue to change, to review their philosophic perception of the changing realities of the world and of its imperatives. Otherwise there is no point in drawing up a joint programme of practical action.

The Soviet leadership, both in the centre and in the republics, as well as a large part of the Soviet public understand this need, although in some parts of our society not everyone is receptive to such ideas. There are some flag-wavers who claim a monopoly of patriotism and think that it means 'not getting entangled' with the outside world. Next to them are those who would like to reserve the course altogether. That kind of patriotism is nothing but a self-serving pursuit of one's own interests.

Clearly, as the Soviet Union proceeds with perestroika, its contribution to building a new world will become more constructive and significant. What we have done on the basis of new thinking has made it possible to channel international cooperation along new, peaceful lines. Over these years we have come a long way in the general political cooperation with the West. It stood a difficult test at a time of momentous change in Eastern Europe and of the search for a solution to the German problem. It has withstood the crushing stress of the crisis in the Persian Gulf. There is no doubt that this cooperation, which all of us need, will become more effective and indispensable if our economies become more integrated and start working more or less in synchronised rhythm.

To me, it is self-evident that if Soviet perestroika succeeds there will be a real chance of building a new world order. And if perestroika fails the prospect of entering a new peaceful period in history will vanish, at least for the foreseeable future.

I believe that the movement that we have launched towards that goal has fairly good prospects of success. After all, mankind has already benefited greatly in recent years, and this has created a certain positive momentum.

The cold war is over. The risk of a global nuclear war has practically disappeared. The Iron Curtain is gone. Germany has united, which is a momentous milestone in the history of Europe. There is not a single country on our continent which would not regard itself as fully sovereign and independent.

The USSR and the USA, the two nuclear superpowers, have moved from confrontation to interaction and, in some important cases, partnership. This has had a decisive effect on the entire international climate. This should be preserved and filled with new substance. The climate of Soviet-US trust should be protected, for it is a common asset of the world community. Any revision of the direction and potential of the Soviet-US relationship would have grave consequences for the entire global process.

The ideas of the Helsinki Final Act have begun to acquire real significance; they are being transformed into real policies and have found a more specific and topical expression in the Charter of Paris for a New Europe. Institutional forms of European security are beginning to take shape.

Real disarmament has begun. Its first phase is nearing completion, and following the signing – I hope shortly – of the START treaty, the time will come to give practical consideration to the ideas which have already been put forward for the future. There seems, however, to be a need to develop a general concept for this new phase, which would embrace all negotiations concerning the principal components of the problem of disarmament and new ideas reflecting the changes in Europe, the Middle East, Africa and Asia, a concept that would incorporate recent major initiatives of President Bush and President Mitterrand. We are now thinking about it.

Armed forces and military budgets are being reduced. Foreign troops are leaving the territories of other countries. Their strength is diminishing and their composition is becoming more defence-oriented. First steps have been taken in the conversion of military industries, and what seemed inconceivable is happening: recent cold war adversaries are establishing cooperation in this area. Their military officials exchange visits, show each other military facilities that only recently used to be top secret and together consider ways to achieve demilitarisation.

The information environment has changed beyond recognition throughout Europe and in most of the world, and with it the scale and intensity and the psychological atmosphere of communication among people of various countries.

De-ideologising relations among states, which we proclaimed as one of the principles of the new thinking, has brought down many prejudices, biased attitudes and suspicions and has cleared and improved the international atmosphere. I have to note, however, that this process has been more intensive and frank on our part than on the part of the West.

I dare say that the European process has already acquired elements of irreversibility, or at least that conflicts of a scale and nature that were typical of Europe for many centuries and particularly in the twentieth century have been ruled out.

Should it gain the necessary momentum, every nation and every country will have at their disposal in the foreseeable future the potential of a community of unprecedented strength, encompassing the entire upper tier of the globe, provided they make their own contribution.

In such a context, in the process of creating a new Europe, in which erstwhile 'curtains' and 'walls' will be forever relegated to the past and borders between states will lose their 'divisive' purpose, self-determination of sovereign nations will be realised in a completely different way.

However, our vision of the European space from the Atlantic to the Urals is not that of a closed system. Since it includes the Soviet Union, which reaches to the shores of the Pacific, and the transatlantic USA and Canada with inseparable links to the Old World, it goes beyond its nominal geographical boundaries.

The idea is not at all to consolidate a part of our civilisation on, so to say, a European platform versus the rest of the world. Suspicions of that kind do exist. But, on the contrary, the idea is to develop and build upon the momentum of integration in Europe, embodied politically in the Charter of Paris for the whole of Europe. This should be done in the context of common movement towards a new and peaceful period in world history, towards new interrelationship and integrity of mankind. As my friend Giulio Andreotti so aptly remarked recently in Moscow, 'East-West rapprochement alone is not enough for progress of the entire world towards peace. However, agreement between them is a great contribution to the common cause.' Asia, Africa, Latin America, the Near and Middle East, all of them, are to play a great role in this common cause whose prospects are difficult to forecast today.

The new integrity of the world, in our view, can be built only on the principles of the freedom of choice and balance of interests. Every state, and now also a number of existing or emerging regional interstate groups, have their own interests. They are all equal and deserve respect.

We consider it dangerously outdated when suspicions are aroused by, for instance, improved Soviet-Chinese or Soviet-German, German-French, Soviet-US or US-Indian relations, etc. In our times, good relations benefit all. Any worsening of relations anywhere is a common loss.

Progress towards the civilisation of the twenty-first century will certainly not be simple or easy. One cannot get rid overnight of the heavy legacy of the past or the dangers created in the post-war years. We are experiencing a turning point in international affairs and are only at the beginning of a new, and I hope mostly peaceful, lengthy period in the history of civilisation.

With less East-West confrontation, or even none at all, old contradictions resurface, which seemed of secondary importance compared to the threat of nuclear war. The melting ice of the cold war reveals old conflicts and claims, and entirely new problems accumulate rapidly.

We can already see many obstacles and dangers on the road to a lasting peace, including:

- Increased nationalism, separatism and disintegrational processes in a number of countries and regions.
- The growing gap in the level and quality of socio-economic development between 'rich' and 'poor' countries; dire consequences of the poverty of hundreds of millions of people, for whom informational transparency now makes it possible to see how people live in developed countries. Hence, the unprecedented passions and brutality and even fanaticism of mass protests. Poverty is also the breeding ground for the spread of terrorism and the emergence and persistence of dictatorial regimes with their unpredictable behaviour in relations among states.
- The dangerously rapid accumulation of the 'costs' of previous forms of progress, such as the threat of environmental catastrophe and of the depletion of energy and primary resources, uncontrollable overpopulation, pandemics, drug abuse, and so on.
- The gap between basically peaceful policies and selfish economies bent on achieving a kind of 'technological hegemony'. Unless those two vectors are brought together, civilisation will tend to break down into incompatible sectors.
- Further improvements in modern weaponry, even if under the pretext of strengthening security. This may result not only in a new spiral of the arms race and a perilous overabundance of arms in many states, but also in a final divorce between the process of disarmament and development, and, what is more, in an erosion of the foundations and criteria of the emerging new world politics.

How can the world community cope with all this? All these tasks are enormously complex. They cannot be postponed. Tomorrow may be too late.

I am convinced that in order to solve these problems there is no other way but to seek and implement entirely new forms of interaction. We are simply doomed to such interaction, or we shall be unable to consolidate positive trends which have emerged and are gaining strength, and which we simply must not sacrifice.

However, to accomplish this all members of the world community should resolutely discard old stereotypes and motivations nurtured by the cold war, and give up the habit of seeking each other's weak spots and exploiting them in their own interests. We have to respect the peculiarities and differences which will always exist, even when human rights and freedoms are observed throughout the world. I keep repeating that, with the end of confrontation, differences can be made a source of healthy competition, an important factor for progress. This is an incentive to study each other, to engage in exchanges, a prerequisite for the growth of mutual trust.

For knowledge and trust are the foundations of a new world order. Hence the necessity, in my view, to learn to forecast the course of events in various regions of the globe by pooling the efforts of scientists, philosophers and humanitarian thinkers within the UN framework. Policies, even the most prudent and precise, are made by man. We need maximum insurance to guarantee that decisions taken by members of the world community should not affect the security, sovereignty and vital interests of its other members or damage the natural environment and the moral climate of the world.

I am an optimist and I believe that together we shall be able now to make the right historical choice so as not to miss the great chance at the turn of centuries and millennia and make the current extremely difficult transition to a peaceful world order. A balance of interests rather than a balance of power, a search for compromise and concord rather than a search for advantages at other people's expense, and respect for equality rather than claims to leadership – such are the elements which can provide the groundwork for world progress and which should be readily acceptable for reasonable people informed by the experience of the twentieth century.

The future prospect of truly peaceful global politics lies in the creation through joint efforts of a single international democratic space in which states shall be guided by the priority of human rights and welfare for their own citizens and the promotion of the same rights and similar welfare elsewhere. This is an imperative of the growing integrity of the modern world and of the interdependence of its components.

I have been suspected of utopian thinking more than once, and particularly when five years ago I proposed the elimination of nuclear weapons by the year 2000 and joint efforts to create a system of international security. It may well be that by that date it will not have happened. But look, merely five years have passed and have we not actually and noticeably moved in that direction? Have we not been able to cross the threshold of mistrust, though mistrust has not completely disappeared? Has not the political thinking in the world changed substantially? Does not most of the world community already regard weapons of mass destruction as unacceptable for achieving political objectives?

Ladies and gentlemen, two weeks from today it will be exactly 50 years since the beginning of the Nazi invasion of my country. And in another six months we shall mark 50 years since Pearl Harbor, after which the war turned into a global tragedy. Memories of it still hurt. But they also urge us to value the chance given to the present generations.

In conclusion, let me say again that I view the award of the Nobel Prize to me as an expression of understanding of my intentions, my aspirations, the objectives of the profound transformation we have begun in our country, and the ideas of new thinking. I see it as your acknowledgment of my commitment to peaceful means of implementing the objectives of perestroika.

I am grateful for this to the members of the Committee and wish to assure them that if I understand correctly their motives they are not mistaken.

The year 1991 was tumultuous for the USSR and for Gorbachev. Having been unable to attend the actual award ceremony the previous year, this lecture was an important opportunity for Gorbachev to speak in depth about his vision for peace. He calls on the world not to miss the unique opportunity opened up by the end of the cold war to build a new world order based on values, trust and the balance of interests not balance of power. His faith in the need for new political thinking is unwavering, and at this watershed moment in history he hoped that solidarity and transformation would be embraced by the entire world as they faced new global challenges.

Gorbachev has been immensely disappointed that, after a brief 'honeymoon' period during the 1990s, new tensions and old misconceptions rose again and the peaceful, effective multilateral world order he envisaged has not yet become a reality. This Nobel message continues to form the backbone of his tireless, ongoing campaigns for peace.

Final Televised Address as President of the USSR

25 December 1991

Addressing you for the last time as President of the USSR, I find it necessary to state my position with regard to the path we have embarked upon since 1985 – especially since controversial, superficial and biased judgements abound.

Fate had decided that, when I became head of state, it was already obvious that there was something wrong in this country. We had plenty of everything – land, oil, gas and other natural resources – and God has also endowed us with intellect and talent, yet we lived much worse than people in other industrialised countries and the gap was constantly widening.

The reason was apparent even then – our society was stifled in the grip of a bureaucratic command system. Doomed to serve ideology and bear the heavy burden of the arms race, it was strained to the utmost.

All attempts at implementing half-hearted reforms – and there have been many – failed, one after the other. The country was losing hope. We could not go on living like this. We had to change everything radically.

For this reason, I never regretted that I did not use my position as General Secretary merely to 'reign' for a few years. This would have been irresponsible and immoral.

I understood that initiating reforms on such a large scale in a society like ours was a most difficult and risky undertaking. But even now, I am convinced that the democratic reforms started in the spring of 1985 were historically justified.

The process of renovating this country and bringing about fundamental changes in the international community proved to be much more complex than originally anticipated. However, let us acknowledge what has been achieved so far.

Society has acquired freedom; it has been freed politically and spiritually. And this is the most important achievement, which we have not fully come to grips with, in part because we still have not learned how to use our freedom. However, a historic task has been accomplished:

- The totalitarian system, which prevented this country from becoming wealthy and prosperous a long time ago, has been dismantled.

- A breakthrough has been made on the road to democratic reforms. Free elections, freedom of the press, freedom of worship, representative legislatures, and a multi-party system have all become realities.
- We have set out to introduce a pluralistic economy, and the equality of all forms of ownership is being established. In the course of the land reform, the peasantry is reviving, individual farmers have appeared and millions of hectares of land have been allocated to urban and rural population. Laws were passed on the economic freedom of producers, and free enterprise, shareholding and privatisation are under way.
- Shifting the course of our economy towards a free market, we must not forget that this is being done for the benefit of the individual. In these times of hardship, everything must be done to ensure the social protection of the individual – particularly old people and children.

We live in a new world:

- An end has been put to the cold war, the arms race and the insane militarisation of our country, which crippled our economy, distorted our thinking and undermined our morals. The threat of a world war is no more. Once again, I should like to stress that I have done everything in my power during the transition period to ensure safe control over nuclear weapons.
- We opened ourselves up to the rest of the world, renounced interference in the affairs of others and the use of troops beyond our borders. In response, we have gained trust, solidarity and respect.
- We have become a major stronghold for the reorganisation of modern civilisation on the basis of peaceful, democratic principles.
- The peoples and nations of this country have acquired genuine freedom to choose their own way towards self-determination. The quest for a democratic reform of our multinational state has led us to the point where we were about to sign a new Union treaty.

All these changes demanded the utmost exertion and were carried through under the conditions of an unrelenting struggle against the growing resistance from the old, obsolete and reactionary forces – the former Party and state structures and the economic management apparatus – as well as our patterns, our ideological prejudices, our egalitarian and parasitic psychology. The change ran up against our intolerance, a low level of political culture and a fear of change. That is

why we have wasted so much time. The old system tumbled down before the new one could begin functioning. And our society slid into an even deeper crisis.

I am aware of the dissatisfaction with today's grave situation, the harsh criticisms of the authorities at all levels and of my personal role. But I would like to stress once again: in so vast a country, given its heritage, fundamental changes cannot be carried out without difficulties and pain.

The August coup brought the overall crisis to a breaking point. The most disastrous aspect of this crisis is the collapse of statehood. And today I watch apprehensively the loss of the citizenship of a great country by our citizens – the consequences of this could be grave, for all of us.

I consider it vitally important to sustain the democratic achievements of the last few years. We have earned them through the suffering of our entire history and our tragic experience. We must not abandon them under any circumstances, under any pretext. Otherwise, all our hopes for a better future will be buried.

I am speaking of this frankly and honestly. It is my moral duty.

Today I want to express my gratitude to all those citizens who have given their support to the policy of renovating this country and who participated in the democratic reforms.

I am thankful to statesmen, political and public leaders and millions of ordinary people in other countries – to all those who understood our objectives and gave us their support, meeting us halfway and offering genuine cooperation.

I leave my post with concern – but also with hope, with faith in you, your wisdom and spiritual strength. We are the heirs of a great civilisation, and its revival and transformation to a modern and dignified life depend on all and everyone.

I would like to express my heartfelt thanks to those who stood by my side, defending the right and good cause over all these years. We certainly could have avoided certain errors and done better in many ways. But I am convinced that, sooner or later, our common efforts will bear fruit and our peoples will live in a prosperous and democratic society.

I wish all the best to everyone.

On 26 December 1991 the USSR ceased to exist. An agreement between the leaders of the Russian Federation, Belarus and the Ukraine to create the Confederation of Independent States effectively dissolved the Soviet Union, and led to Gorbachev stepping down as its President. With this public statement Gorbachev left a 'political will' to his successors, urging them to continue to transform the country into a true democracy and lead the transition to a new world order. It was also a message to Russian citizens to be proud of the achievements of the end of the cold war and the new freedoms and opportunities they have acquired, and to keep faith in the democratisation process no matter how painful.

This process is still under way in Russia today and has faced many problems in the past 20 years, including the growing gap between rich and poor, privatisation of natural resources, organised crime, conflicts in Chechnya and Georgia, terrorism, and new restrictions on freedom of expression and the media. The road to freedom has never been smooth. And Gorbachev, having reached 80, is still not ready to give up responding to standard questions about his role in history with the words 'Don't consign me to history!'

Speech at the Opening of the Fourth International Global Forum of Spiritual and Parliamentary Leaders

Kyoto, Japan, 20 April 1993

Distinguished members of the Presidium and distinguished delegates to the Global Forum, I would like to welcome all of you who have gathered here in the wonderful city of Kyoto, a city that is now in bloom. The cherry blossoms are a reminder to all of us that we have met at a time when people are inspired by new hopes – when they are thinking about a better tomorrow. I am sure that from Kyoto will be heard not only the voice of wisdom and the voice of concern but also the voice of hope.

I thank you for all your words of welcome and greetings addressed to me, and also to the members of the Board of Trustees who have gathered, responding to your appeal, in order to launch here at the Global Forum, after long preparation, a new global organisation – the International Green Cross. As you can see, the baby has been born on time, in term, exactly nine months after you called last June for the creation of this organisation. I thank you for your congratulations, and I hope we will be working together, hand in hand, thinking about our common future and looking for answers to the most difficult questions that we must face.

The theme of my speech today is the values and the imperatives of the philosophy of survival.

Today, everyone seems to agree that mankind is at a watershed in its history. The present-day global landscape is one of profound crisis, which could end either in the death of humankind or in the breakthrough to a new civilisation. The one that has existed for many centuries is close to exhausting its potential, unable to sustain and manage life on planet Earth.

It is true that a crisis of civilisation was announced many times in the past. But today's crisis is qualitatively different. This time, we are speaking not just about something that causes widespread malaise or about people's protest against inhuman conditions of their existence, but about a threat – for the first time ever – to the very existence of the human race.

Of late, tensions between man and nature have degenerated into an outright conflict between them. A real threat has emerged that could threaten the very foundations of human existence, threatening life on nationalisation of the economy, we are witnessing an unprecedented outbreak of nationalism and clear tendencies towards autarchy, separatism and ethnic and religious isolation. The most archaic syndromes are resurfacing, bringing to the fore hidden ethnic conflicts accompanied by violence and unprecedented cruelty.

We have so far failed to find ways of harmonising the principles that form the basics of international relations. We have yet to develop mechanisms of harmonising the democratic principle of state self-determination of nations and the fundamental principle of international relations, that of the inviolability of borders, of the integrity of existing states.

All too often, the idea of development, of progress, conflicts with the need to preserve our planet, to assure mankind's survival. The idea of cooperation, of working together, often conflicts with the instinct of rivalry. Too often, modern nations, in pursuing their selfish aims, undermine the global conditions necessary for life on Earth – thus bringing closer their own destruction.

There is no doubt that the liberation from communist totalitarianism and the end of the cold war were great blessings, for they have significantly reduced the threat of nuclear catastrophe. But we have to see that even this great event of the twentieth century – the end of the cold war – has not diminished conflicts and tensions in the world.

In Russia and in many countries of Eastern Europe, we can see an abrupt swing to the right in social attitudes, a growth of nationalistic sentiments, and increasing influence of fundamentalism in its various forms. Conflicts of one kind are being replaced by new conflicts, underscoring even more dramatically how little we know about society and about humankind.

It has now become clear that the death of totalitarianism, in and of itself, does not lead to democracy. People who fought against totalitarianism have not always proved capable of strengthening and nourishing democracy.

Political freedom is of the greatest value. But our experience has also shown that the growth of freedom, in and of itself, does not automatically result in a growth of morality, in ennobling the motives of people's behaviour. The world community must see, for example, that the breakup of the Soviet Union has resulted in the aggravation of crime-causing factors in CIS countries, in an explosion of crime and drug addiction in Russia. We have come face to face with phenomena whose nature we find hard to understand.

Overall, we can say that the current crisis of the natural environment and of the entire human civilisation is taking place against the background of the crisis of traditional methods of resolving social tensions. Social sciences and, even more, political thinking are still not free from ideological preferences and bias; we are still going around in a vicious circle based on attitudes of class, nation and state, and even partisan attitudes.

So what is the way out? What should we rely on in our efforts to assure the survival of mankind?

The first and most important conclusion is obvious. When science and reason cannot help, there is only one thing that can save us – our conscience, our morality. There is a need for moral strengthening of the roots of the humanism of the eighteenth century, which provides most of the underpinnings of our contemporary civilisation.

The survival of humankind will be impossible without solidifying and insisting on a simple thought: life as such is the greatest moral value which should underlie modern civilisation. Today, it is not enough to say, 'Thou shall not kill.' Ecological education implies, above all, respect and love for every living being. It is here that ecological culture interfaces with religion.

Another important thought that was present during our meetings here is that the beauty and uniqueness of life have as their foundation unity in diversity. The self-identification of every individual and of the many different nations, ethnic groups and nationalities is the crucial condition for preserving life on Earth.

Gorbachev with the founder of GC Russia, the late Nikita Moiseev

The philosophy of survival rests upon the philosophy of diversity. If life itself is the greatest value, then of no less value is the special character of every nation and every race as a unique creation of nature and of human history.

We must abandon the philosophy and the imperatives of man conquering nature, which nourished modern industrial civilisation, in favour of a philosophy of limits, which makes us wake up and see the abyss of probable disaster. We need a philosophy that curbs man's pride and passions. At present, it is not enough to insist on what is already obvious – the organic unity of mankind and nature. Today we must make sure that Kant's moral imperative is applied to man's attitude towards life and nature. Even in his thoughts, man must not wish for nature what he does not wish for himself.

No man has the right to live and enjoy life at the expense of others. Man has no right to see well-being at the expense of poor, developing nations or big nations at the expense of small ones. But the most important thing is that man must not live at the expense of nature, for when we plunder nature we steal from ourselves.

The time has come to formulate the conditions of the ecological imperative – to draw a line which mankind must not cross under any circumstances. If the human race proves capable of fulfilling these conditions, then it will have a chance to refashion its niche in the environment and to adjust its way of life to the needs of the environment.

The ecology of moral and spiritual health presupposes an absolute rejection of racism, chauvinism and national arrogance in any form.

Today, it is not enough to understand that man is an element of nature and that his destiny depends on a reasonable coexistence with nature. We must also understand that there are certain things that man cannot accomplish in principle. During our meetings, we spoke at length about the need to change motivation, to shift the emphasis from technological to spiritual progress. Another important goal is to improve our way of life so as to resist consumerism. But at the same time, we have no right to demand the impossible – the slogan of changing human nature is no less destructive than the slogan of man conquering nature.

Today, a caring attitude towards nature implies, above all, a caring attitude towards man with all his contradictory passions, strengths and weaknesses. Yes, we must understand human nature in order to live in harmony with ourselves and improve ourselves. But we must not try to recast or remould it; we must not seek the impossible. The idea of man as a kind of deity is one of the most dangerous and fateful ideas.

In conclusion, let me refer to some organisational aspects of our work. First of all, it is quite clear from what I have just said that we need a purposeful programme of studies that would enable us to define much more fully and precisely a set of values and imperatives underlying the philosophy of survival. We have to be aware from the outset of the unique complexity of this task. Research of this kind should be of interest and concern not only to scientists but also to policy-makers.

We need to identify value goals relevant not only to the environmental movements but also to policy-makers and international organisations. We cannot lay claim to the role of world government. But it is our duty to clarify for mankind the evolving environmental situation and to reveal the zones that are off limits to human activity.

The scope of such research should go beyond purely academic interests. It should be similar to the kind of programme that the international community is trying to implement in the area of disarmament, the elimination of nuclear weapons and nuclear safety.

Political leaders must begin to assume that the issues of the harmonious development of mankind and of the rest of the biosphere will become part of their duties. The environment will increasingly become a matter of the highest priority in foreign as well as domestic policies. The main efforts in the environmental area should be implemented at the international level. Many environmental problems can only be solved through joint efforts of all countries. Furthermore, states must bear moral, legal and financial responsibility depending on whether they understand the meaning of the ecological imperative and whether they are addressing local environmental problems in the context of the problems of overall human survival.

Our research must be largely independent of governments, whose actions inevitably carry the element of national selfishness. We need objective knowledge, objective information not affected by changing political winds. Those who pursue this knowledge should be independent of national, religious, geographic and other constraints. They must be responsible to humankind as a whole.

To affirm a new morality, we have at our disposal some effective means of education and training. At their basis lies knowledge anchored in credible information and in the cultural context of our time. Mankind must find enough courage to change the way it educates young people, to instil new literacy, a new language for communicating with nature and new meanings of traditional concepts.

Here we will have to begin many things from scratch. We need to immediately launch a competition for a high school ecology textbook and to train teachers in the area. Another extremely important task is to create a global network linking the world's environmental organisations.

The emerging 'environmentalisation' of our civilisation and the need for vigorous action in the interest of the entire global community will inevitably have multiple political consequences. Perhaps the most important one of them will be a gradual change in the status of the United Nations. Inevitably, it must assume some aspects of a world government. Indeed, such a process has already begun. One day, however, the entire structure of the organisation will have to be reconsidered.

The twentieth century has been, in effect, a century of warning. Due to the logic of historic development, its vocation was to caution mankind and to prepare it for the need to develop a new consciousness and new ways of living and acting. Has it fulfilled this role? No, at least not completely.

To repeat, the twentieth century will become either a century of the extreme aggravation of the deadly crisis or one of mankind's recovery and revival. At present, we are running a race against time. What will happen next – a critical escalation of global threats and the collapse of our civilisation or a critical growth of hope, of the willingness and ability of the international human community to develop new, truly humane ground rules of living together, capable of saving civilisation through its renewal?

It is up to all of us who live today on this planet to answer this question.

Kyoto 1993 saw the birth of Green Cross International, today a strong organisation with affiliates in over 30 countries and programmes on all continents. While the activities of GCI have responded to changing global and regional threats – water conflicts, energy crisis, climate change – the mission has continued to be guided by these inaugural words of its Founding President, to help build a harmonious relationship between humankind and nature.

The global financial crisis and ever more urgent threat – and reality – of climate change has today brought this challenge to the political forefront, and citizens around the world are considering the very choices posed by Gorbachev in 1993: consumption and unchecked growth leading to disaster, or respect for the limits of nature.

What Made Me a Crusader

Time magazine special issue: Our Precious Planet, November 1997

I'm often asked why I lead the International Green Cross. And the first question is always about the 1986 nuclear accident at Chernobyl: was that disaster the defining moment for my concern about ecological issues?

Chernobyl did have a tremendous impact on my thinking about the environment and nuclear weapons. But my understanding of the importance of the natural environment came much earlier. I am of peasant stock, and as a young man I worked on a collective farm in Stavropol. A large part of my life was spent on the land. I saw the effects of such problems as soil erosion, the spread of the deserts, and air and water pollution. I saw that man's intrusions in nature were often imprudent and harmful to man himself. Acting as the master and even king of nature, man gave no thought to the consequences. But the consequences came without fail – at once or a little later.

When I came to Moscow in the late 1970s, I learned even more. As a secretary of the Central Committee and member of the Supreme Soviet working for the natural resources commission, I saw how hasty construction and wasteful operation of huge irrigation systems blighted the Central Asian region, destroying the Aral Sea and depleting the rivers Syr Darya and Amu Darya. In Russia, hydroelectric projects built with little thought for their consequences flooded millions of hectares of fertile land. A similarly careless approach to locating industrial projects jeopardised Lake Baikal, the world's largest body of fresh water.

Alas, man does not always learn from his mistakes. I was involved in the debate over redirecting the waters of Russia's northern rivers to the south.

Our reform policies – perestroika – gave scientists and activists a chance to challenge this project and show that it would not work. That put a stop to it.

And then came the thunder of Chernobyl. During that accident's first days, many scientists – even some respected ones – argued that it was 'no big deal', that we would get by. From day one, however, it was our policy to get to the bottom of it. We decided that people must know the truth. The power of the atom had gone out of control, and it took the

Gorbachev speaking at the Green Cross General Assembly in 1998 in Kyoto, Japan

nation's supreme effort to cope with it. It was a watershed in our understanding of many things.

The new era of glasnost and free speech brought people's concerns out into the open. Protests led to the emergence of a grass-roots environmental movement, which made us review a number of decisions taken previously – not just on constructing new nuclear power plants but also on other projects that threatened the environment. In the late 1980s, the reformist government agreed to close hundreds of industrial facilities, despite the impact on the economy.

When I came to the United Nations in October 1988, I brought a package of environmental initiatives. One of them called for creating a global non-governmental organisation to help save the environment. Named the International Green Cross, at my suggestion, it is based near Geneva and has affiliates in dozens of countries. Our main goal is to help set in motion a value shift in people's minds. Our environmental education programmes, in cooperation with the UN Educational, Scientific and Cultural Organisation and several governments, aim at helping people understand a simple truth: man is not the master of nature but just a part of it. After all, the environment has existed for millions of years without man and could, *in extremis*, do so again. So this is the challenge: we need environmentally sustainable development if new generations are to succeed us on earth.

Modern civilisation has given decent living standards to people in advanced Western nations. But how do we assure economic well-being and human dignity for the rest of mankind without ruining the environment? This problem has no purely technological solution. A political and moral choice will have to be made.

Green Cross organisations are developing specific programmes of 'environmental healing'. Among the most important is Legacy, an educational project that addresses the environmental consequences of the cold war, including the discharge of toxic wastes by military bases and the stockpiling of chemical weapons. Another research initiative concerns a problem at the intersections of ecology, economics and politics: the issue of fresh water. We recently brought to Geneva a group of water experts, many of whom predicted that this diminishing resource may ignite some of the next century's most dangerous conflicts.

The Green Cross is off to a good start, but the more I think about it, the more I realise that we are just at the beginning of the road. Last March I attended a conference in Rio de Janeiro that took stock of what has happened in the five years since the Earth Summit.

There is very little to cheer. Governments are in no hurry to implement even the modest pledges made in 1992, even though the time we have to transform our way of living is quickly shrinking. Still, I remain an optimist. I reject defeatism and frustration. But I also reject the view that things will somehow work themselves out. I am convinced that mankind can meet the environmental challenge if all of us join this cause, if all of us act.

© *TIME* Magazine

Ten years after the Chernobyl nuclear accident, Gorbachev is disappointed with the pace of development of alternative energy sources. Five years after the Rio Earth Summit, he is appalled by the lack of action in implementing its pledges. Gorbachev and GCI worked around the world to combat the global apathy and inertia that threatened to block the path to sustainable development. Fortunately, the international community rallied again and in 2000 committed to the visionary Millennium Development Goals, setting ambitious new strategies for combating poverty and environmental destruction by 2015. But, as usual, for Gorbachev words are not enough: with less than five years remaining to meet the MDGs on schedule he is adamant that there can be no excuse for breaking this promise to the world's poor, and that human values and solidarity must prevail.

Nature Will Not Wait

World Watch magazine, March–April 2001

The fall of the Berlin Wall and the political storm that swept across the world a little over a decade ago was above all else a testament to the power of the human spirit to tackle adversity. The cold war had posed a threat to security, liberty and development everywhere, creating a seemingly insurmountable barrier between the peoples of the planet. Yet the right mixture of human vision and courageous leadership brought this dark period in our history to a peaceful end. Today we are faced with another threat, already the cause of great suffering for millions: the degradation of the environment. To meet this global challenge we again need a clear and unified vision, determination and decisive leadership.

The impact and forecasts of global warming are worsening, desertification is advancing, deforestation and pollution are endangering our ecosystems; and more than 1.2 billion people do not have access to clean drinking water. We have seen environmental disasters with untold destruction of both human lives and nature: in the short term, during the past months there have been devastating floods across much of Europe and South Asia and the wreck of tankers off the natural treasures of the Galapagos Islands and Australian barrier reef; in the long term, vast areas of the Earth have been irrevocably scarred by the loss of ancient forests, mismanagement of river basins and contamination.

Many environmental experts warn these trends are now far too advanced for us to achieve real sustainability by means of gradual change; they believe we have 30 to 40 years in which to act. Time is short and we are already lagging behind.

While there are an increasing number of bold initiatives led by government and corporate leaders to protect the environment, I do not see emerging the leadership and willingness to take risks at the scale we need to confront the current situation. While there are an increasing number of people and organisations dedicated to raising awareness and provoking change in the way we treat nature, I do not yet see the clear vision and united front which will inspire humankind to respond in time to correct our course.

The example of the failure of leadership at the climate change talks in The Hague last November is disturbing. This failure lies at the hands of our political leaders, particularly the United States which has not yet even ratified the Kyoto Treaty, and, to a lesser extent, the business community which has increasing influence over government policies. Another worrying example of how we are going about things the wrong way is the increasingly closed nature of the annual World Economic Forum in Davos isolating delegates and pushing other interest groups further from the mainstream. In The Hague and in Davos we saw divisions into camps: North versus South, and pro- versus anti-'globalisationists'.

This is a very grave situation. It is critical that we find a way to bring about rapid, sweeping change of human consciousness and actions worldwide – something that enables us to provoke a large-scale shift of course in a very short time. This cannot be achieved if we remain divided.

The end of the cold war offers an example of people-powered change that positively altered the course of history. We need a similar shift – a fundamental shift in values – to ensure that we do not miss this window of opportunity to save our beautiful planet, and ourselves. First among the threats we must face are those posed by nuclear and other weapons of mass destruction, the freshwater crisis, and the impact of climate change.

A new way of thinking, a new world order that is based more on justice and equality and less on profits is needed. We thought the fall of the Berlin Wall would usher this in, but instead a more complicated world has resulted and, more worrying still, we are now even seeing signs of resurgence in militarisation.

What can be done? What kind of leadership do we need? I consider five points to be vital in this respect:

1. Reform the UN system in order to give more power for actions and the enforcement of UN decisions for peace and stability.
2. International Agreements, Conventions and Protocols relevant to disarmament, climate change, biodiversity, desertification, international watercourses, and others should be ratified without delay, and implemented with courage and determination.
3. Environmental objectives should be integrated from the beginning into development planning and any form of economic activity.
4. Political leaders – and businesses – should acknowledge and act on their responsibility to turn rhetoric into action and achieve environmental compliance.

5. Reverse the decline of international development, allowing developing nations to reduce their crippling debt, cover basic human needs, and access technologies to use materials and energy efficiently, with a minimum of waste.

If nothing is done to achieve sustainability in the first part of this new century, the prospects for humankind's survival will diminish. Still, if I thought it were hopeless, I would not join you in the environmental movement as President of Green Cross International.

Nature is giving us all the signs we need to develop a common vision for the future; we must grasp this message and act now. Governments, individuals and business – let us move together, with bold leadership, to solve the environmental crisis. Nature will not wait.

© *World Watch* magazine

Although armed with the common vision of the Millennium Development Goals, the world in 2001 was increasingly divided between 'North' and 'South', and the barriers at G8 and WTO summits were growing ever higher as the anti-globalisation movement gained strength. Gorbachev was concerned that these tensions were hindering the action so desperately needed to achieve sustainable development. Six months after this article was written, the September 11 terrorist attacks in the USA resonated around the world, deepening divisions and bringing new threats to the forefront. Security, rather than sustainability, became the absolute focus, particularly in the USA.

But, faltering multilateral processes were contrasted by a huge surge in support for addressing sustainable development, climate change and the fight against poverty amongst citizens all over the world. In the age of mass communication, world public opinion truly became a power in its own right, echoing Gorbachev's message that neither nature nor the world's poor, could wait.

A World Free of Weapons of Mass Destruction

The Most Burning Issue on Earth

Mikhail Gorbachev has always been serious about disarmament. As early as 1984, before he assumed the leadership of the Soviet Union, in an address to the UK Parliament Gorbachev declared: 'The nuclear age inevitably dictates new political thinking. Preventing nuclear war is the most burning issue for all people on Earth.'

Once he became Soviet leader in 1985, Gorbachev stepped up his attack on nuclear weapons; though his position was considered by many to be utopian, his approach was entirely pragmatic and determined. Faced with the 'self-destruction of the human race', he stressed that it was time to 'burn the black book of nuclear alchemy' and make the next century one 'of life without fear of universal death'. The 'nuclear era requires new thinking from everybody', he argued and 'the backbone of the new way of thinking is . . . humankind's survival'. Gorbachev's ideas resonated with the tumultuous popular campaign against nuclear weapons that was sweeping around the world during the 1980s, lending political credibility and weight to a position at the time considered by many nothing but a utopian pipe dream.

Gorbachev not only changed Soviet rhetoric, but Soviet policy. He appointed sharp critics of the nuclear arms race as his key advisors on foreign and military affairs. In April 1985, he announced the cessation of the controversial SS-20 nuclear missile deployments in the Soviet Union and Eastern Europe. That July, he proclaimed a unilateral Soviet moratorium on nuclear testing and implored the US Government to join it. By early 1986, this 'new thinking' had produced a Soviet blueprint for a nuclear-free future. Announced by Gorbachev on 15 January of that year, it consisted of a three-stage plan to eliminate all nuclear weapons around the globe by the year 2000. This was not 'another Soviet propaganda trick' but a sincere effort to prevent nuclear war and create a peaceful world.

Given that Gorbachev's activity on arms control and disarmament while in office is well documented, this section covers his more recent statements in this area.

The Importance of Chemical Weapons Abolition

Address at the Geneva Forum on the Worldwide Destruction of
Chemical Weapons, Palais des Nations, Geneva, 26 June 2003

I am pleased to share this morning's panel with Mayor Andre Hediger and
Council President Laurent Moutinot of Geneva, and with Director-
General Rogelio Pfirter from the Organisation for Prohibition of
Chemical Weapons in The Hague. Let me briefly make several key points.

First, our mutual goal to abolish chemical weapons is a very important and historic prize which we must not lose sight of as we debate all of
the implementation challenges we face every day. Recall the shocking
pictures we have all seen of the Kurdish victims of chemical attack in
Hala, Iraq, in 1988, or the terror on the faces of the Japanese victims of
the 1995 terrorist nerve agent attack on the Tokyo subway. We cannot
and will not allow these horrific attacks to happen again.

We all have a mission, and that is to prevent the use of chemical
weapons from ever again being used in either warfare or terrorist attacks
anywhere in the world. This is a formidable goal, and one that will take a
great deal of time and money. But, with the signing of the Chemical
Weapons Convention in 1993, about which my colleague Rogelio Pfirter
will speak more, we have truly begun the process of making this whole
class of inhumane weapons of mass destruction globally taboo.

Second, Russia is fully committed to abolishing its 40,000 tonnes of
chemical weapons but the country very much needs financial and
technical support from the United States and the West. The commitment of the USA eight years ago to fully fund the design and construction of a nerve agent destruction facility at Shchuch'ye in the Kurgan
Oblast was a breakthrough in the Russian chemical weapons demilitarisation programme. I know that my Green Cross colleague Paul
Walker was on the 1994 congressional delegation which visited Moscow, Kurgan and Shchuch'ye and performed an on-site inspection of the
Shchuch'ye stockpile. The Assistant to the Secretary of Defence, Dr
Harold Smith, promised Russia on that trip that the USA would follow
through with this important project. This commitment, estimated at
almost 900 million US dollars, is a central and essential part of the entire
global abolition campaign. Germany's help in constructing the first
Russian chemical weapons destruction facility at Gorny in the Saratov
Oblast has likewise been a vital part of the Russian programme.

But the whole chemical weapons programme in Russia is likely to cost upwards of 6 billion dollars according to current estimates. This means that Russia and other donor nations must contribute some 5 billion dollars over the coming decade. I realise that this will not be easy, but the commitments by the G8 members and other countries of some 20 billion dollars overall for disarmament will certainly meet this need to a large extent. And Russia has itself increased its commitment to weapons destruction, including chemical weapons, over the past two years.

I thank you all for your ongoing pledges to nuclear, chemical and biological weapons destruction programmes in Russia. I am well aware of the work of Italy and the United Kingdom on infrastructure projects at Shchuch'ye, the potential commitments of Canada and Switzerland to Shchuch'ye, and the pledge of Germany to help with Kambarka. You all deserve much credit for this timely international campaign and I am delighted that Green Cross can work with you all.

Third, we must take a comprehensive approach to weapons destruction projects if they are to be truly successful. These weapon destruction projects are for the most part very large, expensive facilities with potentially large socio-economic impacts on local communities and regions. They are also being constructed in formerly secret cities and restricted areas, which have had little investment or development outside of cold war weapons projects, and remain suspicious and mistrusting of both Russian federal officials and foreign governments.

We must therefore be careful to approach these projects, for example, the billion-dollar investment in the Siberian region of Shchuch'ye and neighbouring villages, with a sensitivity and commitment to the needs of the local community. These Russian citizens have lived with the local 'monkey on their back', in this case 5400 tonnes of chemical weapons in two million artillery shells and 760 short-range missile warheads, for decades and now expect that there will be some daylight in community development.

We learned an expensive and tough lesson at Chapeyevsk in 1989 when local factories went on strike simultaneously and over 7000 citizens mobilised at the front gates of a military base to block the opening of a new, centralised chemical weapons destruction facility. The Soviet Ministry of Defence made the strategic error of not involving the public in any serious consideration of this project, nor had they tried to help the local community. To this day, this first facility is used only for training and will never be able to handle chemical weapons destruction activities.

We also learned the hard way most recently in Votkinsk, a 200 million dollars project in the Udmurt Republic to destroy strategic missiles. After almost 100 million dollars had been spent on preconstruction, engineering and design activities, the project was cancelled due to lack of land allocation by local authorities. And local and regional authorities balked because of lack of any investment by either Moscow or Washington in the local community. So, for want of one million or less in community investment, we lost 100 times that amount.

While, on the one hand, these public and community issues can be frustrating for project construction engineers and managers, I am happy to say that they reflect the emerging democratic voice of Russian society. Glasnost and perestroika have clearly unlocked public demands for a voice in major decisions, not unlike what we see in the West. We need to applaud these social movements in the direction of civil society, rule of law, public involvement and democratic decision-making processes, rather than oppose them, and make good use of them in our projects.

In practice, what this means is that our weapons destruction projects – whether nuclear submarine decommissioning in the Barents Sea, fissile material storage at Mayak, missile destruction in Udmurtia or the Altay Kray or chemical weapons destruction in Kambarka, Shchuch'ye, Kizner, or elsewhere – must take into account the need to help local communities actively participate, and to create sustainable economies so that the projects turn into win-win efforts rather than 'boom and bust' cycles.

While it may be easy for foreign politicians to say that such work – public involvement, infrastructure investment and local community development – should be a Russian responsibility, in reality we must ask ourselves what it takes to make these important projects successful. If it requires, which it usually does, a few per cent of total project costs in local investment, and another few per cent in public facilitation, is this too high a price to pay for eliminating thousands or even millions of weapons of mass destruction?

Fourth, we all must overcome political and bureaucratic obstacles to our larger goals of safe and sound weapons destruction. When one puts together multiple projects, each involving international, national, regional and local levels of politics, each involving multiple donors and funding mechanisms, each involving high risk processes which place the environment and public health at risk, and each embedded in old cold war stereotypes and ideologies, we have to recognise that there is a compelling need to keep our eyes on the ultimate prize – the destruction of dangerous weapons.

I might cite, for example, the dozen or more US congressional conditions that have been placed on Cooperative Threat Reduction monies over the past few years. While I am sympathetic with countries wanting accountability on their investments, I am not supportive of linking weapons destruction projects with broad political criteria. For example, one US condition on CTR monies states that the US President must certify to Congress annually that Russia is abiding by all human rights treaties; another requires presidential certification that Russia is abiding by all arms control treaties. While we all support national adherence to international norms and conventions, certainly on human rights and arms control, these broad conditions remain open to political interpretation and abuse. In practice, they have served only to disrupt the timely implementation of cost-efficient CTR projects, annoyed Russian ministries and officials, and have not had the intended policy impacts on Russia.

More recent conditions placed on CTR support for the chemical weapons destruction project at Shchuch'ye have unnecessarily stalled construction funds for two years. It is frustrating to me that, on the one hand, one would promote an accelerated destruction schedule for Russian chemical weapons and, on the other hand, curtail or constrain funding for the project. The recent congressional condition, for example, that the US Defence Secretary certify annually to Congress that Russia has 'fully and accurately' declared the size of its chemical weapons stockpile seeks to undermine the partnership that Russia and the United States has built over the past decade.

Should there be questions about the size and location of Russian chemical weapons, beyond the seven declared stockpiles, there are other diplomatic venues, both bilateral and multilateral, including OPCW inspections, which afford productive discussions and resolutions. To stall the destruction of millions of nerve agent artillery shells, vulnerable to theft and diversion, on the Kazakhstan border is the height of folly. Who will take responsibility for the deaths of innocent citizens if one of these weapons winds up in terrorist hands, perhaps because we failed to destroy or secure them in time?

I am grateful to President Bush, and to other CTR advocates such as Senator Richard Lugar and former Senator Sam Nunn, for waiving these inappropriately linked congressional conditions last year and thus freeing up 160 million US dollars in construction funds for Shchuch'ye just three months ago. I also congratulate them for opposing new congressional conditions and CTR funding cuts which came out of the

other states and terrorists, we must also work, as pledged in several internationally binding treaties, to destroy existing arsenals. This discriminatory structure cannot continue much longer without recognising its natural consequences – 'have-nots' will want to become 'haves', more than likely at the expense of global security.

The signing and entry into force of the Chemical Weapons Convention was a major step in the right direction. Two more nations have just acceded to the Convention this month, now totalling 153 state parties. This is an enormous accomplishment and I am delighted to have the OPCW Director-General Rogelio Pfirter here with us today. But 43 nations still remain outside of the Convention. These include North Korea, Egypt, Iraq, Lebanon, Libya, Somalia, Syria and Israel. I know that the recent Five-Year Review Conference in The Hague reiterated the importance of universality, that is, the need to convince these non-member states to join. I must especially emphasise the need for the Middle East, on the heels of the Iraq War, to become a chemical weapons free region and wish Mr Pfirter and his OPCW colleagues good luck in bringing these countries fully on board.

But we must not only outlaw weapons of mass destruction; we must engage in the tough business of safely destroying them. I fully support these efforts, and thank you all for your time, energy and financial support in pursuit of this goal. We just last month celebrated the tenth anniversary of Green Cross, which I and other colleagues founded in 1993, and we were pleased to note that some 8000 tonnes of chemical weapons have been destroyed to date. I hope in another ten years, when we celebrate our twentieth anniversary, that the remaining 64,000 tonnes are also gone and we have 196 parties to the CWC.

In the year following this speech, Mikhail Gorbachev personally spearheaded the Green Cross 'Destroy Chemical Weapons, Now!' campaign, addressing special sessions of many parliaments – including the UK, French and European – and writing and appealing directly to heads of state. The – at the time – stalled process was subsequently unblocked and the implementation of the Chemical Weapons Convention was given far higher priority. The world continues to benefit from the reinvigoration of this key disarmament objective. In November 2010, Russia opened its sixth major CW destruction facility and announced that it had eliminated half of its stockpile; the United States has destroyed 80 per cent of its chemical weapons to date; there are 188 state parties to the CWC. The work of Green Cross continues.

Message Sent to the Second Rally for International Disarmament: Nuclear, Biological and Chemical

Saintes, France, 6–8 May 2006

I wish to commend the organisers of this event for raising awareness about one of the most acute challenges of our time: ensuring global security – a challenge that cannot be successfully realised without the elimination of the world's nuclear, biological and chemical weapons.

Humankind has a unique opportunity to make the twenty-first century one of peace and security. The true 'peace dividend', opened up to us by the end of the cold war some 20 years ago, provided a new-found freedom to turn from containment and confrontation to consultation and cooperation. Together, we must not waste but rather seize this occasion.

Yet force and threats continuously retort as instruments of foreign policy, particularly among 'nuclear club' member states. Within the international arena, obsolete double standard politics are increasingly gaining a stronger ground. Why, for example, do Russia and the United States still maintain thousands of nuclear warheads on constant alert, pointed at one another from across the globe, when we are now allies and partners? Why do we continue to spend tens of billions of dollars annually on nuclear weapons, but are trying to convince North Korea, Iran and other countries not to build their own nuclear weapons? Why does the Moscow Treaty, signed several years ago by Russia and the USA, propose such a slow drawdown in nuclear weapons that it will take until 2012 – another six years or more – to significantly reduce our strategic nuclear arsenals?

It is clear that global security requires new thinking, free from outmoded military planning and the animosities of the past. Modern international relations can no longer be based on the conventional principle of balance of power, but must be reoriented towards a balance of interests, deeply engaged in an active dialogue between cultures and civilisations. Politics must concentrate on avenues of cooperation and ways to break through deadlocks by promoting just, sustainable and real-world solutions, rather than quick fixes or inequitable compromises.

The danger of a remilitarisation of international relations diverts our common efforts, resources and energy from addressing the world's most acute problems: poverty, environmental degradation, proliferation of AIDS, and a critical lack of drinking water.

While the main responsibility for meeting these challenges rests on governments, the role that civil society can and must play should not be underestimated. I am convinced that government transparency, coupled with coherent communication and a general education of populations, especially the youth, is of utmost importance for this complicated issue.

I sincerely wish the organisers and participants of this Second Rally for International Disarmament the utmost success with this significant event.

The Nuclear Threat

Wall Street Journal, 31 January 2007

The essay 'A World Free of Nuclear Weapons', published in this newspaper on 4 January, was signed by a bipartisan group of four influential Americans – George Shultz, William Perry, Henry Kissinger and Sam Nunn – not known for utopian thinking, and having unique experience in shaping the policies of previous administrations. It raises an issue of crucial importance for world affairs: the need for the abolition of nuclear weapons.

As someone who signed the first treaties on real reductions in nuclear weapons, I feel it is my duty to support their call for urgent action.

The road to this goal began in November 1985 when Ronald Reagan and I met in Geneva. We declared that 'a nuclear war cannot be won and must never be fought'. This was said at a time when many people in the military and among the political establishment regarded a war involving weapons of mass destruction as conceivable and even acceptable, and were developing various scenarios of nuclear escalation.

It took political will to transcend the old thinking and attain a new vision. For if a nuclear war is inconceivable, then military doctrines, armed forces development plans and negotiating positions at arms-control talks must change accordingly. This began to happen, particularly after Reagan and I agreed in Reykjavik in October 1986 on the need ultimately to eliminate nuclear weapons. Concurrently, major positive changes were occurring in world affairs: a number of international conflicts were defused and democratic processes in many parts of the world gained momentum, leading to the end of the cold war.

As US-Soviet arms negotiations got off the ground, a breakthrough was achieved – the treaty on the elimination of medium- and shorter-range missiles, followed by agreement on 50 per cent reduction in strategic offensive weapons. If the negotiations had continued in the same vein and at the same pace, the world would have been rid of the greater part of the arsenals of deadly weapons. But this did not happen, and hopes for a new, more democratic world order were not fulfilled. In fact, we have seen a failure of political leadership, which proved incapable of seizing the opportunities opened by the end of the cold war. This glaring failure has allowed nuclear weapons and their proliferation to pose a continuing, growing threat to mankind.

The ABM Treaty has been abrogated; the requirements for effective verification and irreversibility of nuclear-arms reductions have been weakened; the treaty on comprehensive cessation of nuclear-weapons tests has not been ratified by all nuclear powers. The goal of the eventual elimination of nuclear weapons has been essentially forgotten. What is more, the military doctrines of major powers, first the US and then, to some extent, Russia, have re-emphasised nuclear weapons as an acceptable means of war fighting, to be used in a first or even in a 'pre-emptive' strike.

All this is a blatant violation of the nuclear powers' commitments under the Non-Proliferation Treaty. Its Article 5 is clear and unambiguous: Nations that are capable of making nuclear weapons shall forgo that possibility in exchange for the promise by the members of the nuclear club to reduce and eventually abolish their nuclear arsenals. If this reciprocity is not observed, then the entire structure of the treaty will collapse.

The Non-Proliferation Treaty is already under considerable stress. The emergence of India and Pakistan as nuclear-weapon states, the North Korean nuclear programme and the issue of Iran are just the harbingers of even more dangerous problems that we will have to face unless we overcome the present situation. A new threat, nuclear weapons falling into the hands of terrorists, is a challenge to our ability to work together internationally and to our technological ingenuity. But we should not delude ourselves: in the final analysis, this problem can only be solved through the abolition of nuclear weapons. So long as they continue to exist, the danger will be with us, like the famous 'rifle on the wall' that will fire sooner or later.

Last November, the Forum of Nobel Peace Laureates, meeting in Rome, issued a special statement on this issue. The late Nobel laureate and world-renowned scientist Joseph Rotblat initiated a global awareness campaign on the nuclear danger, in which I participated. Ted Turner's Nuclear Threat Initiative provides important support for specific measures to reduce weapons of mass destruction. With all of them we are united by a common understanding of the need to save the Non-Proliferation Treaty and of the primary responsibility of the members of the nuclear club.

We must put the goal of eliminating nuclear weapons back on the agenda, not in a distant future but as soon as possible. It links the moral imperative − the rejection of such weapons from an ethical standpoint − with the imperative of assuring security. It is becoming

clearer that nuclear weapons are no longer a means of achieving security; in fact, with every passing year they make our security more precarious.

The irony — and a reproach to the current generation of world leaders — is that two decades after the end of the cold war the world is still burdened with vast arsenals of nuclear weapons of which even a fraction would be enough to destroy civilization. As in the 1980s, we face the problem of political will — the responsibility of the leaders of major powers for bridging the gap between the rhetoric of peace and security and the real threat looming over the world. While agreeing with the 4 January article that the USA should take the initiative and play an active role on this issue, I believe there is also a need for major efforts on the part of Russian and European leaders and for a responsible position and full involvement of all states that have nuclear weapons.

I am calling for a dialogue to be launched within the framework of the Nuclear Non-Proliferation Treaty, involving both nuclear-weapon states and non-nuclear-weapon states, to cover the full range of issues related to the elimination of those weapons. The goal is to develop a common concept for moving toward a world free of nuclear weapons. The key to success is reciprocity of obligations and actions. The members of the nuclear club should formally reiterate their commitment to reducing

I am referring to the 1987 Intermediate-range Nuclear Forces (INF) Treaty, which eliminated two classes of nuclear missiles, and the 1991 START treaty, which launched the biggest cutbacks of nuclear weapons ever. Thousands of tactical nuclear weapons were destroyed in accordance with the US-Soviet agreement of October 1991.

We have to admit that nothing fundamentally new has been achieved in the past decade and a half. The pace of nuclear arms reduction has slowed. The mechanisms of arms control and verification have weakened. The Comprehensive Test Ban Treaty has not entered into force. The quantities of nuclear weapons held by Russia and the United States still far exceed the arsenals of all other nuclear powers taken together, thus making it more difficult to bring them into the process of nuclear disarmament. The regime of nuclear non-proliferation is in jeopardy.

The two major nuclear powers — the United States and Russia — bear the greatest responsibility for this state of affairs. I have to note, however, that it was the United States that abrogated the ABM Treaty, has failed to ratify the Comprehensive Test Ban Treaty and refused to conclude with Russia a legally binding, verifiable treaty on strategic offensive arms.

It is only recently that the first signs have appeared that the major nuclear powers understand that the current state of affairs is untenable. The presidents of the United States and Russia have agreed to conclude before the end of this year a verifiable treaty reducing strategic offensive arms and have reaffirmed their countries' commitment to obligations under Article 6 of the Non-Proliferation Treaty. The joint statement approved by the two presidents calls for a number of other steps to reduce the nuclear dangers, including the ratification by the United States of the Comprehensive Test Ban Treaty. These are positive, encouraging steps. And yet, we have to recognise that the problems and dangers are still more numerous than the achievements. The road to a nuclear weapons free world is filled with multiple obstacles.

Nuclear weapons are an extreme manifestation of the militarisation of international relations and of political thinking. We have so far failed to overcome this dark legacy of the twentieth century. In fact, over the past decades, things have become even worse.

The root cause of this is the erroneous evaluation of the events leading to the end of the cold war. They were seen in the United States and some other countries as the victory of the West — and a green light for unilateralist policies.

Instead of creating a new architecture of international security based

Gorbachev at the Overcoming Nuclear Dangers Conference in April 2009

on real cooperation, as called for in the Charter of Paris for a New Europe, signed in 1990, an attempt was made to impose on the world a 'monopoly leadership' of the sole remaining superpower and of the institutions and organisations, such as NATO, inherited from the cold war and not reformed after it.

The use of force and the threat of force — which, of course, is also illegal under the UN Charter — were reasserted as a 'normal' way of solving problems. Official documents rationalised the doctrines of pre-emptive strike and the need for US military superiority.

Today, we are facing the real possibility of a new arms race. Priority is still being given to financing military programmes; 'defence' budgets which far exceed reasonable security requirements keep growing, as does the weapons trade. The United States spends almost as much as the rest of the world put together on military purposes.

Disregard for international law and for peaceful ways of settling disputes, for the United Nations and its Security Council, is being proclaimed as a kind of policy.

As a result, we have witnessed a war in Europe (in Yugoslavia), something that had seemed inconceivable, a long-term deterioration in the Middle East, the war in Iraq, an extremely severe situation in Afghanistan, and — something that we are particularly concerned about here — the increasingly alarming nuclear non-proliferation crisis.

Its main cause is the failure of the members of the nuclear club to fulfil their obligations under NPT Article 6 – to move towards the elimination of nuclear weapons. While this fact remains, there will be a continued danger that other countries will acquire nuclear weapons. Today, dozens of states have the technical ability to do so.

In the final analysis, the nuclear danger can only be removed by abolishing nuclear weapons. But could one regard as realistic the prospect of one country retaining quantities of conventional weapons that exceed the combined arsenals of practically all other nations – the prospect of one country achieving absolute global superiority?

Let me be very frank here: such a situation would be an insurmountable obstacle on the path to a world without nuclear weapons.

Unless we address the need to demilitarise international relations, reduce military budgets, put an end to the creation of new kinds of weapons and prevent the weaponisation of outer space all talk about a nuclear weapon free world will be just inconsequential rhetoric.

Our assessments, judgements and proposals could be a contribution to overcoming the current shortage of practicable ideas, a real help to political decision-makers and government leaders. Let me therefore offer a couple of suggestions.

First, concerning the need for an international discussion of the problem of militarisation. Some of its aspects are addressed by the United Nations Conference on Disarmament in Geneva. Its work should certainly be re-energised – and I welcome the participation here of UN Under-Secretary General Ordzhonikidze – and the valuable proposals of the UN Secretary-General should be given support.

Furthermore, the discussion of this subject should be given impetus through the G20. That forum must not be limited to the role of a 'fire brigade' in the current crisis. I believe it is inevitable that the G20 will have to deal with political problems. The G8, too, needs to address the problem of demilitarising world affairs, lest they be marginalised in a rapidly changing world.

My second proposal concerns nuclear issues directly. After the recent speech by President Obama in Prague there is a real prospect that the United States will ratify the test ban treaty. This would be an important step forward, particularly in combination with a new strategic arms reduction treaty between the United States and Russia.

Following this, I believe that other nuclear powers – both the 'official members of the club' and others – will have to, at the very least, declare a freeze on their nuclear arsenals and their readiness to engage in negotiations on their limitation and reduction. If the holders of the largest stocks of nuclear weapons embark upon real reductions, others will no longer be able to sit it out, concealing their arsenals from international control.

This is an issue that we must raise now if we are to have the kind of trust without which common security cannot be achieved.

As we start our debate I hope that it will produce ideas to advance the process of moving towards the goal that I trust we all share. Let us go beyond rhetoric to bring this goal closer and ultimately make it a reality.

Conference organised by the World Political Forum, the Italian Ministry of Foreign Affairs and the Nuclear Security Project.

Made just a few months after Barack Obama was sworn in as President, this speech encouraged the United States and Russia to systematically – and urgently – engage in nuclear disarmament. Mikhail Gorbachev also urged President Obama to use the goodwill generated by his election to launch a serious disarmament programme during their White House meeting in March 2009. Later in the year, President Obama's pledge to do just that, and the agreement he reached with Russian President Dmitry Medvedev to negotiate a new nuclear disarmament treaty, were instrumental in him being awarded the Nobel Peace Prize. In a letter welcoming the President to the family of Nobel laureates, Gorbachev described the award as an expression of the hopes of the world, but stressed that implementing Obama's vision of peaceful relations between nations will require strong will, statesmanship and communication.

Disarmament Lessons from the Chemical Weapons Convention

By President Mikhail Gorbachev and OPCW Director-General
Rogelio Pfirter
Bulletin of the Atomic Scientists, 16 June 2009

The recent joint declaration by US President Barack Obama and Russian President Dmitry Medvedev to negotiate a new treaty reducing their countries' nuclear stockpiles as a first step towards 'a nuclear weapon free world' has spurred hopes for renewed progress in global disarmament after a decade of gridlock. An excellent example of how nations can work together effectively within a multilateral framework to eliminate weapons of mass destruction is the Chemical Weapons Convention (CWC).

The convention is unique in the sphere of disarmament and nonproliferation – an international treaty that abolishes an entire class of weapons of mass destruction under a stringent regime of inspections to verify compliance. Since its entry into force in April 1997, the convention has attracted 188 states parties representing 98 per cent of the world's population and chemical industries, the fastest rate of accession for any arms control treaty in history.

In this time, 43 per cent of the chemical weapons declared by seven 'possessor' states have been verifiably destroyed, and three of these states have eliminated their stockpiles altogether. At the current pace, the global figure will more than double to at least 90 per cent by 2012. In addition, all of the facilities that produced these deadly weapons have now been dismantled or converted to peaceful uses.

Parallel to these historic disarmament measures, a regime of industrial inspections has been established under the convention to ensure that new chemical weapons do not emerge and to prevent the illicit spread of toxic chemicals that could be used for weapons. The global chemical industry has been a valuable partner in these efforts by actively promoting adherence to the convention and helping to sustain the effectiveness of the industrial inspections, which have been conducted in more than 80 countries to date.

The convention's implementing agency, the Organisation for the Prohibition of Chemical Weapons (OPCW), offers important additional benefits to member states. It has mobilised significant resources to build

their capacities to protect against the possible use of chemical weapons and advanced the peaceful uses of chemistry for economic development by facilitating the exchange of scientific knowledge and expertise. These programmes are based on an ethos of mutual support and have attracted increased interest as a means to reduce the risk of terrorists using chemical weapons.

The CWC has several distinctive virtues that in our view are directly relevant to the goal of eliminating both nuclear and biological weapons. The first is its comprehensive nature. Previous treaties on chemical weapons demonstrated that so long as they were allowed to exist they would be used. The convention aims to remove this threat by obligating the destruction of all existing chemical weapons and banning the development and production of new ones. While this goal remains a work in progress, the possession and use of these weapons has been delegitimised by an overwhelming majority of countries.

Another virtue of the convention is its non-discriminatory character. All member states share the same rights and obligations, and those with chemical weapons must declare and destroy them, without exception. As well, every member with a chemical industry covered by the convention must subject it to international inspection for non-proliferation purposes. A third virtue is that OPCW policy decisions are rendered by consensus, which requires competing interests to be reconciled to reach agreement on all policy issues. This process can be difficult and time-consuming, but over time it has returned great dividends in sustaining the trust and commitment of members.

These virtues have enabled rivals to find common ground for strengthening international peace and security. The United States and Russia, which held the vast bulk of chemical weapons at the end of the cold war, led the way in concluding the multilateral negotiations on the convention and have shown impressive commitment to completing the destruction of their entire stockpiles.

Significant challenges remain to the complete abolition of chemical weapons. Seven countries remain outside the convention, including several suspected of having active chemical weapons programmes. The United States and Russia will both need to accelerate their efforts in order to meet the convention's legally binding deadline of April 2012 for completing stockpile destruction. And advances in science and technology pose constant challenges to the effectiveness of the OPCW's industrial inspections regime.

World leaders should not see the virtues of the CWC as a panacea for nuclear and biological weapons, which have different strategic and technical dimensions. But the convention has demonstrated that, given the political will, eliminating weapons of mass destruction in an equitable and verifiable manner is feasible.

The United States and Soviet Union decisively put the abolition of nuclear weapons on the international agenda more than 20 years ago, which led to major nuclear force reductions in Europe and legitimised the international goal of eliminating nuclear weapons altogether. With review conferences scheduled for the Nuclear Non-Proliferation Treaty, the Biological Weapons Convention, and the CWC during the next three years, the international community should seize the moment and move decisively to rid the world of all weapons of mass destruction.

Two First Steps on Nuclear Weapons

New York Times, 25 September 2009

Yesterday, President Obama presided over the United Nations Security Council meeting that passed a resolution seeking to strengthen the international commitment to limiting the spread of nuclear weapons. A week ago, he announced that the United States will not deploy – at least, not in the foreseeable future – a missile defence site in Central Europe, including powerful radar in the Czech Republic and interceptor missiles in Poland.

Is there a link between the two events? I believe there is. Yet initial comments by many political figures and journalists have for the most part ignored this key relationship.

Instead, many are asserting that cancelling the Eastern European missile defence was simply a concession to Russia, which must now reciprocate with a concession of its own. But President Dmitry Medvedev of Russia had already said last November that if the United States made changes to its missile defence plans his nation would refrain from counter-measures like deploying its own missiles. Soon after President Obama's decision was announced, this position was reaffirmed.

Many of President Obama's critics in the United States insist that he 'caved in' to Russian pressure, virtually leaving America's NATO allies to fend for themselves. There is nothing behind this argument other than the old stereotype of 'bad Russia', a Russia that is always wrong.

Consider the merits of the case. Russia's leaders have been saying for some time that the fear of Iran developing effective long-range missiles in the near future was not grounded in fact. Now, after a thorough review by intelligence and defence officials, the United States Government has come to the same conclusion, holding that Tehran is perhaps at least five years or even a decade away from such capacity.

The initial reaction by some politicians and commentators in Poland and the Czech Republic is no less odd. They seem to enjoy the role of a spoiler in relations between other countries and Russia. Voices of realism and caution are routinely rejected, and the opinion of their own citizens, who by and large have no use for radars and missiles, is brushed aside.

In Russia, President Obama's decision has been well received. It also met with support in Europe, with Chancellor Angela Merkel of Germany

and Prime Minister Nicolas Sarkozy of France lauding it. The Polish Prime Minister, Donald Tusk, called it 'a chance to strengthen European security'. Indeed, if the President's decision is followed by further serious steps, it will provide an opportunity for us to strengthen global security as well as reach a new level of cooperation in ridding the world of nuclear danger.

At their meeting in Moscow in early July, Presidents Obama and Medvedev reaffirmed the relationship between strategic offensive weapons and missile defence. The two nations continue arms reduction talks and, judging by cautious diplomatic statements, they seem to be on course to complete them by 5 December, when the first Strategic Arms Reduction Treaty – which I signed with President George H.W. Bush in 1991 – is due to expire.

This week's United Nations meeting marks the next stage of progress. It is vital that other nations come away from the meeting believing that America and Russia are moving towards verifiable nuclear arms reductions, and that by the time the Nuclear Non-Proliferation Treaty review conference is held at the United Nations next May they will have made progress towards the eventual elimination of nuclear weapons.

Unless they show the world they are serious, the two major nuclear powers will be accused, again and again, of not keeping their word and told that if it is acceptable for five or ten countries to have nuclear weapons as their 'ultimate security guarantee', why should it not be the case for 20 or 30 others?

It is vital that the two presidents themselves monitor the negotiations closely, sometimes plunging into minute details. I know from experience how difficult it is to deal with such technical details on top of constant political pressures, but it is necessary to avoid misunderstandings that could undermine trust.

Some questions that will need to be clarified are evident now. The American Secretary of Defense, Robert Gates, has said that the SM-3 missiles that are to be used under the new missile-defence plan could later be perfected to intercept long-range intercontinental missiles. Yet he has also raised the possibility of cooperating with Russia on missile defence. To me, these two ideas seem incompatible. The sooner such issues are cleared up the better.

As I see it, there is only one way to move forward. Washington should agree to the Russian proposal for a joint assessment of missile threats. Let the experts from both countries have a frank discussion that would reveal which threats are real and must be dealt with, and which are imaginary. This would help to avoid misguided projects like the Polish-Czech missile shield, and could help move us from a state of mutual deterrence to a goal of minimum nuclear sufficiency for self-defence.

This is a big agenda. Realistically, it would take two or three years of intense negotiation. But Russia and the United States must set big tasks for themselves. What is needed is nothing less than a change in the strategic relationship between the two major nuclear powers – in their own interests and in the cause of world peace.

Resetting the Nuclear Disarmament Agenda

Third Geneva Lecture, United Nations, 5 October 2009

Thank you very much Mr Secretary-General of the United Nations and Mr Director-General.

This very representative gathering demonstrates the interest in the subject of the new agenda of nuclear disarmament, and also the interest in searching for multilateral collective approaches to this problem. Here in Geneva, where one of the most important centres of UN activities is located and where the principal multilateral disarmament mechanism of the UN Disarmament Commission is working, such an approach is particularly appropriate.

I am one of those who has always been a determined supporter of the UN, and I believe that the global financial and economic crisis which is still, I believe, very far from its end has reminded us of the fact that in the world in which we live only multilateral approaches are effective. They will be needed not only to respond to the immediate crisis but also in order to move towards the new model of development which the world needs. Because the old model, based on super-profits and hyper-consumption, and on social and ecological irresponsibility, has run its course and has become dangerous for mankind.

And the same is certainly true of the old model of security. To an even greater extent, the concepts or doctrines on which that model is based have become outdated and are becoming increasingly dangerous. The weapons that emerged from those doctrines are still being produced, tested and improved, are becoming increasingly deadly and very often actually used.

The militarisation of international politics is the onerous legacy of the twentieth century. And as a result of militarisation, instead of addressing the urgent social economic problems, governments spend their resources on the acquisition of weapons. The weapons business, with its propensity for corruption, which we increasingly learn of from the media, is flourishing and is continuing to ruin our economies and society. We have recently read in the media information to that effect about corruption on a shocking scale.

At the forefront of this generally unsatisfactory picture, in terms of the danger to mankind, are of course nuclear weapons. It is their arsenals, the danger of their proliferation, the danger that they could be seized by terrorists, the danger of technical failure or an explosion as a result of an accident. All of this should be of enormous concern to us. I will go even further. Knowing all this, we really should not be able to sleep quietly.

In the mid-1980s there was a combination of extreme tension in relations between the nuclear powers and the size of the nuclear arsenals. That led the world to a very dangerous point. And it was at that very dangerous moment that the leaders of the USSR and the United States were able to transcend the obstacles, the prejudice, and the old stereotypes to initiate a process of real reductions of nuclear weapons.

In 1985, here in Geneva, President Reagan and I declared that a nuclear war cannot be won and must never be fought. Less than a year later, in Reykjavik, we declared the need to eliminate nuclear arsenals. That was the next step. And I still value what we did in Reykjavik. Because this is when we looked beyond the horizon. And even though the path to an agreement at that time was blocked by the US plans to create a global ballistic missile defence system, the movement towards that goal began. Two classes of medium-range missiles were eliminated. A treaty was signed to reduce by one half, that is to say thousands of weapons, all strategic arms. Then, in October 1991, we agreed on decommissioning and liquidating a large portion of tactical nuclear weapons.

We agreed on an enormous set of verification and confidence-building measures. We started military to military contacts and we started to review our military doctrines, And all that we agreed at that time has today been implemented. However, after the Soviet Union left the political scene, the movement towards nuclear disarmament stalled, despite the fact that the ending of the confrontation seemed to create better conditions to accelerate that process.

In effect, what we have now in terms of reducing nuclear weapons is the result of agreements, of implementing agreements that were signed at the end of the 1980s and early 1990s. Twenty years after the end of the cold war, thousands of nuclear warheads are still in the arsenals of the nuclear powers.

Nuclear weapons are still deployed on the European continent, and the pace of nuclear arms reduction has slowed. There are new nuclear weapon powers and the problem of the proliferation of nuclear weapons has become increasingly urgent. The verification mechanisms have been weakened. Instead of a system of on-site inspections, we have seen a rather doubtful, questionable idea of taking on faith the implementation of nuclear and biological weapons commitments.

Gorbachev speaking at the UN in 2009

The favourite Russian proverb of Ronald Reagan 'trust but verify' has been conveniently forgotten. The treaty on the complete ban on nuclear tests has not come into force. The nuclear arsenals of the United States and Russia still far exceed the combined arsenals of all other countries, rendering it more difficult to convince certain countries to become involved in the process of nuclear disarmament.

There is a real threat of a new arms race and of the weaponisation of outer space.

Recently there have there been concrete signs that the leading nuclear powers are becoming aware that the current situation is untenable, but I believe that today there are more problems and dangers than achievements. The road to a nuclear weapons free world is currently blocked by a myriad of obstacles and, if we do not want this peaceful future to remain 'a mountain-top covered in fog', we must talk about these obstacles very honestly.

There are critical situations in the Middle East and Afghanistan, and we have seen a worsening of the situation in terms of nuclear weapons proliferation. Let me emphasise that proliferation is a problem that should not be seen just in the context of Iran and North Korea. The core of this problem is the non-implementation by the members of the nuclear club of their obligation, under Article 6 of the Non-Proliferation Treaty, to move towards the elimination of nuclear weapons. While this situation continues there will be a continued danger of the emergence of new nuclear powers.

Today dozens of countries are technically capable of it. Indeed, absolute security for some ultimately means insecurity for everyone else. If a handful of countries are permitted to retain nuclear weapons as their ultimate security guarantee, then why not 20 or 30 more?

This question has been repeated again and again, but repetition doesn't make it irrelevant. There are at least 40 threshold nuclear powers now. It is an issue that is becoming increasingly urgent. We can only eliminate the nuclear danger by eliminating nuclear weapons.

While giving credit to my colleagues, the veterans of US politics George Shultz, Henry Kissinger, Sam Nunn and William Perry, whose article in *The Wall Street Journal* in 2007 reminded the world of the goal of eliminating nuclear weapons, I thought it was important, it was necessary, to put this question in a broader context.

If we do not address the need to demilitarise international politics, to reduce military budgets, to put an end to the development of new weapons, to prevent the militarisation of outer space, then all talk of a nuclear weapons free world will be just a lot of hot air.

Now there is an opportunity to break the vicious cycle of the past few years and to start moving in the right direction. Over the past weeks we have seen significant steps and breakthroughs on nuclear issues. President Barack Obama announced changes in the US missile defence plans. This is a decision that was positively perceived by the leaders of Russia, Germany, France and Poland, among others.

This certainly creates a more favourable atmosphere for nuclear arms talks, even though some issues remain. The best forum to discuss those issues would be the joint consultations on the Joint Assessment of Missile Threats that are being proposed by Russia. We have also seen some positive steps in the negotiating process on the Iranian nuclear programme, and we may expect that recent contact with the People's Democratic Republic of Korea will not be fruitless.

Those are first steps. They must be consolidated and further developed. As we move forward there will be setbacks and disappointments, but it is clear that constructive multilateral approaches are beginning to bear fruit. In this regard, the role of the United Nations is of fundamental importance.

With all due respect for the bilateral efforts of the leading nuclear powers, who were responsible for the arms race in the past and are therefore of course responsible for curbing it now, the UN is indispensable. I have said many times that attempts to sideline the UN and its Security Council and supplant it with other organisations and bodies such as NATO, G8 or even the emerging G20 must be rejected. It is because of this that, from the start, I suggested that there should be a clear link between the G20 and the UN, with the G20 submitting regular reports to the General Assembly.

Paraphrasing the words of Winston Churchill, we could say that the United Nations may be imperfect. It needs reform. But no one has been able to invent anything better and will not be able to invent anything better because there is no other universal world organisation. And that means that it should play a more important role in disarmament issues.

The recent Security Council Summit on Nuclear Disarmament and Non-proliferation was an important step in this direction. The resolution that it adopted is a strong and balanced document that reflects the urgency of the problem and considers the questions of disarmament and security as an interconnected complex, and that is the way it should be.

The fact that top leaders are paying attention to these issues makes it possible to expect that there will be the political will necessary to overcome the selfish interests and parochialism that often derailed disarmament initiatives.

I welcome the reinvigoration of the UN Disarmament Commission and also appreciate the initiatives of Secretary-General Ban Ki-moon, and his five-point programme in particular. This sets an agenda both for the members of the Nuclear Club and for other countries that are capable of contributing to disarmament, for the demilitarisation of international politics, and the creation of a new security architecture.

I believe that the idea of building a United Nations Arms Convention similar to the conventions on prohibition and elimination of chemical and biological weapons is promising. I believe that in preparing this, the Commission could play a stronger mobilising role in getting a broad range of countries involved in the nuclear disarmament process and in reaching agreements.

It is within the UN that we should raise issues such as getting the so-called second tier nuclear powers involved in nuclear disarmament.

After the United States and Russia conclude a new agreement for the legally binding and verifiable major reduction of their nuclear arsenals, and the ratification by the United States of a Comprehensive Test Ban Treaty, this issue will become particularly relevant and important.

I believe, after that, all nuclear powers must at the very least declare a freeze of their nuclear arsenals.

If those who possess the biggest arsenals start real reductions, the others will no longer be able to sit on the sidelines, hiding their arsenals from international control.

Another important and promising multilateral issue is the need for a global ban and elimination of the medium range and shorter-range missiles that the United States and Russia have already eliminated. This is a dangerous, destabilising kind of weapon that does not strengthen anyone's security.

And finally, the question of the concepts and doctrines that we inherited from the era of uncurbed nuclear arms race. This is a subject that should no longer be taboo. The discussion of the subject could be started within the framework of the Military Staff Committee in the Security Council. The Military Staff Committee that I suggested should be revived from the comatose state it has been in since 1988, when I spoke at the UN General Assembly.

To summarise, our goal should certainly be the movement towards a nuclear free, non-violent and demilitarised world where everyone is secure. I believe that this is in the interest of all countries and all people.

But it is important, at all stages of moving towards that goal, for all participants to be confident that their security is not being diminished, that it is getting stronger. This is not easy to achieve, but this is the only way to advance. We should move forward in the context of efforts to resolve regional conflicts, to reduce conventional arms, to prevent a new arms race, whether on Earth or in space, and through a combination of bilateral and multilateral efforts.

In achieving this goal, the importance of multilateral efforts will be growing. The UN is an indispensable forum for harmonising the efforts of big and small states. And it can and it must play a key role in this process.

I hope that all of you gathered here will work actively for this goal. All of us can make our own contribution. And I am sure that together we will be able to create the critical mass of political will needed to make sure that the new nuclear disarmament agenda becomes real and irreversible.

The Ice Has Broken

New York Times, 22 April 2010

A remarkable sequence of events in April has turned the spotlight on the subject of nuclear disarmament and global security. I am referring to the signing by Presidents Obama and Medvedev of the New START treaty, the presentation of the Obama administration's nuclear doctrine and the nuclear security summit meeting in Washington attended by leaders of several dozen countries.

The ice has broken. The situation today is dramatically different from just two years ago. But has it changed enough to say that the process now under way is irreversible?

Let's first look at the New START treaty. It has been deemed irrelevant and the reductions it calls for described as 'creative accounting'. Though the cuts are indeed modest compared to those made under the treaty the first President Bush and I signed in 1991, the treaty is a major breakthrough.

First, it resumes the process initiated in the second half of the 1980s, which made it possible to rid the world of thousands of nuclear warheads and hundreds of launchers.

Second, the strategic arsenals of the United States and Russia have once again been placed under a regime of mutual verification and inspections.

Third, the United States and Russia have demonstrated that they can solve the most complex problems of mutual security, which offers hope that they will work together more successfully to address global and regional issues.

Finally, and perhaps most importantly, with the New Strategic Arms Reduction Treaty the two biggest nuclear powers say to the world that they are serious about their Nuclear Non-Proliferation Treaty obligation to move towards eliminating nuclear weapons.

By reviving the goal of a world free of nuclear weapons, the treaty is a powerful tool for political pressure on those countries, particularly Iran and North Korea, whose nuclear programmes have caused legitimate concern within the international community. It also reminds other nuclear weapon powers that they, too, must join in the process of nuclear disarmament.

I have often been asked, in Russia and elsewhere, whether the process of nuclear disarmament could be scuttled by a build-up in the arsenals of other countries – for example China, Pakistan and India. This is a legitimate question. The least that the other members of the 'nuclear club' must do now is freeze their arsenals.

Further progress along the path of disarmament and non-proliferation would be facilitated by a statement from nuclear powers saying that the sole purpose of nuclear weapons is to prevent their use. Unfortunately, the new US nuclear doctrine does not go that far. Nevertheless, this document, as well as Russia's military doctrine, signals a tendency towards reduced reliance on nuclear weapons.

The new US doctrine emphasises that Russia is no longer an adversary. It declares the Obama administration's intent to secure ratification of the treaty banning all nuclear testing and states that the United States will not develop new nuclear weapons.

The Obama administration has proposed bilateral dialogues on strategic stability with Russia and China. Such a dialogue must include missile defence issues. After all, the interrelationship of strategic offensive arms and missile defence is recognised in the New START.

The dialogue on strategic stability is certainly in Russia's interest. To conduct it with confidence, we in Russia need a serious debate on the problem of missile defence, involving experts, members of Parliament and the military. What kind of missile defence does Russia need? Should it be linked with the US missile defence system? These are political rather than 'agency' issues. Decisions on such issues will be with us for decades to come.

Yet the proposed dialogue should not be limited to strategic weapons. More general problems must also be addressed if we are to build a relationship of partnership and trust. Foremost is the problem of military superiority.

The US national security strategy, adopted in 2002 and still in effect, clearly proclaims the need for US global military superiority. This principle has in effect become an integral part of America's creed. It finds specific expression in the vast arsenals of conventional weapons, the colossal defence budget and the plans for weaponising outer space. The proposed strategic dialogue must include all these issues. Reaching mutual understanding will take a sense of realism and long-term vision.

NATO is now discussing a new 'strategic concept', and for the first time it is consulting with Russia. I welcome this. Does it mean that NATO is ready to renounce the claim to include the entire world in its 'zone of responsibility' and instead work together with others within multilateral institutions vested with real authority and powers? The recent opinion essay by George Shultz and William Perry (IHT April 12) seems to suggest that influential Americans are now seriously considering such issues.

I am sure that Russia is ready to engage in such a discussion, and not Russia alone. For whether we like it or not, the world today is multipolar.

There has been much disingenuous talk that 'multipolar structures are inherently unstable', citing examples of Europe in the nineteenth and early twentieth centuries and blaming multipolarity for conflicts and wars, including world wars. Such talk is pointless, because multipolarity is now a reality.

We have seen in recent months that power centres like China, Russia and the European Union have responded to the global financial crisis responsibly. While defending their own interests they have taken into account the interests of other players and of the world community as a whole. This is multipolarity in action, helping to mitigate the crisis and move towards addressing longer-term measures. But it's only a beginning.

The Middle East peace process is in a deep crisis. The world is still paying for the mistakes of US strategy in Iraq and Afghanistan. Efforts to agree on a global climate policy are stalled. The mechanisms for fighting poverty and backwardness are dysfunctional. In the final analysis, it all comes down to the lack of political will and failure of leadership.

We need collective leadership. We have recently seen examples of what it can achieve. But what remains to be done is much more than what has been done. Too much time was wasted after the end of the cold war. The legacy of mutual suspicion, narrow self-interest and domination is still very much with us. The struggle between this legacy and new thinking will define international politics in the twenty-first century.

Address Sent to the Nobel Peace Laureates Forum

Hiroshima, Japan, 12–14 November 2010

The Nobel Peace Laureates Summit in Hiroshima is an event of special significance. Its venue is a reminder of our responsibility, of our duty as Laureates, which is to work towards a more just, more humane and more secure world. And that, of course, means a world without nuclear weapons.

Ever since nuclear weapons first made their appearance, the need for their abolition has been discussed. Billions of words have been uttered and tens of thousands of books, speeches and articles written about nuclear disarmament. But it is here that the gap between words and deeds, so typical of the twentieth and, unfortunately, still in the twenty-first century, is at its widest.

The problem of eliminating nuclear weapons has moral, legal and practical dimensions. I am convinced that as Peace laureates we must, above all, take a moral stand. Nuclear weapons are unacceptable because of their unique inhumanity and their ability to destroy human civilisation as we know it. Such weapons never existed before, and they must not exist.

Yet for many years nuclear weapons were produced, perfected and stockpiled on a truly incredible scale. What is more, military concepts and doctrines considered them to be a legitimate means of waging war. The nuclear arms race resulted in the production of tens of thousands of nuclear weapons for all types of warfare – strategic, tactical and 'battlefield'. The process of nuclear disarmament could only start after the leaders of the two biggest nuclear powers showed the political will to initiate it.

We needed to break out of the vicious circle of 'nuclear thinking' and take the moral position that had always been clear to most ordinary citizens. This position was reflected in simple words, unusual in diplomacy, that were included in the Joint Statement of the leaders of the Soviet Union and the United States adopted in Geneva in November 1985, exactly 25 years ago: 'Nuclear war cannot be won and must never be fought.' This proposition combined morality and politics – something that many people had considered and still consider impossible.

Proceeding from that principle, we needed to embark upon practical deeds. For if nuclear war was inconceivable and unacceptable it had to

Gorbachev speaking at the 10th Nobel Peace Laureates Summit in Berlin in November 2009

be made impossible, and ultimately the only way to make it impossible is to reduce and destroy the accumulated huge stockpiles of nuclear weapons.

I think we must be proud of what we were able to achieve within a historically short span of time. In accordance with international agreements, such as the US-Soviet INF and START treaties and the agreement to eliminate most of the tactical nuclear weapons, thousands of warheads have been decommissioned and destroyed, and some categories of nuclear weapons have ceased to exist. We must also commend specific actions such as the elimination of South Africa's nuclear arsenal and the decision of Belarus, Ukraine and Kazakhstan to give up all the nuclear weapons they possessed after the breakup of the USSR.

Yet we must also note that after the end of the cold war the process of nuclear disarmament slowed down and continued mostly on the momentum of the agreements reached before. The Comprehensive Nuclear Test Ban Treaty was not ratified and the number of nuclear weapons powers grew. This makes it necessary to reiterate the moral position of condemning nuclear weapons and to remind everyone that while such weapons exist there will also exist the possibility of nuclear war starting either by design or by accident.

I want to note that as Nobel laureates we have been taking this stand, which is the only one that is right and just, throughout all these years, reminding the leaders of nuclear powers of their responsibility.

This year has witnessed an event that could mark the resumption of the nuclear disarmament process. We should commend the signing, by Presidents Medvedev and Obama, of the New START treaty and call for its early ratification. A great deal is at stake. If the nuclear weapons lobby succeeds in derailing ratification, it will deal a heavy blow to the Nuclear Non-Proliferation Treaty, the obligations of which, as we have constantly insisted, are mutual and concern both non-nuclear states, which pledge to renounce nuclear weapons, and the nuclear weapon powers, which commit themselves to nuclear disarmament.

The practical goal for the medium term should be to have other nuclear powers join the process of nuclear disarmament and to reduce the stockpiles to a minimum level, i.e. a few dozen warheads. Even that, however, should be an interim solution on the path towards the complete elimination of nuclear weapons.

As we work on practical steps to reduce nuclear weapons, their abolition must remain our ultimate objective. Therefore, we should support the initiative of the United Nations Secretary General to start work on a universal convention or treaty to prohibit the use, development, production, stockpiling and transfer of nuclear weapons and related technologies and components.

While taking a moral stand and demanding the prohibition and elimination of nuclear weapons, we should also be realists and recognise the obstacles on the way to our goal.

Nuclear weapons are still built into the security policies and strategic planning of all nuclear weapon states. Practically all of them not only regard nuclear weapons as the ultimate 'security guarantee' but also see them as a measure of their geo-political weight in the world arena.

This inevitably influences other nations' policies. Hence the continuing danger of a new arms race and of the appearance of new kinds of weapons, particularly space weapons, and of the growth of military budgets and the weapons trade.

Efforts by one country or a group of countries to achieve superiority in conventional weapons are also incompatible with a nuclear weapons free world. The Geneva joint statement adopted in 1985 stated that the USSR and the United States would not seek military superiority. However, after the end of the cold war we have witnessed a build-up of US conventional forces and their use in a number of regions.

I therefore must repeat what I have been saying for some time: absolute military superiority of one nation would be an insurmountable obstacle on the way to a world without nuclear weapons. This is why it is so important, even as we strive for nuclear disarmament, to insist on the demilitarisation of international relations and political thinking, on the need to reduce military budgets, curb the weapons trade and prevent the development of new kinds of weapons. We must also work relentlessly to resolve the disputes and conflicts that engender and feed the arms race.

Militarism, the painful legacy of the twentieth century, which in the past repeatedly brought our planet to the brink of disaster, must be forever relegated to the past, while the principle of peaceful settlement of disputes must become the imperative norm of international relations. It is only then that a world without nuclear weapons would be safe and just.

Today, the main challenges to mankind's future are the threat of catastrophic climate change, the degradation of the environment, massive poverty that breeds extremism, migration flows and state failure, diseases and epidemics, organised crime, drug trafficking and massive violations of human rights. There are no military responses to these challenges. Therefore, we cannot be indifferent to the fact that instead of effectively addressing these problems governments continue with wasteful expenditures on weapons of war, particularly nuclear weapons.

With these remarks I wanted to propose an approach that, while based on a moral position, is also realistic in confronting the problems that we face today. I believe such an approach could provide guidance for our actions in the coming years and I hope it will be reflected in the appeal to world leaders and citizens that will be adopted by the forum.

The 'Hiroshima Declaration on the Abolition of Nuclear Weapons' issued by this forum of Nobel Peace laureates reiterated Gorbachev's disarmament plea to world leaders. The year 2010 ended on a positive note when the US Senate voted to ratify the New START treaty on 22 December, but Gorbachev stresses that more is needed to really get disarmament processes on the right track. Thousands of nuclear warheads remain on high alert, and the USA, Britain and France all voted against changing this highly dangerous and outdated situation at the UN in October 2010. Gorbachev will continue to speak out on nuclear weapons until this most burning threat to our civilisation is finally consigned to the past.

The Senate's Next Task:
Ratifying the Nuclear Test Ban Treaty

New York Times, 28 December 2010

Just a few weeks ago, the fate of the New START nuclear arms treaty seemed to hang by a thread. But since last week, when the United States Senate ratified the treaty, which reduces the size of the American and Russian nuclear stockpiles, we can speak of a serious step forward for both countries. I hope this will energise efforts to take the next step to a world free of nuclear weapons: a ban on all nuclear testing.

In the final stretch, President Obama put his credibility and political capital on the line to achieve ratification. That a sufficient number of Republican senators put the interests of their nation's security, and the world's, above party politics is encouraging.

The success was not without cost. In return for the treaty's ratification, Mr Obama promised to allocate tens of billions of dollars in the next few years for modernising the American nuclear weapons arsenal, which is hardly compatible with a nuclear-free world.

Missile defence remains contentious. During the ratification debate, many senators objected to the treaty's language about the relationship between offensive and defensive arms, which the new agreement takes from the first START treaty, signed in 1991. Others tried to scuttle ratification by complaining that New START did not limit tactical nuclear weapons.

These attacks were fended off. Nevertheless, these problems clearly need to be discussed. There must be an agreement on missile defence. Tough negotiations are ahead on tactical nuclear weapons, and a realistic agreement is needed on the deployment of conventional forces in Europe. We shall see very soon whether all these issues were raised just for the sake of rhetoric, as a demagogical screen to maintain military superiority, or whether there is a real readiness to conclude agreements easing the military burden.

The priority now is to ratify the separate treaty banning nuclear testing. The stalemate on this agreement, the Comprehensive Nuclear Test Ban Treaty, has lasted more than a decade. I recall how hard it was in the second half of the 1980s to start moving in this direction. At the time, the Soviet Union declared a unilateral moratorium on nuclear testing. However, when the United States continued to test, we had to respond.

The Green Agenda

The New Path to Peace and Sustainability

El Pais, 30 January 2004

The forthcoming Earth Dialogues (co-hosted by my own organisation Green Cross International and the city of Barcelona) to be held in Barcelona on 5–6 February will be the official launch event for the Universal Forum of Cultures Barcelona 2004.

The Earth Dialogues are not intended as a mere 'talk shop', but as a dynamic and highly interactive forum that brings together not just world leaders and captains of industry but also the actors who really count: members of civil society.

The Dialogues' main focus will be the identification of the concrete strategies that are needed to operationalise the new global agenda for peace and sustainability.

Increasing tensions on the world scene, escalating terrorism, religious intolerance, environmental degradation, and the systematic violation of human rights have reached an explosive threshold. The resolution of all these problems cannot be delayed.

But first of all, in order to respond effectively to these new problems, we must understand the diverse roots of conflicts, as well as the links between poverty, environmental deterioration and scarcity, and peace and security. Above all, the world needs a global vision of common values, which must underlie the new forms of dialogue and cooperation needed among nations and civilisations.

As never before, the 'post-Iraq' world community beckons a new understanding of the global situation. Indeed, a central message of the seven US Democratic presidential candidates is the need to build a new security and sustainability paradigm. The timing of their messages could not be more relevant since the beginning of the twenty-first century has added new and deadly dimensions to the challenge of maintaining global peace and security. Most recently in a *Der Spiegel* interview published on 26 January, Mohamed El-Baradei, Director-General of the International Atomic Energy Agency, pronounced that the world is now closer to the threat of nuclear war than ever before, in particular because of the growing illegal trade in nuclear technologies. However, despite the pervasive threat of international terrorism and the terrifying prospect of nuclear war in the twenty-first century, the reality is that security in this new millennium is not just about protection from aggression but also from disease, economic shocks, environmental degradation and resource scarcity.

For most of the world, security tensions centre less on geo-political boundaries and external might than on internal conflict that stems from poverty, social exclusion, dispossession and marginalisation, as well as economic instability and competition over shared resources such as water and arable land.

Another important phenomenon is that in the globalised world governments alone can no longer provide adequate security to their citizens, let alone protect increasingly porous geo-political borders.

How then does the world move forward to respond to the new global survival challenges of the new millennium?

Well, as a first important step, I maintain that we must replace the overriding culture of violence and conflict with a new culture of peace. This means not just strengthening and democratising our institutions of peace and security to better respond to and prevent violence, war and conflict. It means developing, at all levels and in all spheres of life, a complex of attitudes, values, beliefs and patterns of behaviour that promote not just the peaceful settlement of conflict but also the quest for mutual understanding, and opportunity for individuals to live harmoniously with each other and the larger community of life. Above all, it means promoting a new global security and sustainability ethic.

By a global ethic, I do not mean a new ideology or superstructure. A new global ethic is not intended to make the specific ethics of the different religions superfluous. Neither is it intended to be a substitute for the Torah, the Sermon on the Mount, the Koran, the Bhagavadgita, the Discourses of the Buddha or the Sayings of Confucius.

Rather, a global ethic, as reflected in the Earth Charter, an authoritative statement of ethical principles for sustainable development and recognised by thousands of organisations and millions of individuals, constitutes a core of belief which is indeed acceptable to all.

As one of the participants in the development of the Earth Charter, I stressed that the global ethic enshrined therein should not impose one vision or legislate away important cultural differences. This is particularly important for nascent democracies around the world, which I

assert must be free to define for themselves their own democratic paths to sustainability and security.

Contrary to the arrogant display by the world's one remaining superpower of not only its self-acclaimed political, social and religious superiority but also its systematic attempts to dictate its will upon the rest of the world, the Earth Charter respects an important balance between the goals of unity and solidarity amidst the very real diversity that characterises the global community of civilisations.

The new global ethic also asserts that real security and sustainability can only exist in a world where finite ecological and economic resources are protected in a spirit of stewardship to enable all to meet their basic human needs and to live a life of material and spiritual well-being.

In a world increasingly besieged by corruption, greed and self-interest, we need leaders who have the moral courage to ground their decisions in this new global ethic. We need leaders who understand that, in the words of the Earth Charter, 'when basic needs have been met, human development is primarily about being more, not having more'.

We also need global leaders who understand that attending to the growing environmental, economic and cultural stresses are just as critical as the political and military factors in the maintenance of international peace and security.

And in a year in which there will be an unprecedented number of national elections we especially need leaders who care not only about the results of yet another election campaign, but who take decisions that respect the increasing interdependence of the community of nations and civilisations. This means leaders who have the moral rectitude to transcend narrow national self-interests and to recognise that the new generation of global survival problems are only resolvable through multilateral channels, and in a true spirit of global solidarity that recognises that the culture of peace and sustainability is really the only viable path forward.

© *El Pais*

Divisions between 'the establishment' of governments and big business – represented by WTO, G8 and Davos – on the one hand, and the 'anti-globalisation' movement – represented by the World Social Forum – on the other had deepened in the early 2000s and been joined by growing tensions between Islam and the West, and by mass protests against the invasion of Iraq in 2003. Gorbachev, with GCI and other partners, sought to create a new forum for dialogue, transparency and the elaboration of innovative and practical solutions to the world's most important challenges: this gave rise to the Earth Dialogues, held for the first time in Lyon, France, in 2002, and subsequently in Barcelona in 2004. At that time, to bring all parties – from farmers and writers to religious leaders to CEOs and government ministers – together in intimate round-tables was truly unique and a credit to Gorbachev, who personally led the initiative. The principal goal was to integrate ethical concerns into sustainable development, economic and security policies.

In Barcelona, hundreds of participants, from every branch of society and all continents, came together to propose concrete ways of building peace, stability and sustainability in the Middle East – at an extremely volatile time. The dialogues concluded that the peace process must understand the expanding frontiers of the security agenda – and respond to the social and environmental factors at the root of many problems. The recommendations of the Earth Dialogues were delivered to heads of state, key players in the region, and the UN and other international actors, and closely followed up by Gorbachev. Since then, the need to look beyond conventional security concerns has been increasingly recognised. The Earth Dialogues created space for civil society activists to engage more constructively with decision-makers, and spearheaded the – now popular – notion of 'globalisation with a human face'.

A New Glasnost for Global Sustainability

The Green Cross Optimist, April 2004

It may seem paradoxical, but despite having borne witness to the countless humanitarian and environmental disasters of the past decades I am still an optimist. After all, we have been exposed to an avalanche of grim forecasts regarding our future, seemingly leaving little, if any, room for optimism. But being an optimist does not mean simply looking at the world through rose-tinted glasses, like Voltaire's Candide, and declaring everything to be for the best despite an endless array of misfortunes. Being an optimist, as I see it, means to refuse to make do with the status quo and instead to consciously look for ways to make the world a better place and help address the practical challenges faced by people here and now. I call this 'optimism by action', and I believe that such a philosophy of life could provide the catalyst for the much-needed transformation to sustainable development. The first step is to inform and motivate the people.

Twenty years ago, when glasnost – openness – was used to launch the process of perestroika that transformed the Soviet Union, no one believed that it was doable. But I was driven by the need to 'wake up' those people who had 'fallen asleep' and make them truly active and concerned, to ensure that everyone felt as if they were master of their country, of their enterprise, office or institute – to get the individual involved in all processes. One of the first outcomes of glasnost in the USSR was heightened awareness of the massive environmental problems blighting the country and impassioned public demands to stop the most damaging activities, resulting in the closure of thousands of heavy polluting factories and cancellation of a major project to divert Siberian rivers.

Today I am convinced that the citizens of the world need a reformulated glasnost to invigorate, inform and inspire them to put the staggering resources of our planet and our knowledge to use for the benefit of all citizens of the Earth, not go back to the days of prolific military spending and fear of people whose ways are different from our own. People cannot long tolerate living on a planet where millions of children have no clean water to drink and go to sleep hungry once they know that they have the power to change it. I have faith in humankind, and it is this faith that has allowed me to remain an active optimist.

As the stakes rise higher, with the permanent damage we are doing to our planet and the erosion of global security, there is no time to be lost in addressing the three principle and interlinked challenges of sustainable development: peace and security, poverty and deprivation, and the environment. In the face of international terrorism, the threat of pro-liferation of weapons of mass destruction and frequent local armed conflicts, continuous efforts are needed to ensure peace and security.

The existence of enormous poverty-stricken areas in the world is morally unacceptable and provides the breeding grounds for extre-mism, violence and organised crime unconstrained by any borders. The global environment displays alarming signs of discontent, and problems are no longer localised and manageable. Damage to Earth's atmosphere is causing our climate to change, natural disasters to become more frequent and devastating, glaciers to melt and the polar ice caps to thin; coupled with our irresponsible business practices, ocean fish stocks are depleting, deserts are advancing and thousands of plant and animal species continue to disappear.

We are risking our future for an ephemeral, pollution and exploita-tion based prosperity. Disaster in the form of an oil spill, a chemical leak or even nuclear accident like Chernobyl could strike any day with little being done in the way of prevention. In order not to let this happen we must put an end to the conspiracy of silence of those who are unwilling to change their lifestyles or risk disturbing the foundations of the economic system that pays their bills; we must expose the terrible moral cowardice of those politicians who cover this conspiracy up, refusing to recognise the true extent and nature of modern challenges.

There are clear links between the three sustainable development challenges, both in terms of origin, repercussions and the imperatives they dictate to humankind. One cannot counteract bigotry, crime and terrorism or ensure global security without combating poverty. One cannot address poverty without protecting our human right to fulfil our basic needs and ensuring both environmental protection and equal access to natural resources for all. Human development and environ-mental protection are interdependent objectives. How can one tell the poor of the Amazon basin not to chop down the rainforest to lay a field if this is their only means of making ends meet? How can one demand cost-prohibitive environmental protection measures of a poor country? On the other hand, if nature is not given enough consideration, our efforts to build a more equitable and better world are doomed to founder.

Reflecting upon this, one cannot help wondering what caused the situation we now have on our hands? If the causes are unclear, no rational solution is possible. Our world is becoming rife with conflicts and contradictions, problems with a long heritage whose preconditions have been amassing during the evolution of human civilisation. Today, these conflicts have reached truly global proportions and stand to jeopardise the basic security of humankind. And globalisation, as the prevailing force in world development, must be held responsible. Globalisation lays bare and intensifies all the conflicts and contradictions of the past, and drives them to dangerous degrees.

The world's market-driven globalisation tends to enforce the notion, derived from neo-liberal theory, that economic growth as measured by GNP/GDP indicators is the only way to measure national wealth and progress. Capital accumulation and individual consumption are given a higher status than social and spiritual values or cultural heritage. Ideology and policies of the neo-liberal globalism initiated by the countries that have benefited most from globalisation make this trend that much stronger. The cumulative results of all the individual decisions based on this logic in the long run lead to unforeseen and dangerous consequences.

One often comes across the argument that globalisation, as we know it, is a fait accompli, a process entirely outside our control. Particularly vociferous with this argument, unsurprisingly, are those who want to instil in the public mind the futility and pointlessness of any opposition to globalisation. In the meantime, several highly influential researchers have argued convincingly about the role of political choices as a factor used to harness globalisation and make it work for the benefit of major players in the global marketplace.

That politics lie behind globalisation is unquestionable. In recent years this has been clearly illustrated by the neo-conservatives in the USA seeking to take advantage of globalisation to pursue an imperialist policy of force and impose their will upon the rest of the world. The reason why the force factor comes to the fore possibly lies in the realisation of a few simple facts: natural resources are finite, their use has already exceeded a critical point, and the capture of the lion's share by a smaller (and decreasing) portion of humanity deprives the rest of the world (and growing majority) of equal access to such resources and, in many cases, to the essential means of subsistence.

Is there an alternative to the existing situation? It is my conviction that our history is not predetermined and there is room for an alternative in any situation. It was this pursuit of an alternative development model that led to the elaboration of a sustainable development programme for the world. Agenda 21 was supported by the United Nations and endorsed by the heads of state and government of most states in 1992. For the first time in history, the world community managed to map out and agree a general strategic plan designed to address people's vital problems. However, serious obstacles emerged as implementation started. The governments of industrialised countries chose to retract from their commitments, in particular regarding increasing their development aid, in favour of the philosophy of economic liberalism, deregulation and accelerated economic growth.

Opponents of the sustainable development paradigm have spared no effort in trying to discredit the idea in the public mind. And yet the interest is still there. The so-called 'anti-globalisation movement' (in effect, it is the movement against market-driven fundamentalism) is in favour of an alternative development model. Their motto is: 'Another World is Possible'. International social democracies, rural people, 'green' movements worldwide, and thousands of NGOs representing millions of members also stand behind the sustainable development principle. We are talking about a powerful force whose pressure is being increasingly felt by the ruling elite.

So, what can we do to make a difference? First of all, we need to scrutinise the structural factors inhibiting the transition to sustainable development. We need to better understand the mechanisms of globalisation that are directing development on such a dangerous course. We need to bridge the gap between our moral consciousness and the challenges of the times. Consumerism and national egocentrism continue to pose a serious threat to achieving sustainable development goals. A turn-around will not be possible unless the breach between the objective need to reverse currently prevalent behavioural patterns and the subjective unwillingness of states, communities and individuals to do so is crossed. This turn-around must begin with changes in the human spirit, a reprioritisation of our value system, including relations between people and the interrelationship of human beings with nature.

Currently, politics lags behind the pace of change. Greater analysis of global issues and corresponding recommendations to politicians are needed, and hence the role of science and education ought to be enhanced. There is an urgent need for environmental education and the respect for nature. All this gives science, education and the mass media a special role and responsibility. Prominent scientists have been cautioning us about the dangers looming over humankind for many years. Sadly, they have been paid little heed to, often ignored, and even forgotten altogether.

Facts about global threats gathered by scientists should become public knowledge, and the main vehicle for translating scientific conclusions into terms we can all understand is the mass media. The mass media are needed to build a bridge between civil society and political and economic leaders. The anti-globalisation movement simply says that a different world is possible – the Socialist International adopted a special document on promoting globalisation with a human face. Moreover, the media have an exceptionally important role to play in building a 'society of knowledge'. Interaction of science and the mass media is becoming crucial today. The more society relies on true knowledge, the more desperately it needs it.

But the media are not always consistent; they are often controversial, and sometimes even counterproductive. Scientists and the media both suffer from a 'credibility gap'. Too often the media not so much inform viewing, reading or listening audiences as mislead them. Cheap sensationalism is used to satisfy raw tastes and thus manipulate the public mind. Scientists themselves could use a little help coordinating their actions, and getting the truth across.

Apart from science and the media, the education system is another essential channel of knowledge regarding global challenges and sustainable development. Practically every activity in our times requires knowledge in the area of environmental protection. It is important that people learn, starting in school, how to respect nature, save energy and water resources, and manage domestic waste. Schools of all levels are called upon to instil the concepts of human togetherness, world integrity and the culture of solidarity and peace in their students.

Glasnost could be put to service as a catch-all phrase for all of these weapons in the struggle for transparency and awareness. Glasnost is more than transparency; it is a demanding, long-term process of awakening, which inevitably leads to calls for fundamental changes. In the field of sustainable development, such a process is needed to combat apathy, to engage the people to the task of choosing more equitable and sustainable lifestyles, and to address the dominance of short-term interests and lack of transparency at the decision-making level. A process of glasnost would tackle both aspects of this dangerous blend of indifference and concealment, and ultimately rebuild trust between people, business and government, desperately needed if we are going to stand any chance of achieving the Millennium Development Goals to combat poverty, disease and deprivation by 2015.

The escalation of global problems is in many ways attributable to world politics lagging behind the real processes unfolding in the world. World politics is skidding, proving to be incapable of responding to the challenges of globalisation. I am personally enormously disappointed that, more than a decade after it was given a new lease of life with the end of the cold war, multilateralism is floundering. We have squandered much of the capital of trust and cooperation that emerged at the end of the twentieth century. I am convinced that contemporary world politics is not to be based on the conventional principle of balance of powers, but rather on the balance of interests, and that dialogue between cultures and civilisations must become its primary tool. Politics should concentrate on avenues of cooperation and ways to break through deadlocks by promoting just and long-term real-world solutions, not quick fixes or inequitable compromises.

For several years, a number of prominent civil and political leaders have gone to great lengths to develop moral frameworks for sustainable development. These efforts bore fruition in the form of the Earth Charter (2000), a code of ethics for the planet. The Earth Charter outlines the interrelationship between humans and the rest of nature – it spells out a new set of ecological principles as guidelines for human behaviour. The Charter has become an important document in the sustainable development field and the Earth Dialogues is part of the process of promoting an understanding of the 16 principles of the Earth Charter. Today, the Earth Charter is endorsed by more than 8000 organisations that represent hundreds of millions of people.

Under current circumstances, it is becoming an extremely pressing task to have this code of basic moral principles observed by governments, business and NGOs simply in order give future generations and our planet a chance to survive. In a world increasingly besieged by corruption, greed and self-interest, we need leaders who have the moral courage to ground their decisions in this new global ethic and sustainable development principles.

Among these principles, solidarity takes a special place. The principle of solidarity has played a vital role at all times, especially in small groups, communities and social movements, but in this day and age the imperative of global solidarity moves to the foreground. This means solidarity of a higher order, to meet the requirements of globalisation as the dominant trend of modern world development. It is solidarity that

Energy Shift, NOW!

Address at the Green Cross Energy Dialogues, Universal Forum of Cultures, Barcelona, 2 June 2004

One of the greatest challenges facing our planet and humanity is finding radically new and clean energy solutions for sustainable development. The generation and consumption of energy is quite simply the foundation of modern economies. While the harnessing of energy by humankind has brought with it many benefits – transportation, heating, cooking, industrial development and now this infant information economy – it has also come with very heavy environmental impacts, including air pollution, oil spills, massive habitat devastation, nuclear waste problems which will be passed on to a multitude of human generations, and finally the ever-growing and more severe problem of climate change.

It is clear that the world must embark on a new energy path, for transportation, electricity, industry, and our homes and offices too. Consumerism is becoming rampant in the world – particularly in the United States – and is creating an unsustainable lifestyle and standard of living. At our current rates, we cannot support the energy demands of our society – we see the tensions in the Middle East over the need to secure supplies of oil for the West, China is quickly becoming one of the largest importers of oil, and all this to secure oil supplies for a very short time, some estimating 40 to 50 years left of oil supply.

At this current rate, without radical reductions in energy use and emissions, we are on the course for a disaster, not too unlike the Hollywood movie that was just released around the world, *The Day After Tomorrow*, which is about an extreme scenario for climate change that destroys the United States and much of the world.

To change our course, a global value shift in the minds and actions of humanity is necessary and should start as soon as possible. But nature will not wait. So we face a conundrum: how do we help the developing countries lift out of poverty without using the same Victorian age technologies that built the wealth of Europe, Russia and, particularly, America? How do we provide clean power to the two billion people without access to electricity (a major stumbling block to breaking the cycle of poverty)? At the same time, how do we maintain the economic engine of OECD countries without creating a major climate change

Gorbachev announcing the launch of the Global Solar Report Card in San Antonio, Texas in March 2009

disaster, how do we move our goods around the world or from region to region without polluting our air, and how do our cities maintain their vibrant nature if blackouts become the norm?

So it is clear — we face two different yet related challenges. The first is the over-consumption of energy by the developed world. OECD countries account for 53 per cent of the world's energy usage with less than 20 per cent of the world's population.

On the other side of the scale is the great need for energy in the developing economies of the world. We can see very plainly energy use is the equivalent of economic development. Unfortunately, this use in developed economies is extremely wasteful and the first step to an energy solution for developed economies is to become more efficient, much more efficient.

Secondly, developed economies have an advantage in that they have been able to use oil as a primary inexpensive energy source for many years, but now we are coming to a point of increasingly tight oil supplies — not to mention its detrimental environmental impacts from habitat destruction to oil spills, air pollution and of course climate change. Worldwide, oil remains the greatest energy source. It supplies 35 per cent of the world's current energy needs, over 40 per cent in the industrialised nations. We are seeing the value of this 'black gold' grow now to 40 dollars a barrel, while reserves are drawn down and demand increases. We are also seeing increased instability and threats of war grow in areas that have the remaining world reserves. We only need to look at Iraq and other regions where tensions mount.

We must create a radical shift – in our values, technologies, and lives – that rethinks how we produce and deliver energy. We need an energy shift for not just the developed world, but the developing world as well. The old ways are not working. We need to open up our energy systems from the control of oil companies that too often dictate foreign policy and electric utilities that resist distributed energy like solar power, and allow for innovation to free our bonds from this addiction to fossil fuels.

We must radically increase our use of energy efficiency to improve technologies – to produce and live with less energy. Buildings use 40 per cent of the world's energy, so we must start with the design of our appliances, buildings, transportation and our cities. As OECD economies were able to develop using the world's oil supplies, they now bear the economic and moral burden to develop and implement the next generation of clean fuel technologies for both themselves and – just as importantly – the developing economies.

We must also find a way to reach a substantial goal for clean energy and achieve it within 10 to 15 years; 20–25 per cent of our world's energy use should come from renewable energy by 2020. The composition of renewable energy should include solar, wind, geothermal and tidal, and there should be standards for appropriate biomass technologies. Large dams are controversial solutions as we know, but small hydropower solutions should be considered and developed.

This goal for renewable energy is important not only for the environment – it is important for our world's security. We can reduce many of the current tensions and security issues that arise from oil dependence. We can reduce military spending and conflict around the world while maintaining a strong economy. To succeed in fighting terrorism, we must reduce our dependence on oil from the Middle East and Central Asia.

In addition, the changes that are happening in the global climate are threatening international peace and stability. One of the leading causes of conflict, poverty and disease is the shortage of fresh water. Hydrology around the globe is being changed by climate change – climate change is causing severe and more frequent drought in some regions, and droughts in places where we didn't have droughts before, while creating massive flooding and the displacement of millions of people in other parts of the world. This is why Green Cross acts on this issue with such urgency.

If droughts continue and the food resources of the world are undermined (even today more than a billion people are hungry on a daily basis), we will see a situation that will deteriorate; we will see social tensions that threaten to spiral out of control adding fuel to extremism.

We have seen in Russia, in the Arctic, that the ice has thinned. We know that Africa is not the same as it used to be, as the glacier on Kilimanjaro has receded at rapid rates.

The Kyoto Protocol is important. We have heard good news from Moscow and President Putin that Russia will accelerate the ratification of the Kyoto Protocol. But we must push the USA to take action. They alone can undo the progress of the current signatories to the Kyoto Protocol.

To solve climate change, however, a new energy era is needed, one that is more in tune with the rhythm of the planet. The unsustainable burning of fossil fuel must end. The damming of the world's great rivers and the mass destruction of habitats must be mitigated. Women across the planet must be freed from the shackles of collecting fuel for cooking meals.

The planet and the sun, in their natural cycles, provide an abundance of energy, and we need to use it. For electricity, wind, solar, geothermal, marine and biomass are all technologies whose time has come. For transportation, solar created hydrogen for fuel cells could be viable as well.

We hope the leaders in Bonn at the Renewables 2004 meeting, which grew out of the WSSD in Johannesburg, will heed this call by embracing a vision and action plan for renewable energy to achieve 20 to 25 per cent.

As part of this solution, Green Cross proposes the creation of a Global Solar Fund. The Global Solar Fund presents a vision, a vision for helping the energy-impoverished developing world, as well as creating concentrations of solar energy in cities that can be used to prevent blackouts, lower energy bills for the poor, and provide a source for creating renewable hydrogen.

The Global Solar Fund would provide 50 billion dollars over the next ten years to install solar photovoltaic energy around the planet, driving down the price and creating a mass market for a clean fuel technology. We should focus on those with no access to electricity.

There are positive signs already. In 2002, 48 million dollars was provided by the Spanish Government to provide solar electrification for

400,000 homes in the Philippines. The solar systems in the Philippines will reduce the dependence of villages on non-renewable energy sources. The systems will also slow deforestation as less wood will be cut to meet daily needs, and contribute to improved water supplies and better health and education facilities. Solar powered pumping and irrigation systems will free women and children from spending much of their time gathering food.

The fundamental element to all sustainable economies is clean, renewable energy. We need a value shift, to change the paradigm of energy use. We need an openness of the electricity grid to allow for solutions such as solar, a transparent solution to provide electricity for the energy impoverished, and democratisation of energy solutions for transportation that all increase our energy independence. Let political leaders in Bonn hear from the voice of the people from our meeting today that we must act now.

Gorbachev was frustrated by the slow pace and lack of investment in renewable energy development and wanted to send a strong message to the International Conference on Renewable Energies that was taking place in Bonn, Germany, the same week as the GCI Energy Dialogue in Barcelona, Spain.

Led by Global Green USA, GCI launched a variety of practical initiatives to promote the switch to solar power, including the Global Solar Fund proposal and, since 2008, the 'Solar Report Card' which is designed to give an accurate and essential perspective on progress – or lack thereof. Though there remains a long way to go, since this speech was made worldwide photovoltaic installations have increased at an average annual rate of 60 per cent, and there are now six times as many as in 2004.

When Gorbachev in his speech called for states to aim for renewables to make up at least 20–25 per cent of their total energy mix, many thought he was unrealistic. But, in 2007, the EU adopted a target of 20 per cent by 2020, and in January 2011 announced that they expect to exceed this goal.

The Third Pillar of Sustainable Development

Foreword to *Toward a Sustainable World: The Earth Charter in Action*, 2005

The current millennium started with the recognition by the international community of the many critical situations it faces, the most appalling of which are addressed in the United Nations Millennium Declaration: hunger, poverty, gender inequality, child mortality, water crisis and environmental decline. In more general terms, I believe that the world is confronted today with three major challenges which encompass all other problems: the challenge of security, including the risks associated with weapons of mass destruction and terrorism; the challenge of poverty and underdeveloped economies; and the challenge of environmental sustainability.

No national government, even that of a super-powerful state, no group of countries, even the richest ones, can meet these challenges alone. The deadly terrorist attacks in London in July 2005 came as the latest tragic reminder of this reality. We must and will fight terrorism, but one should not forget that we might lose this war if we do not eradicate its roots. The only answer is a universal coalition of informed, responsible and active citizens. Hence the importance of initiatives like the Earth Charter which, from an idea shared by a handful of like-minded individuals, has developed into a mass movement supported by millions of people worldwide.

The book in front of you is not simply another activity report that any organisation regularly compiles — far more than five years of work lie behind it. Movements like the Earth Charter Initiative do not come to life spontaneously or out of the blue. The fact of their creation is preceded by a more or less long prenatal period during which the people concerned come to understand their needs, formulate their demands, organise themselves, and get ready for action. In this sense, the book *Toward a Sustainable World: The Earth Charter in Action* is a testimony to the process of all humanity becoming mature, aware of the dangers it faces, and of the responsibilities it will inevitably have to assume vis-à-vis future generations if it continues to treat the environment as 'business as usual'.

The subjects dealt with and opinions expressed in the book are as varied and complex as our reality itself, and range from more global

*Maurice Strong
and Gorbachev
at the Rio +5
Summit in 1997*

concepts like democracy, non-violence and peace to very practical issues of youth employment and gender equality. Another very impressive feature revealed by the book is the multitude of purposes for which the Earth Charter can be used: promotion of equitable employment, citizen participation in environmental and educational programmes, creating global dialogue on sustainable development, working with ex-combatants from war-torn regions, and even local campaigns against genetically modified organisms. This list can be continued.

One of the main themes of the Earth Charter, and of the book, the theme particularly dear to me as Founding President of Green Cross International, is ecological integrity and our common responsibility for its preservation. I was not born an ecologist, but the environment has always meant a lot to me. I grew up in a village and perceived the dying of rivers and land erosion as personal pain. Right after coming to power in the Soviet Union, I had to deal with a huge project of reversing the flow of the rivers from north to south. If not stopped, it would have resulted in a tremendous ecological disaster. I thought this was a tough school. Yet I still had Chernobyl to face. This catastrophe of planetary scale shook the world and showed, in the harshest form, that nature does not forgive human mistakes.

The Earth Charter is an unusual document since it reflects a new, universally shared level of understanding of the interdependence between humans and nature. It also corresponds to the stage of globalisation at which we find ourselves.

Coming back to the three challenges I mentioned earlier, two global documents are called to help the human community to cope with them.

The first pillar is the Charter of the United Nations, which regulates the relations among states and thus sets the rules for their behaviour in order to secure peace and stability. The second pillar is the Universal Declaration of Human Rights, which regulates the relations between states and individuals and guarantees to all citizens a set of rights, which their respective governments should provide. The importance of these two documents cannot be overestimated. But it has become obvious that another document is missing, one which would regulate the relations among states, individuals and nature by defining the human duties towards the environment.

In my opinion, the Earth Charter should fill this void, acquire equal status, and become the third pillar supporting the peaceful development of the modern world. The process of its endorsement has already begun – it is endorsed by the United Nations Educational, Scientific and Cultural Organisation (UNESCO), a growing number of local and national governments, and many non-governmental organisations. However, we founders and supporters should consider our mission accomplished only when the Earth Charter is universally adopted by the international community.

In this Foreword, Gorbachev reveals what the Earth Charter means to him, as one of its original founders, and what he hopes it will mean for the world. There is a direct line of thought going back to his speech at the Issyk-Kul Forum in 1986, in which he referred to the primacy of universal human values for the first time, to the final text of the Earth Charter, which so perfectly embodies these values in union with nature. In 2010, the Earth Charter celebrated ten years since it was launched after the most partici-patory drafting process of any document in history.

Today the Earth Charter has been formally endorsed by over 4500 orga-nisations, representing millions of people. Endorsement has come from environmental groups like IUCN, over 250 universities, religious groups, mayors of cities and local and regional authorities, political parties, citizen and youth groups, the UN agency UNESCO, and countless individual sup-porters. The importance of the Earth Charter is acknowledged in many UN and other inter-governmental documents, and some international lawyers consider that it is acquiring the status of a 'soft law' document alongside the Universal Declaration of Human Rights, as Gorbachev envisaged from the beginning.

The Lessons of Chernobyl

To mark the twentieth anniversary of the Chernobyl disaster, Mikhail Gorbachev was interviewed in Moscow by Galia Ackerman, a Russian translator and writer. The English version of the interview was published in *The Green Cross Optimist* magazine in 2006.

Q: Mr President, how did you find out about what happened at Chernobyl? What were your first decisions?

MG: I received a call at five o'clock in the morning on 26 April 1986, informing me that a serious accident, followed by a fire, had just occurred in the fourth block of the Chernobyl nuclear power station, but that the reactor was still intact. I should clarify that in those early hours, until the evening of 26 April, we had not yet realised that the reactor had actually exploded and that there had been a huge discharge of radioactive materials into the atmosphere. Nobody had any idea that we were facing a major nuclear disaster.

Nevertheless, I ordered that a government commission be immediately created, charged with the task of determining the causes of the accident and coordinating the activities necessary to liquidate the damage. Later in the morning experts from Moscow and Kiev arrived on site, and in the evening they were met by the government commission, presided over by Boris Shcherbina, vice-president of the Council of Ministers. I was in permanent contact with Shcherbina and with the academician Valery Legasov, vice-director of the Kurchatov Institute in Moscow, who regularly informed me of everything that was happening on the site. During the first days we also set up a special group at the Politburo to coordinate the work of the government commission and other departments and ministries involved. Gradually, as we became aware of the magnitude of the disaster, its liquidation also assumed greater and greater dimensions. Naturally, we can regret, today, after the fact, that we did not grasp everything more quickly.

Q: And what was your first reaction to what had just happened?

MG: I was astounded: how was such a thing possible? Nuclear scientists had always assured the country's leadership that our nuclear reactors were completely safe. The academician Anatoli Alexandrov, for example, used to boast that we could install an RBMK reactor in the middle of Red Square, as they were no more dangerous than a samovar.

Q: Scientists were afraid that a second explosion would occur in the heart of the damaged reactor. What other threats did you consider to be particularly serious?

MG: Immediately after the accident, the management of the station gave the order to flood the reactor with water, because, I repeat, they were not aware of the fact that the reactor had exploded and that there was nothing left to extinguish (several fires had broken out in various parts of the station, but the reactor itself was not on fire). Finally, the pool under the reactor, and some underground locations were filled up with water. Scientists were afraid that if the hot mass of nuclear fuel and graphite were to rupture the bottom of the reactor's tank and fall into radioactive water this would create the conditions for a nuclear explosion.

We were not panicking. The probability of such an explosion was in the order of five to ten per cent, but we urgently needed to pump out this water. This was completed at the beginning of May. In this way, such an explosion, as slight as its probability may have been, was effectively prevented.

There were other threats that needed to be eliminated with the utmost urgency. There remained the danger that the mass at the heart of the reactor would rupture its tank and even blast through the foundations of the building housing the reactor, thereby coming into contact with the soil and leading to a major contamination of groundwater. We also had to prevent the radioactive waste and debris from around the plant from contaminating the waters of the Dnieper and Desna rivers. You must appreciate that this required operations on a massive scale.

Firstly, at the proposition of the government commission, and with the approval of the Politburo, we called for help from the miners of Donbass and Toula. Under extreme conditions, they dug a tunnel under the reactor and installed a thick slab of concrete, equipped with cooling pipes, which measured 30 by 30 metres. Thus, thanks to the prowess of engineers and the heroism of these miners, we were able to isolate the reactor from any groundwater.

Secondly, we built a ten kilometre long dyke along the right bank of the River Pripyat, as is often done in order to prevent flooding. We then dug an 'underground wall' several kilometres long; this was a very deep trench which was filled with bentonite, an isolating material intended to prevent any infiltration of contaminated waters from the power station.

Moreover, planes were circling the area around the power station to who was extremely well informed on the situation at Chernobyl and suffered very much. By the way, he did propose some very important measures for the liquidation of the consequences of the disaster, including the idea of dumping sand and lead on the reactor. Perhaps he considered that he did not always make the right evaluations? You know, the human soul is difficult to penetrate, and he did not leave a note before his suicide. The fact that he committed suicide practically on the anniversary of the disaster, 27 April 1988, and that he had dictated five audiotapes with his account of the events at Chernobyl, leaves one to suppose a link between these two tragic events.

Q: You write in your book *My Manifesto for the Earth* that Chernobyl changed you into a different man. Could you explain this?

MG: I've always had a link with the earth. I grew up in a peasant family, and since my childhood have always worked in the fields. At 16 I helped my father driving tractors. My higher studies at university were not only in law, but also in agricultural management. Later on, I was governor of the region of Stavropol, which had experienced 52 droughts in the last century. That is where my passion for ecology stems from.

However, it was only on my arrival at the Kremlin, when I became Secretary-General of the CPSU, that I understood the dimensions of the ecological disaster in the USSR and the urgent need to improve the situation. It is not a coincidence that glasnost manifested itself for the very first time in the field of ecology – the first mass movements were born out of protest against industrial pollution. Thanks to these popular demonstrations, we were able to stop several toxic industrial processes; among other things we closed hundreds of chemical factories that were destroying the environment, and we also put an end to the insane project of diverting the great Siberian rivers.

Nevertheless, Chernobyl profoundly shocked me. I have just said that it altered my perception of our planet and rendered the cold war more obsolete than ever. But it is not the only lesson that I have drawn from this disaster, far from it.

Q: And what were the other lessons of Chernobyl?

MG: Chernobyl clearly demonstrated that each disaster is unique and that no country can be prepared for every eventuality. That is why we must deploy the maximum amount of effort to prevent disasters. One must not compromise on nuclear safety. The social, ecological and economic consequence of this kind of disaster is much too heavy, in

1. Gorbachev with the Rt Hon. Margaret Thatcher in Oxfordshire in December 1987

2. Gorbachev throws the first pitch of the game as President Bush watches at Tiger Field in College Station, Texas, April 2001

3. Gorbachev with Shoo Iwasaki and Rabbi Soetendorp at the launch of Green Cross International, the Hague, 1993

4. Green Cross International's General Assembly, Kyoto, 1998

5. *Meeting of the Green Cross International Board, October 2009, Geneva*

6. *Gorbachev with the winners of Green Cross Japan Environmental Diary Contest, Tokyo, December 2009*

7. Gorbachev with the then UN Secretary-General Kofi Annan, 2001

8. Gorbachev with the Dalai Lama at a Peace Nobel Laureates Summit, Rome,
December 2007

9. *Gorbachev with Franco Frattini and George Shultz at the Overcoming Nuclear Dangers Conference, Rome, April 2009*

10. *Gorbachev and Ted Turner at Global Green's 5th Annual Sustainable Design Awards, New York, October 2003*

11. *Gorbachev introduces UN Secretary General Ban Ki-moon to members of the Climate Change Task Force, Geneva, October 2009*

12. *Gorbachev with GCI President Alexander Likhotal, Moscow, July 2010*

13. *Gorbachev presenting the International Green Film Award to Leonardo DiCaprio at the Cinema for Peace Awards, Berlin, February 2009*

14. *Gorbachev accepting the Globe Energy Award at the European Parliament, Brussels, May 2008*

15. *Gorbachev and Global Green President and CEO Matt Petersen visiting the levee in New Orleans following Hurricane Katrina, October 2007*

16. *Gorbachev at the UN, Geneva, October 2009*

every sense of the word. We can therefore see what enormous responsibility is placed not only on politicians, but on scientists, engineers, and designers — their mistakes could cost the life and health of millions of people.

Q: Was it the Chernobyl disaster that prompted you to create Green Cross International?

MG: When I assumed leadership, in 1993, of a new non-governmental organisation baptised Green Cross International, I had been prepared for this decision by the entire story of my life, and Chernobyl certainly contributed to that. Today it is a very resolute NGO with affiliates in 30 countries.

Naturally, providing help to the victims of Chernobyl, especially to children and adolescents, constitutes an important part of our activities. Our programmes, carried out by our national organisations in Belarus, Russia and Ukraine, and financed by Switzerland and other European countries, concentrate on providing help to children and adolescents living in the contaminated regions. These young people have a weakened immune system, and suffer from a number of health pathologies. For them Green Cross International organises therapeutic holiday camps, from which over 12,000 young people have already profited in the last ten years.

We cannot separate the ecological consequences of Chernobyl from the socio-economic aspects, and issues of health. The victims of Chernobyl continue to suffer both physically and mentally; it is our moral duty to help them while continuing to limit the ecological consequences of this disaster.

The Chernobyl nuclear accident was a watershed moment, not only for the USSR and Gorbachev's leadership but also on a more personal level. The event, and its aftermath, not only spearheaded glasnost (transparency), but also moved Gorbachev deeply and was a decisive factor in his decision to devote his time to promoting sustainable development and environmental responsibility. The seeds of the Green Cross concept were sown that week in 1986 as Gorbachev realised in the most painful way that we are the guests and not the masters of nature.

Interview with The House Magazine

2006

The House Magazine: Are environmental issues too long-term to be embraced by election-seeking politicians?

MG: I think there is a considerably overstated, apparent contradiction between long-term environmental issues and election-seeking politicians. Strategically, any political activity – whether related to economics, foreign policy or social issues – depends heavily on the prevailing discourse circulating within society at that given time. In this sense, long-term environmental issues are the same as any other; if a nation believes that environmental challenges are a real issue, a politician – particularly one seeking office – cannot ignore this sentiment ...

HM: How do the environmental threats to the Earth compare to the nuclear threats of two decades ago?

MG: In this regard, I agree with Hans Blix who believes that the challenge of the environment today is more ominous than that of war, and that global warming is a bigger threat than even a military conflict. In this regard we must take seriously the Intergovernmental Panel on Climate Change's recent report, which affirms that an overall increase in temperature of just three degrees Celsius would so substantially diminish proper water and soil that 400 million people would face the risk of death. Globally, whether a population is developed or developing, we must thus work together to combat these challenges and preserve our world's future ...

I feel that civil society, which in the last years has evolved from an abstract notion into a real force, should embrace a more pro active stance in solving these mounting problems, rather than simply blaming governments for their inertia and lack of political will. One good example is the recent UK-based initiative Make Poverty History.

Nearly one trillion dollars is spent each year on the world's militaries, a fifth of which is borne by developing countries. In contrast, analysts estimate that 50 billion dollars in additional annual funding could achieve the Millennium Development Goals.

HM: What do you hope to be agreed at the G8 summit in July?

MG: The G8 Summit in St Petersburg will address energy security as a top priority. GCI believes that this should be seized as an opportunity for the world's largest industrialised nations to make strong commitments to a truly secure and sustainable energy future. Energy security is an issue that affects every person on the planet, whether in developed countries facing the need to ensure reliable supplies and reduce greenhouse gas emissions, or in developing countries struggling to meet basic needs and enhance their opportunities. Decisions made related to energy today will also have major consequences on future generations. Therefore, there is too much at stake to allow short-term political considerations to dominate proceedings. We are concerned that different signals from preparatory sessions seem to be concentrated on securing the supply routes of oil and gas, and facilitating a renewed growth in nuclear power. This approach lacks vision, and if renewable energy and energy efficiency are relegated to secondary status in their discussions the G8 will fail to move forward on providing real solutions to the energy and climate change crises.

G8 nations have a global responsibility to lead the advancement towards a sustainable energy future. This is too important to be left to leaders and ministers alone: parliaments must play a stronger role in pushing for concrete action, reflecting the will of the majority of citizens in G8 states to address climate change. In this regard, we welcome the creation of the Climate Change Dialogue between parliamentarians and business leaders.

HM: How can the G8 countries encourage fast-growing nations like India, China and Brazil to adopt environmental policies? Is this fair?

MG: These countries are emerging as economic powerhouses, opening up considerable opportunities for their own citizens and the entire global community, but at what cost to the environment and global stability? The enormous increase in demand for energy and natural resources that is driving their growth represents a major risk. If India and China – with their population of 2.5 billion – replicated the energy consumption models of the West, experts claim that we would need the equivalent of three planets Earth to meet the world's needs. Obviously we don't have three planets. I commend the leaders of these two nations for recognising that they cannot follow a resource-intensive model of development in the twenty-first century; though far more needs to be done, they are already making strides in sustainable energy and agriculture.

While recognising that the per capita consumption of energy and resources in North America and Europe is far higher than in China or India, I believe it is the responsibility of all business and political partners and leaders in these emerging economies to follow the principles of sustainable development, and to develop and implement international standards for environmental protection, non-proliferation, and global security. For example, environmental issues must be incorporated into the framework of the GLOBE G8+5 Legislators Dialogue, where leaders from India, China, Brazil, Mexico and South Africa will unite with G8 participants prior to the Summit. I hope that the developed world will recognise that all our futures are at stake and pledge to support these nations in their development of clean and renewable energy, recycling solutions, and resource efficient technologies.

And to reiterate, of course double standards should not be tolerated: the West must take its share of responsibility and refocus its development as well.

Look at the recent dispute between Argentina and Uruguay over the construction of two paper mills on Uruguay River. The authorities of Argentina and environmentalists in both countries are concerned that it will lead to the pollution of air and water. In fact, their arguments convinced the World Bank to suspend its loan of 400 million US dollars until a new environmental impact assessment. I am very pleased that the authorities of Argentina, with the consent of their counterparts in Uruguay, invited Green Cross International to contribute to the resolution of this conflict – but what is most important is that these kinds of problems can and should be resolved jointly.

HM: Should the failure of the Kyoto agreement be a cause for alarm?

MG: I am generally not one to panic. The Kyoto Protocol represented an opportunity for a minimum progress, which meant that it would be necessary to dramatically increase the objectives of CO_2 reduction in the future. If enacted, the Kyoto Protocol would give industrialised countries until 2012 to reduce their combined emissions of carbon dioxide and other heat-trapping gases slightly more than five per cent below 1990 levels. That means that the Protocol would only constitute a first small step in the right direction, though a much bigger effort is needed. According to the Intergovernmental Panel on Climate Change, humanity must reduce carbon emissions by about 70 per cent to stabilise the climate. In reality, the Kyoto process has already moved beyond naive ideas of emission trading and towards joint projects where European countries, for example, invest in the introduction of cleaner technologies.

But whatever the fate of the Protocol, it has already achieved a success in one sense, by putting the world on a path towards solving this long-term problem. The process of advancing towards limiting releases of gases, after more than a century of relentless increases, has clearly begun. The European Union had already passed a law requiring a cap and credit-trading system for the heat-trapping gases in 2005, which follows the pattern outlined in Kyoto, regardless of what happens with the treaty itself.

Spurred by the prospect of international curbs on emissions, many corporations with long-term business plans have started changing practices and adjusting investments to focus on improving energy efficiency. Even in the United States, where the President and the Republican-controlled Congress strongly oppose the treaty, legislation that would require stronger restrictions on emissions than those in the Kyoto pact has gained some momentum. Does it mean then that the 'don't worry, be happy' approach is acceptable? Unfortunately no, business as usual does not work any more. A Chinese proverb warns, 'If we do not change direction, we are likely to end up exactly where we are headed.'

Applied to contemporary humanity, this would be disastrous. Without a change in direction we are on the way to: a world of increasing population pressure and spreading poverty; increasing the potential for social and political conflicts; accelerating climate change; and augmenting water, food and energy shortages.

HM: Should environmental policies be funded by the state through tax and not private investment?

MG: One of the primary principles of Green Cross is the belief that environmental challenges are a universal problem and their resolution must engage all actors of society, whether private or otherwise. Often, however, the question of funding this process arises only after governments make the appropriate political decisions. Thus, while I believe that we all maintain a certain level of responsibility, the government must take the lead in implementing the necessary decisions and creating a system that would encourage private businesses to invest in sustainable development while simultaneously dissuading environmentally damaging ventures. The 'green taxes' applied in the USA are a good example of this.

HM: Is investing in a new generation of nuclear power stations a short-term fix or a long-term solution?

MG: I don't think it is a question of time: for me, it is simply a matter of approach. This past June, I had the opportunity to address the British Parliament's All-Party Parliamentary Group on Climate Change where, in my capacity as Chairman of Green Cross International, I discussed energy security issues. In this speech, I tried to emphasise how problematic it would be to build a new generation of nuclear power stations as a solution to the energy crisis. In my judgement, nuclear power is not a panacea for dealing with the world's energy deficit, nor is it an instrument for fighting climate change. Having intimately experienced the Chernobyl disaster I am rather well informed on this issue; during my time in office and even to the present, millions have been spent on repairing the damage, thousands of human lives have been lost and are continuously affected, and the inflicted areas have been badly contaminated for several generations.

At the same time let's be realistic; four hundred nuclear reactors are active around the world and new plants are anticipated. China, Japan, France, the US, the UK and Russia maintain a similar approach, implying that nuclear energy is the ultimate enduring solution to the energy crisis and ensuing complexities of climate change. I certainly do not share this view. But we cannot expect the dismantling of nuclear power in a fortnight. Even if it is an evil, at this moment, it is a necessary one. However, we must clarify that it is not the only solution and major investments in the development of renewable and safe energy sources must be advanced.

HM: What is the Global Solar Fund and how will it make a difference?

MG: The Global Solar Fund is a recent initiative of Green Cross International that reflects our vision for how to help the energy deficit and resulting problems currently afflicting the developing world. Through an endowment of 50 billion dollars over ten years the Global Solar Fund would develop solar photovoltaic equipment for global use which, if successful, could reduce energy prices and create a mass market for clean fuel technology. In addition, through decreasing subsidies for fossil fuels like oils and coals – which the World Bank estimates equals about 210 billion dollars annually – the total sum of the Global Solar Fund could increase over time. Considering that the International Energy Agency has approximated that a total of 17 trillion dollars should be invested in the energy sector prior to 2030, allocating a portion of this savings into the Global Solar Fund is logical. When one considers that oil company profits hit 100 billion dollars last year alone, Green Cross International's 50 billion dollars investment really pales in comparison.

HM: If money can be raised so quickly for war, why can it not be found for environmental innovation?

MG: Good question. Indeed, it took just two weeks for the US Government to raise 70 billion dollars to start a war in Iraq. At the same time, according to the estimates of UN specialised agencies, if governments allocated an amount equivalent to 20 dollars per capita towards solving the water crisis every year it would take only 10 years to solve the problem. Moreover, according to a recent assessment by the WHO, every dollar invested in reaching the Millennium Development Goals could bring from 3 to 34 in revenue. Just 20 dollars per person – how can anyone claim that is unattainable? And yet it is not happening, and millions of people, especially children, continue to die from a lack of water or from water-related diseases. What a shame! Why is it so? I share Kofi Annan's view – it is the paralyses of political will, inertia, and short-sightedness of decision-makers. Hence the particular importance of civil society. This is the position of Green Cross International, and if you share it I invite everyone to support our action.

Published by Dods

As the emerging economies of China, India, Brazil and other rapidly developing states began to take centre stage in discussions about climate change and other challenges, Gorbachev made clear in this interview that the West must take their fair share of responsibility for the damage that they have already caused.

He strongly condemns using the rise of these new economic powers as an excuse on the part of the US and other industrial states not to take decisive action on climate change, though stressing that the emerging economies, especially India and China, must adopt sustainable development strategies. Disputes over this very issue set the stage for tense climate negotiations in the following years as attempts to chart the post-Kyoto climate agenda reached fever pitch in the run-up to the Copenhagen Climate Summit in 2009.

Antarctica: The Global Warning

Foreword by Mikhail Gorbachev to book by Sebastian Copeland
(October 2007)

In January 1991, I received a message from Jacques-Yves Cousteau who
was sailing to Antarctica for a scientific mission and public awareness
campaign designed to protect the white continent for future generations
and to create a World Peace Park in Antarctica. At the time, certain
groups wanted to exploit the hypothetical underground mineral
resources of the Antarctic. A Convention had been negotiated between
parties of the Antarctica Treaty that would guarantee a fair and clean
exploitation. Captain Cousteau, who along with many NGOs was aware
of the risk of accidents and their potentially drastic consequences for
such a fragile and unique environment, proposed to replace the unen-
forceable Convention with a Protocol that aimed to truly protect the
environment. In 1992 this Protocol was adopted in Madrid: Antarctica
was declared 'Land of Science, Land of Peace' and protected for 50
years. It was a wise decision taken by politicians heeding the call of
millions of citizens around the world.

Nevertheless, today, Antarctica is once again threatened: this time not
by oil or coal exploitation, but by global warming. The impact of climate
change is most apparent in the Antarctic, where global warming has
driven significant changes in the physical and living environment,
causing ice to melt faster than anywhere else in the world. Antarctic
surveys have clarified several key issues in the field of the science of
climate change and unveiled the clearest link between greenhouse gas
levels in the atmosphere and surface temperatures. If all the ice captured
in Antarctica were to melt, sea level would rise by a terrifying 60 metres.

Climate change is happening now and will remain with us for a long
time to come. As a result, in the past decade, the number of floods,
hurricanes, tropical storms and other natural disasters has quadrupled
in comparison with the 1960s. Scientists have already calculated that —
if the carbon gas concentration continues to grow at current rates —
during the course of the present century the average temperature of the
earth will rise by between 1.1 and 6.4 degrees Celsius. It is time to act to
avoid the clearly forecast global climatic catastrophe; now is the time to
develop efficient solutions on a local, national and global level.

More than an indicator of the effects of human activity on global

warming, I truly believe that Antarctica should become a powerful symbol to raise awareness of the urgent need to save our planet while there is still time.

It is in this essence of hopefulness that *Antarctica: The Global Warning* came into being. It depicts the ephemeral and austere beauty of Antarctica through stunning photographs of the largest remaining wilderness on Earth. But, while Antarctica appears to be the last unspoiled place on Earth, its balance is being systematically endangered by rising temperatures caused by greenhouse gases emitted thousands of miles away.

I hope from the heart that this book will inspire you to further explore the issues surrounding climate change and its impact at the farthest reaches of our planet.

Gorbachev has been lending his voice to 'global warnings' from both Poles since the first Green Cross-led expedition in 2005. This book was the result of a groundbreaking 2006 multinational expedition of scientists, researchers and photographers, which brought back unique images from Antarctica, illustrating the melting ice shelf. The expedition team, including Global Green USA board member and renowned photographer Sebastian Copeland and GC Argentina representatives, sent a stark SOS message on the imminent danger of warming trends. At the other end of the Earth, missions to the Arctic have included the 2008 voyage of young 'Arctic Ambassadors' to document the changing climate in northern Canada, organised by Global Green USA, and 'Pax Arctica', a series of expeditions to the Arctic led by Green Cross France in conjunction with GC affiliates in Canada, the USA, Denmark, Russia and Sweden. All of these missions had a strong educational focus, engaging everyone from children, to climatologists, to Hollywood stars, and have been at the forefront of raising international awareness on the effect that climate change is already having in the fragile polar regions.

The World Food Crisis

Rossiskaya Gazeta, 13 May 2008

The world food crisis seems to have caught political leaders and even specialists in the field off guard. First called a 'silent tsunami', it is no longer silent. Many countries, including some that are critically important for regional and global stability, have already seen unrest and even food riots.

Several causes of the crisis stand out: growing food consumption in rapidly developing China and India; increased demand for biofuels like ethanol, mostly made of grain; and changes in weather conditions caused by global warming and water shortages.

The first is an inescapable trend, and we must rejoice that hundreds of millions of people are pulling themselves out of poverty and can afford decent food. Our planet is quite capable of feeding them: experts estimate that with existing agricultural technologies, global production should be enough for eight billion people.

The main reasons for the sudden crisis are man-made, resulting from action or inaction by politicians.

Were they not warned about global warming and the need for measures to fight it and adjust to it? Production of ethanol was presented as an environmentally beneficial way to reduce dependency on oil. But it was not carefully thought through, and the result has been ironic: taxpayers in a number of countries subsidise the conversion of grain into ethanol, thus reducing food resources. This creates a vicious circle, which proves once again that there are no simple solutions or magic wands.

The Director-General of the UN Food and Agriculture Organisation, Jacques Diouf, was right to point out recently that the crisis had been building up for decades and was the result of 'inappropriate policies over the past 20 years'. While aid to agriculture in developing countries was cut in half between 1990 and 2000, the industrialised world maintained generous subsidies for its own farmers. So that's the way it is: let 'them' sink or swim on the waves of the free market while 'our people' will get help.

Now that the food crisis is with us, and in all likelihood is here to stay, two things need to be done. First, emergency measures must be taken. Second, lessons must be learned and directed towards long-term action.

As the situation evolves, will nations follow the principle of 'every man for himself' or will they finally show the strength and ability to work together and act effectively?

The answer is not yet clear. Some food-producing countries have already imposed limits on export to keep prices down and avoid popular anger. That is an understandable reaction, but over the long term it won't work. Solutions are needed at an international level.

The UN Secretary-General recently convened a meeting of the heads of 27 international organisations to coordinate the response of the world community. A special task force was created, which is a good first step. Wealthy countries have allocated about half a billion dollars for urgent food aid – not a lot of money, but still a beginning.

The agenda of the G8 summit meeting to be held in Japan in early July has been revised: Japan's Prime Minister has proposed discussing the 'threat of hunger and malnutrition' in the world.

The global civil society is also pitching in, with non-governmental humanitarian organisations offering aid.

That's all well and good, but I still wonder what is being done by the Security Council, which according to the UN Charter 'bears primary responsibility for maintaining international peace and security'. Is the threat to peace and stability not seen from the East River UN building?

'I am surprised,' Diouf said, 'that I have not been summoned to the UN Security Council' to report urgently on the situation. The diplomats there seem too used to working as a fire brigade that responds to crises that have already degenerated into hostilities. That, of course, is necessary work, but developing preventive measures is even more important. When the situation blows up, with the number of hungry migrants swelling as nations fight for water, it will be too late.

Why is it, one wonders, that while national parliaments hold hearings on urgent problems, mobilising all available expertise and inching toward solutions, the same is not happening at the international level?

The Security Council has not yet become a policy-making centre that could focus the minds of world leaders on the real problems, the real priorities rather than the skewed set of priorities that we see today.

Once again, it all comes down to distorted priorities. It is up to the Security Council to correct the world's system of priorities and adapt it to the new challenges. It is imperative to start now, without waiting for the reform of the Council, which is of course necessary. While it is true that the absence of major countries like India, Brazil, Japan, Germany and South Africa from the group of permanent members is wrong and must be corrected, and that the Council's purview should include economic and environmental security, why not change the agenda and begin by bringing those countries into the discussion now?

The problem is inertia. But the food crisis has reminded us once again that inertia kills.

That inertia will keep generating new crises and producing emergencies. It is past time for world leaders to start developing preventive mechanisms. Such mechanisms have been proposed, but the proposals are being shot down by those who like to talk about the ineffectiveness of the UN while doing everything to sideline the world organisation.

While focusing on the food crisis, Gorbachev was also sending a wider message that the world must honour the Millennium Development Goals and not pay lip service to the climate threat. Concerned about faltering multilateral relations at the time, Gorbachev followed this article by joining over 30 other Nobel Prize laureates in sending a strong statement to world leaders after a summit in Petra, Jordan in June 2008 on food security, poverty and peace.

Keynote Address to the Club of Rome

Energy Efficiency, Climate Stabilisation and Economic Recovery,
Amsterdam, 26 October 2009

Your Majesty,
Dear Members of the Club of Rome,
Ladies and Gentlemen,

The theme chosen for discussion at this Assembly, the inter-
dependency of environmental problems, energy and the overcoming
of the global economic crisis, indicates that the Club of Rome continues to be highly responsive to the trends observed in the global
development. It is the interconnectedness of these problems that is of
fundamental importance today. However, by no means everybody has
come to realise this.

The events of recent years and months have shown with renewed
sense of urgency just how tightly all the key challenges and threats
which confronted humanity during the last decades of the past century
are intertwined. Today, they are felt increasingly keenly.

The environmental challenge is the biggest of them.

It has incorporated virtually every problem of concern to humanity.
Today we are no longer talking of a purely environmental agenda. It
relates directly to the problems in the area of security, to the probability
of increasingly dangerous inter-ethnic and international conflicts. It
relates directly to multimillion migration flows that are already having
their destabilising effects on politics and the economy. It relates directly
to the growing poverty and social inequality, water crisis, and the
shortage of energy and food.

The latest climate science is deeply disturbing. It is the last wake-up
call. All the excuses and justifications for inaction as well as the
pseudoscientific arguments of the deniers should be finally discarded.

And another very important point I need to make: all talk about the
efforts to save our environment undermining the economy has been
refuted by life itself. We have seen even more clearly in recent months
that it is not the desire to ensure normal conditions of life for current
and coming generations that undermines the economy. Crippling the
economy are factors of a very different nature: the irresponsible drive for
profit at any cost, the blind faith in the 'invisible hand of the market',

failure of the state to act, and the patterns of consumerism that have been forced onto the world.

The current economic crisis is, in my view, far from over. Those who have been on the periphery of economic development before are yet to fully see and comprehend its consequences. For the rest of us, the implications of the crisis will be severe as well. However, they will be deemed inconsequential compared to the devastation that the threat to the environment might bring to the world. And this devastation is inevitable if the efforts to steer ourselves out of the financial and economic crisis are confined to stopgap measures, leading to the preservation of the old model and business as usual.

We must take action to save our planet. This should be a common task for governments, the business and scientific community and civil society. Each of the stakeholders in this noble cause has a role to play and opportunities that are offered in the process. However, the world today is such that the main burden of responsibility lies with the states and their institutions.

Only the state can enforce the strict standards and norms without which all efforts to tackle climate change are meaningless. Only the state can mobilise resources and funds to encourage and deploy break-through technologies. Only the state can provide adequate support to those who find themselves particularly vulnerable in the context of the changing climate. And this support will definitely be needed. That is already clear today.

However, the states today are all too often doing quite the opposite: spending hundreds of billions on weapons, the trade in which has blown into a corruption scandal on a global scale; subsidising the past century's fossil fuel-based industries, not the energy sector of the future; saving money on social programmes instead of investing in human capital.

A few weeks from now, state representatives will gather in Copen-hagen to usher in a new and important era of cooperation between the states in addressing climate change. It depends on them whether it will be a strong and convincing start or a weak and hope-shattering act.

Green Cross International, of which I am the Founding President, is concerned by the gap between the negotiating process and the latest scientific evidence. Proposals that are now on the table are more con-sistent with a path to 3–4°C warming than the science-based 'maximum of 2°C' endorsed by the leaders of the major economies in L'Aquila. Because of the differences between the industrialised and developing countries the official UNFCCC negotiating process has run into grid-lock.

Much is determined today by the US position. President Obama's personal commitment to success in Copenhagen is obvious; however, his opportunities are limited by the systemic difficulties related to the position of the US Congress. Without meaningful contribution by the United States no success is possible in cutting emissions or assisting developing countries.

A number of countries have already achieved significant progress.

China is on track to meet the energy targets in its 11th Five Year Plan and has announced its intentions to do more.

India has unveiled an ambitious solar programme. Brazil, South Africa, Mexico and other developing countries have also taken far-reaching steps.

The European Union appears to be holding firm on its target, and the new Japanese Government recently announced an ambitious plan to cut emissions by 25 per cent by 2020.

Russia has set for itself ambitious goals in cutting the energy intensity of production and reducing gas flaring.

At the recent UN climate summit, the tone was more positive than it has ever been. The speeches were already about 'how' not 'whether'. The state leaders can no longer fail to hear the alarm bell ringing. A strong, effective agreement in Copenhagen or soon afterwards is feasible. This should be the baseline assumption and the goal to be sought vigorously.

Achieving meaningful progress will require the exercise of political will at the highest levels. Therefore, it is essential that the conference is attended by the heads of state and government. This is required both by the scale and the complexity of the challenge.

A kind of a 'global deal' between industrialised and developing countries is needed. Industrialised countries must lead the way with both deep emission cuts at home and strong financial and technical support for the mitigation of climate change in the developing world.

Developing countries — especially those with large fast-growing economies such as China, India and Brazil — must recognise their growing responsibilities for the health of the planet and the fact that low-carbon development is the only viable future for any economy.

It is clear that the fleshing out of political decisions that are taken is a colossal task. They should be converted into real technologies and mechanisms. A dramatic increase in investment in energy-efficient technology and production, renewable energy sources, and new engi-

the emergence of increasingly more communications channels for this, including the so-called 'social networks'.

This approach forms the basis of an initiative launched by a number of organisations including Green Cross International, the Club of Rome, the Club of Madrid, the Nobel Peace Laureates Summit, and other NGOs, as well as prominent scientists to develop a joint 'beyond Copenhagen' road map. UN Secretary-General Ban Ki-moon, with whom we had a fruitful meeting in Geneva recently, has shown support to our initiative.

We expect that the Task Force we have launched will provide an impetus to the negotiating process as early as at the stage of working out an agreement in Copenhagen. We seek to stir public opinion on the issue by disseminating 'alerts' available to everybody via a cell phone or PC.

I would like to inform you that yesterday the second meeting of the Task Force took place. We had a heated debate, which helped us understand more clearly what we want and what we can do. I hope some of you in the audience would be able to join this initiative.

The other day, my family and I celebrated the first birthday of my first great-granddaughter. She is one of those who will inherit our planet from us. We, who are past our life's meridian, bear responsibility for the disastrous, virtual emergency state of our planet, our home. Therefore, we cannot sit idle. We must take action to assure our grandchildren and great-grandchildren of a future.

The Club of Rome has been warning about the limits of growth since as early as 1967, and – like Gorbachev – had been declaring the need for a new model of development for decades before climate change brought the issue to the political forefront. The financial crisis was a definitive sign that the old system was unsustainable and grossly unjust, and that the wealth generated in the 'boom' years had been largely squandered while having a devastating impact on the environment. Gorbachev also believed that, combined with the climate threat, the financial crisis could provide the impetus for profound change. By 2009, this message had become one of the utmost urgency, and was now shared by the millions of people around the world who were calling for climate action and justice.

Tear Down This Wall! And Save the Planet

The Times, 9 November 2009

There are urgent parallels between the fall of communism and the fight to stop climate change.

The German people, and the whole world alongside them, are today celebrating a landmark date in history: the 20th anniversary of the fall of the Berlin Wall.

Not many events can claim their place in the collective memory as a watershed that divides two distinct periods. The dismantling of the Berlin Wall – that stark, concrete symbol of a world divided into hostile camps – is such an event. It brought incredible hope and opportunity to people everywhere, and provided the 1980s with a truly jubilant finale. That is something to think about as this decade draws to a close, and the chance for humanity to take another momentous leap forward appears to be slipping away.

The road to the end of the cold war was certainly not easy or universally welcomed at the time, but it is for just this reason that its lessons remain relevant. In the 1980s the world was at a historic crossroads. The arms race had created an explosive situation. Nuclear deterrents could have failed at any moment. We were heading for disaster, spending billions on an arms race rather than investing in creativity and people.

Today another planetary threat has emerged. The climate crisis is the new wall that divides us from our future, and today's leaders are vastly underestimating the urgency and potentially catastrophic scale of the emergency.

People used to joke that we will struggle for peace until there is nothing left on the planet; the threat of climate change makes this prophecy more literal than ever. Comparisons with the period immediately before the Berlin Wall came down are striking.

Like 20 years ago, we face a threat to global security and our very future existence that no one nation can deal with alone. And, again, it is the people who are calling for change. Just as the German people declared their will for unity, world citizens are today demanding that action is taken to tackle climate change and redress the deep injustices that surround it. Twenty years ago key world leaders demonstrated resolve, faced up to opposition and immense pressure, and the Wall came down. It remains to be seen whether today's leaders will do the same.

Gorbachev at the 10th Nobel Peace Laureates Summit in Berlin in November 2009

Addressing climate change demands a paradigm shift on a scale akin to that required to end the cold war. But we need a 'circuit-breaker' to escape from the business-as-usual that currently dominates the political agenda. It was the transformation brought about by perestroika and glasnost that provided the quantum leap for freedom for the Soviet Union and Eastern Europe, and opened the way for the democratic revolution that saved history. Climate change is complex and closely entwined with a host of other challenges, but a similar breakthrough in our values and priorities is needed.

There is not just one wall to topple, but many. There is the wall between those states which are already industrialised and those developing countries which do not want to be held back. There is the wall between those who cause climate change and those who suffer the consequences. There is the wall between those who heed the scientific evidence and those who pander to vested interests. And there is the wall between the citizens who are changing their own behaviour and want strong global action and the leaders who are so far letting them down.

In 1989, incredible changes that were deemed impossible just a few years earlier were implemented. But this was no accident. These changes resonated the hopes of the time and leaders responded. We brought down the wall in the belief that future generations would be able to solve challenges together. Today, looking at the cavernous gulf between rich and poor, the irresponsibility that caused the global financial crisis, and the weak and divided responses to climate change, I feel bitter. The opportunity to build a safer, fairer and more united world has been largely squandered.

To echo the demand made of me by my late friend and sparring partner President Reagan: Mr Obama, Mr Hu, Mr Singh, Mr Brown and, back in Berlin, Ms Merkel and her European counterparts, 'Tear down this wall!'

For this is Your Wall, your defining moment. You cannot dodge the call of history. I appeal to heads of state and government to personally come to the climate change conference in Copenhagen this December and dismantle the wall. The people of the world expect you to deliver; do not fail them.

© *The Times/nisyndication*

This was Gorbachev's unabashed outcry on the eve of the Copenhagen summit, when hopes of a positive outcome had reached rock-bottom in the face of deep 'North-South' divides. He personally called on heads of state to attend the conference and meet the call of history – reminding them that their job is to lead us out of this crisis, not send officials to negotiate yet more managerial compromises. Gorbachev is clear that addressing climate change will be painful but insists that making history is not for the fainthearted. At the time, many leaders remained ambivalent about their plans, but in the end 119 heads of state answered the call and participated in person during the crucial final days of the summit.

Failure in Copenhagen would be 'catastrophic risk': Gorbachev

Marlowe Hood, Agence France-Presse, 3 December 2009

PARIS, Dec 3, 2009 (AFP) – The Copenhagen climate summit is a 'test of modern leadership' and a failed outcome would almost certainly condemn the planet to disaster, Mikhail Gorbachev said Thursday in an interview.

The Nobel laureate and last leader of the Soviet Union also told AFP that Russia had put forward serious targets for curbing carbon emissions and should not be cast as a spoiler going into the December 7–18 talks.

World leaders faced an unprecedented challenge in forging a lasting solution to global warming and crafting a fair way of coping with its impacts, Gorbachev said by email in response to written questions.

Compromises on policy 'virtually guarantee a temperature increase of around four degrees Celsius (7.2 degrees Fahrenheit), well into the catastrophic risk range', he warned.

'The "business-as-usual" mindset and incremental approach that dominates the world thinking today is the source of our multiple crises – economic, financial and environmental.

'We are currently in a genuine global emergency that requires a new way of thinking.'

Gorbachev argued that a breakthrough was still possible, even if the summit did not yield the legally binding treaty originally envisioned.

The UN talks have foundered on discord between rich and developing nations over sharing the burden of slashing greenhouse-gas emissions and helping poor countries adapt to climate change.

The first step, Gorbachev suggested, is a 'firm political commitment' that spells out the aims and legal framework of an accord that would take effect after 2012.

The meeting would also have to fix a timetable to secure an international binding agreement next year.

'This two-step process should not be seen as a setback but rather a way to strengthen' the deal, Gorbachev said. 'Copenhagen thus is a test of modern leadership.'

Through his Green Cross International, set up in 1993, Gorbachev has made sustainable development one of his key priorities.

This year, he set up a Climate Change Synergy Task Force, whose members include several top climate scientists and economists, as well as a scattering of former heads of state.

Gorbachev defended the position of Russia, the world's No. 3 polluter. 'Russia is not the bad apple when it comes to climate change,' he said, pointing to what he said was an aim to reduce its emissions by 22–25 per cent by 2020 over 1990 levels, amounting to a doubling of its previous commitment.

Critics, however, say that the huge drop in carbon pollution after the collapse of the Soviet economy has already helped Russia to meet these targets.

They also note Russia has yet to spell out its proposals in the international arena and has a history of taking a hard line, claiming its vast forests as 'carbon sinks' that can be used to reduce its emissions target.

Gorbachev also said that the target of preventing global temperature from climbing more than 2.0°C (3.6°F) – endorsed by rich nations and emerging giants such as China, Brazil and India – is not good enough.

'The science says that temperature increase should be limited to around 1.0°C (1.8°F),' he said, calling on developed countries to cut their collective emissions by 45 to 50 per cent by 2020.

The offers on the table from rich nations currently total a cut of about 12 to 16 per cent, according to experts.

Asked whether these goals were realistic, Gorbachev was upbeat. 'No one believed in the end of the cold war at the close of the 1980s… Politics is not about the art of the possible but about making what is perceived as impossible happen.'

© AFP 2011

In 2009, Green Cross and a host of institutional and expert partners created the Climate Change Task Force (CCTF), aimed at alerting the public and governments of the urgent need to close the gap between what scientific facts were dictating – i.e. very deep cuts in emissions to avoid outright catastrophe – and the stalling, wavering and bickering that was plaguing national and international policy.

Gorbachev and the CCTF made resounding calls for a new energy and development paradigm to lead the world to the low-carbon future essential for our survival, releasing several statements and detailed reports and meeting personally with key delegations preparing for the Copenhagen summit. UN Secretary-General Ban Ki-moon attended the CCTF meeting in Geneva and gave his full support to the initiative.

Playing Russian Roulette with Climate Change

Mikhail Gorbachev and Alexander Likhotal
Project Syndicate, 3 December 2009

Mounting scepticism and deadlocked negotiations have culminated in an announcement that the Copenhagen climate conference will not result in a comprehensive global climate deal. Disappointing? Certainly. But the Copenhagen climate summit was always meant to be a transitional step. The most important thing to consider is where we will go from here.

The phrase 'the day after' is most commonly associated with the word 'hangover'. The absence of a binding agreement could mean a global hangover, and not just for a day. Fed up with apocalyptic predictions, people wanted a miracle in Copenhagen. So a perceived failure may cause a massive, perhaps irreversible, loss of confidence in our politicians. No surprise, then, that governments have sought to manage our expectations carefully.

Decision-makers have not faced up to just how close the world may be to the climate 'tipping point'. But, while a runaway climate remains a risk, runaway politics are already a fact. Official negotiations are removed from reality. According to the latest science, the current proposals under negotiation will result in warming of more than $4°C$ during this century – double the $2°C$ maximum endorsed by the G8 and other leaders. That leaves a higher than 50 per cent probability of the world's climate moving past its tipping point.

An agreement based on the parameters that are now on the negotiating table would thus put us in a position more dangerous than a game of Russian roulette. To avoid both the global hangover of no deal and the self-deception of a weak deal, a breakthrough is needed – and can still be achieved in Copenhagen.

A two-step process is now our best bet. States should make a political commitment to a framework that includes overall objectives, an institutional framework, and specific pledges of early action and financing. The declaration must stipulate that a legally binding agreement must be finalised by COP15 in 2010. That would allow the United States and other countries to enact the necessary legislation, and provide United Nations negotiators time to translate the COP15 Declaration into an appropriate, workable legal structure. If this means a total reworking of the current document, so be it.

In addition, it might be necessary to have a review conference in 2015 to adjust our targets and plans to the new realities. Therefore, it is more important than ever that heads of state attend the Copenhagen conference, as this two-step solution will only work with strong, direct intervention by leaders.

In 1985, during the height of the cold war, when negotiations were bogged down at the US–Soviet Union Geneva summit, the negotiators were told by their leaders, annoyed by the lack of progress, 'we do not want your explanations why this can't be done. Just do it!' And it was done by the morning. Today's leaders must come to Copenhagen and say, 'We want this done!'

To move forward, the Copenhagen meeting must break the political deadlock between industrialised and developing states. Climate injustice must be redressed, as developing countries bear the brunt of the impact and face massive adaptation costs. Rich countries need to put serious money on the table. Claims that they lack the necessary resources ring hollow, as trillions of dollars were found to bail out banks in the financial crisis.

Poor countries are aware of their power to block progress. Veto power is effectively shifting from the UN Security Council to G77 plus China. Who would have imagined in the West ten years ago that the future and their children's well-being would depend upon decisions taken in Beijing or Delhi or Addis Ababa?

So the industrialised countries need to put a real financing offer on the table as soon as possible, to allow time for a positive reaction and announcements of commitments from developing countries. In particular, commitment to an early-start fund – at least 20 billion dollars to immediately assist the least developed countries – is critical. This would help establish the trust that is now sorely lacking, and create the conditions to restart productive negotiations.

Leaders must be honest about the scale of the challenge and recognise that a systemic and transformational change, not incremental gestures, is required. The official response to climate change must be recalibrated to the level and urgency of the threat. A new global agreement must be science-based, not a lowest-common-denominator compromise watered down by vested interests.

Sensible risk management today dictates that atmospheric carbon should be stabilised at 350 parts per million of CO_2 equivalent, not the current pathway of 450–500ppm CO_2e. This requires emission reductions of 45–50 per cent in industrialised countries by 2020, and almost complete de-carbonisation by 2050, not the levels of 15–25 per cent by 2020 and 60–80 per cent by 2050 that are now on the table. Major developing countries must also commit to nationally appropriate mitigation actions. But the rich must move first. Their inaction over the last 20 years does not give them the right to point fingers.

Governments should not withhold the truth from their citizens. Everyone will have to make sacrifices. But do you want your home to be cheap, dirty and dangerous or clean, decent and safe? Are you ready to say, 'Okay, kids, I inherited this house, but I neglected to maintain it, so you will have to worry that the roof might collapse at any time'? That is not the type of legacy that any of us would want to leave our children.

© Project Syndicate

At the eleventh hour, these two articles – one written just before and the other at the very height of the summit – were Gorbachev and the CCTF's final push to salvage a united, workable outcome in Copenhagen. In the end, though disappointing, the summit took the two-stage approach recommended by Gorbachev and others, and managed to keep the hope of a breakthrough in 2010 alive.

We Have a Real Emergency

New York Times, 9 December 2009

As the climate change summit meeting moves forward in Copenhagen, it is increasingly clear that more than just the environment is at stake. The global environmental crisis is at the heart of practically all the problems now confronting us, including the need to create a global economic model grounded in the public good.

It is directly linked to security issues and to increasingly dangerous ethnic and international conflicts; to mass migrations and displacements of people, which are already destabilising politics and economics; to growing poverty and social inequality; to the water crisis and energy and food shortages.

Excuses and pretexts for not taking action on the environment, and assertions that there are more important problems, are simply no longer credible. If we fail on this problem, we'll fail on all the others.

Saving our planet should be a task shared by governments, the business and scientific communities, and civil society. Each stakeholder in this noble cause has a role to play. The main burden of responsibility, however, lies with governments and their institutions.

Governments can set firm standards and norms that are indispensable to fighting climate change. Only the state is capable of mobilising the resources and incentives to implement cutting-edge technologies. Only the state can help those who are the most vulnerable to climate change.

Representatives of governments are meeting in Copenhagen to open a new stage in international cooperation on climate change. Whether it will be a strong and convincing start or a weak, disappointing one is up to them.

The latest scientific research on climate change is extremely disturbing. We have a real emergency. Yet the gap between science and policy keeps widening, as does the gap between the negotiations and the urgency of the issue.

Science indicates that the global temperature increase should be limited to 1 or 2 degrees Celsius. World leaders endorsed this view at the G8 meeting in Italy in July. Even with that limit, major destruction, including the disappearance of most of the world's coral reefs, is likely.

Gorbachev meets with Pax Arctica Youth Ambassadors in Moscow in November 2008

Yet policy compromises agreed to by negotiators involved in the Copenhagen talks virtually guarantee a temperature increase of around 4 degrees Celsius – well into the catastrophic risk range.

Why is this happening? For several reasons, including the inertia of the existing economic model, one based on hyper-profits and excessive consumption, political and business leaders' failure to think long term, and concern that reducing carbon emissions will undercut economic growth. Those who don't want any change are exploiting that concern.

As the global financial crisis has made abundantly clear, efforts to make the world sustainable for present and future generations do not undermine the economy. The culprit is something quite different: reckless pursuit of profit at any price, blind faith in the 'invisible hand of the market', and government inaction.

What is needed is a search for new engines of growth and incentives to economic development. Transitioning to a low-carbon, low-waste economy will create qualitatively new, green industries, technologies and jobs.

A low-carbon economy is just part of a new economic model, one the world needs as badly as the air we breathe.

Overnight changes to the economic model that has prevailed for a half century are not realistic. The transition to a new model requires a shift in values.

The global economy must be reoriented toward the public good. It must emphasise issues like a sustainable environment, healthcare, education, culture, equal opportunities and social cohesion – including reducing the glaring gaps between wealth and poverty.

Society needs this, and not just as a moral imperative. The economic efficiency of emphasising the public good is enormous, even though economists have not yet learned how to measure it. We need an intellectual breakthrough if we are to build a new economic model.

We also need a moral realignment of the business community. Companies and their CEOs tend to define their positions on environmental issues according to the short-term or at best medium-term bottom line. Socially and environmentally responsible business is still the exception rather than the rule. Change is needed in the entire system of taxes, subsidies and incentives.

Civil society must also play a larger role. It must become not just a stakeholder but a full participant in making decisions that will shape the environment and the economy for decades to come.

In Copenhagen, we will closely watch the political leaders. More than 60 heads of state will take a personal leadership test there. We have seen how easy it would be to fail. The weeks and months ahead offer them a chance to show that they can truly lead.

After Copenhagen: A New Leadership Challenge

By Mikhail Gorbachev and Alexander Likhotal
22 December 2009

After a tumultuous fortnight that saw everything from deal-breaking pledges to derailing walkouts, from outright squabbling between the world's most powerful nations inside to clashes in the streets outside, the climate change summit is over and assessments are pouring in from all sides. The United States' participation is being scrutinised most closely of all, closely followed by its fellow top-two polluter, China.

The summit can be described as a last minute diplomatic success, but at the price of a failure of vision. On the positive side, we have Fast Start finance for the next two to three years, a vague blueprint for a Climate Fund for future mitigation action, the promise of greater transparency from major emerging economies, and a reference to the limit of 2 degrees Celsius average global temperature rise, with a review conference by 2016 to decide on a stricter goal in the future. On the negative side, the Copenhagen Accord — tailored to placate emotional concerns and serve short-term political ambitions — ultimately just does not fly, falling dramatically short on how or when most goals will be achieved. We remain firmly on track for a 3–4°C global temperature rise: in other words, climate catastrophe.

A convergence of closely entwined global economic, energy and environmental crises is dictating the complete recalibration of the world's response to climate change to the emergency level. It calls for genuine statesmanship — not the lowest common denominator compromise and business as usual — and this was sorely lacking in Copenhagen. There is not much time left to close the gap between 'politics as usual' and the transformational, collective leadership required to turn the seemingly impossible changes needed to prevent climate catastrophe into reality.

What has the summit failed to achieve?

First, Copenhagen failed to issue firm commitments commensurate with the challenge — according to the latest scientific analysis and political consensus — of restricting average global temperature increase to below 2°C. The declaration that the world 'ought to' limit warming to 2°C does not hold water, as it is not matched with a concrete cap on developed countries' 2020 emission reductions. This is a slap in the face for developing countries, which have been demanding up to 40 per cent reductions. The US emission reduction pledge of 17 per cent below 2005 levels by 2020 translates to just 3–4 per cent below 1990 levels – that is nearly ten times less than the EU has committed to. It is not an offer that puts the United States in a position to expect very much from the major developing economies, and is bitterly disappointing for African and other poor nations already suffering from the impacts of climate change. It is not a leadership position.

Second, the absence of even a goal to reach a legally binding agreement hardly provides the basis for a robust institutional framework for the future climate change system. Besides, it is absolutely critical that the USA equips itself with the necessary corresponding national legislation in the first half of 2010, not only to enable it to implement its pledges but also to avoid the climate change debate becoming completely engulfed by the mid-term elections. The recent EPA Endangerment ruling gives the USA some scope for immediate action to curb emissions, but it is no substitute for a strong national energy and climate change law. Without this, other major stakeholders – including China, India and even the EU – might retract on their commitments.

Third, the financial mechanisms and kick-start packages are not sufficient. A vague call for a 'goal' of 100 billion dollars a year by 2020 to help poor nations cope with climate change, along with 30 billion dollars for the least developed countries from 2010 to 2012, is not nearly enough to actually permit the poorest nations to either cope with the consequences they already face or advance low-carbon development programmes. The industrialised world has a climate debt to the developing nations that must be honoured, not used as a bargaining chip. To be credible, the Fast Start Fund must be followed by at least 200 billion dollars of genuinely additional financing per year in the future.

Fourth, the political bickering completely marginalised specific commitments to early action, and even the agreement on protecting tropical forests fell short of what was hoped for. But while the Copenhagen debates were weak in the practical action department luckily the solutions themselves are far from lacking. Wind power alone has the potential to satisfy a large part of global electricity demand. Since the 1990s, the cost of producing wind energy has fallen by 80 per cent: it is now a bona fide profit and job generating industry, and set to expand 20-fold in the USA alone by 2020.

The USA has many such 'low hanging fruits' to pluck, and huge financial gains to reap, by enhancing its energy efficiency – which is currently many times lower than either Japan or most of Europe – and boosting its long-neglected renewable energy industries. Private investors are already taking note. By some estimates, 1 trillion dollars have been invested in low carbon energy sources and buildings since 2007. But every month that America wavers on its climate and energy legislation it is losing green investment and jobs to its competitors.

Change will happen regardless of what was done – or rather not done – in Copenhagen, or will be decided in Washington. However, the transition to a low-carbon, green economy that must take place for economic and geological reasons – even without putting climate change into the equation – will be much more painful, dramatic and expensive if governments fail to lead the transformation. Global oil supplies will peak within the next decade. If we are not prepared for this transition the global financial crisis of 2008–09 will look like a picnic. It is time to envisage a US economy freed from the 700 billion dollars a year oil bill that it currently pays out to foreign suppliers. It is also worth remembering that while, due to our years of inaction, avoiding a climate catastrophe may now cost up to 4 per cent of global economic output, this is still less than the 5 per cent it cost to bail out the banks.

The world, and especially the American people, have already missed out on 20 years of sorely needed US action on climate change. We cannot turn back the clock. US emissions have risen by 20 per cent since 1997, and the emerging economies of China and India have completely changed the playing field. Meanwhile, the crisis has been mounting and the window of opportunity for avoiding irreversible disaster is narrow. But it is still there. The task is harder now, more complex and far more urgent, but with all nations working together the opportunity to forge a sustainable future is within reach.

Multinational cooperation and the engagement of international organisations are essential preconditions for effective action. Fortunately, the USA has reclaimed its place in global multilateralism. In this regard, President Obama's words at the Nobel Peace Prize acceptance ceremony, that 'America's commitment to global security will never waver', should be recognised as a very important political commitment.

The US President issued a leadership challenge to his global counterparts prior to and at Copenhagen, and to a degree it worked. In brokering a Copenhagen Accord he has thrown down the gauntlet and delivered a similar challenge to the American people and their elected representatives on Capitol Hill. Much depends on how they respond. As the President declared in Copenhagen, 'These international discussions have essentially taken place now for almost two decades and we have very little to show for it other than an increase, an acceleration of the climate change phenomenon. The time for talk is over.' By setting an example, the USA has a historic opportunity to lead, uniting the world to fight climate change. However, leadership has always meant more than just successful politics — it is about leading the change and not just recognising the challenge.

Over-expectation in the run-up to Copenhagen, the limitations of the Copenhagen Accord and the method by which it was reached left a global sense of frustration and threatened the relevance of the UN platform for negotiating a global climate change regime. This discontent and fatigue provided space for vested interests and climate deniers to mount a new wave of attacks on climate science which were fuelled by sensationalism in the press.

Gorbachev did not want this sense of disillusionment to grow after Copenhagen. While judging the outcome harshly, to prevent the momentum from completely dissipating he renewed his plea to the leaders who had signed the interim Copenhagen Accord, particularly the USA, to have the courage to keep their word in 2011. While the BP oil disaster in 2010 again highlighted the dangers of oil addiction, the political climate in the USA became more hostile with the powerful but unsubstantiated climate-change-denier messages reaching new audiences and the mid-term elections effectively shelving the 'Energy Independence and Security Act'. The CCTF and Gorbachev kept the pressure up, pushing for ambitious climate action based on the latest science in this new economic and political landscape.

but needs to be used much more effectively to bring us not only the daily sensations but also a focus on the underlying fundamental challenges of poverty, environmental threats and access to essential services like water, energy and education.

As a contribution to this new glasnost, Green Cross has launched an international magazine – *The Optimist* – to provide decision-makers and opinion leaders with a fresh perspective on how to address the serious socio-economic conflicts and environmental threats that we face today. The magazine seeks to foster transparency, understanding and the resolution of conflicts between different interest groups in order to open up new avenues for partnership and innovation.

A new global glasnost is what we urgently need for the sake of our future.

A global treaty on the right to water

Those without access to water are by definition the poorest and most deprived people on Earth. They are often without a voice, and without a means of asserting their rights. We must give them a voice, give them their humanity and honour our Millennium promises to them.

Meeting the water goals would be a shining example of how it is possible to make a difference – to make things better for everyone, and for the environment, by changing our values, re-evaluating priorities and living up to our commitments as a human family. The alternative – that in 2020 half the countries of the world live in severe water stress, and one third of the world's population is without water and sanitation – is too awful to even contemplate.

We must aim for universal access to water and sanitation – anything less is a violation of our civilisation, our universal human rights, our nature.

I would like to ask you to imagine a scenario. What would happen if one morning the people of the 'rich world' – the USA, Russia, Japan, Germany, Turkey, France, the UK, Italy, Spain, Poland, Canada, Australia, The Netherlands, Greece, the Czech Republic, Portugal, Hungary, Sweden, Austria, Switzerland, Slovakia, Denmark, Finland, Norway, New Zealand, Ireland and Luxembourg – all woke up to discover that they had no running water?

What would happen?

- Bottled water and other drinks in the shops would sell out within hours.

- People would be forced to walk for miles to rivers or lakes.
- People would get sick because the water is not clean enough to drink.
- Because everyone would be flocking to the water sources, the roads would be blocked – so driving wouldn't be an option.
- People would have to carry heavy jugs and not just this one day, but every day until the water supply was restored.

- This could take up to eight hours a day, so people could not go to their normal jobs.
- Without running water, no one's toilets would work any more, and without water the sewage treatment plants would stop working.
- Imagine the smell.
- Imagine what it would feel like to be thirsty, to watch your children go thirsty, and perhaps even to get sick or die as a result of dehydration or contamination.
- Imagine the newspaper headlines.
- Imagine the demonstrations in the streets; imagine the riots, the looting.
- Imagine the demands on government to restore the water supply.

Government officials and experts would make it their number one priority and work around the clock to restore the service and deal with the associated problems – they would spare no effort.

The combined population of the countries in this unthinkable scenario is about 1.1 billion. But 1.2 billion people in the world already live this unthinkable scenario every day with no access to safe drinking water. And 2.4 billion people are without access to sanitation.

According to reliable estimations it would cost 20 US dollars per year per person for 10 years to resolve the water crisis. Somehow we have been unable to find the funds to bring water to the world's poor and suffering, but it was easy to raise 70 billion dollars in a fortnight in order to fight a war! This is a scandal.

Water is not a privilege: it is a RIGHT!

We should be working with the same sense of urgency that we would have if it were our own taps that were running dry, our own children going thirsty. That is what solidarity means.

Every person on Earth should have access to basic essential services, including energy, water, sanitation, education, health and, in today's world, means of communication. Providing these basic services often falls under the domain of competence of local and regional governments. Without rules and regulations formulated and guaranteed by national governments and supported by international solidarity and partnership, it is impossible for many local governments in developing countries and especially in large cities to provide these basic services to everyone.

Supporting the ongoing work of institutions like UN-HABITAT, which are promoting the adoption of a universal declaration on access to essential services, Green Cross and its partners believe that an urgent effort must be made regarding water supply and sanitation.

A Global Treaty on the Right to Water could give all people a tool through which to assert their human right to safe water and sanitation. The rights-based approach to the management of water resources will open the road to access to water for all.

Green Cross and its partners are proposing the negotiation and adoption of a Global Treaty on the Right to Water. The fundamental principles of this Treaty have been discussed over the past three years, and agreed to in June during the Water for Life Dialogue here in Barcelona.

And now, with other international, national, regional and local organisations, we are launching an international public campaign in order to convince national governments to start the negotiation of this Treaty. Citizens around the world will be encouraged to sign a global petition and become actively involved. Our target is to present the world with a petition of at least 10 million signatures at the MDG+5 Review in 2005.

Mr Mohamed Elyazghi, the Minister of Territorial Management, Water and Environment of Morocco, who came to Barcelona in June, represents the first government supporting the Treaty initiative. We hope that many other governments, national and local, will soon be joining this essential movement for the survival of humankind.

I encourage and invite all of you to become ambassadors for this global citizens' initiative in your countries, your communities, your organisations.

This speech was Gorbachev's most powerful to date on the water crisis. It was a call to arms for people everywhere to stand up against injustice and demand a new world order that focuses on people not profit. Incensed by the waning progress towards the MDGs, and the war in Iraq which he had vehemently opposed, Gorbachev used the example of the most vital element, water, to shame governments and the entire international community for their lack of action and failure to find the relatively modest resources needed to end extreme poverty – to fulfil their promises. In an eerie premonition of the impending global financial meltdown, Gorbachev also admonishes governments for blindly prioritising economic liberalism over sustainable development and human rights.

Our Common Future

Opening Address at the La Plata Basin Earth Dialogues, Iguassu Falls, Brazil, 12 September 2005

I am very pleased to have the opportunity to launch, together with you all, this exciting international process – the La Plata Dialogues. I stress the word *process* very deliberately because the essence of our programme consists not in organising various separate events, but in establishing a permanent platform for communication and the exchange of opinions between all stakeholders: government representatives from five nations, residents of this region and entrepreneurs.

This is my third visit to Brazil, but the first one to Iguassu, and I cannot express how amazed I am by the beauty of this place. But I am also well aware that Iguassu is not merely a big waterfall, but also the site of one of the world's largest dams, an enormous enterprise that inevitably affects the environment and communities in this vast region. There are also unresolved problems with the other three dams located in the Upper Parana, producing power that is of such great importance for Argentina, Paraguay and southern Brazil. I am also informed about the difficult situation regarding Aquifero Garani Bay, the main reservoir of clean groundwater in the region, shared by Argentina, Brazil, Paraguay and Uruguay. There are many unsolved problems, made even more complex by the necessity that their effective resolution must combine economic considerations with politics, ecology, ethics, culture and social issues. Nevertheless, I believe that all governments that are able to see beyond their national borders will benefit from the spirit of cooperation and integration so perfectly symbolised by the shared water resources, which are the subject for these dialogues.

I address you today in my capacity as Chairman of the Board of Green Cross International, a non-governmental organisation that works in the field of sustainable development. At the same time, I remain a politician. But besides this, I am also a father, a grandfather and simply a human being who loves life and possesses quite a wealth of experience. That is why I will be approaching all the issues, which I wish to discuss with you today from three points of view.

As you undoubtedly know, two days from now, at the UN Headquarters in New York, the World Summit will open, bringing together more than 170 heads of state and government – the largest gathering of world leaders in history. The main issue on the agenda – assessing the progress made so far towards implementation of the Millennium Development Goals, to which world leaders pledged their commitment in the UN Millennium Declaration in 2000. The unavoidable question of how to enhance financing for development will also take centre stage. Both the further development of the international community and the future of the UN itself will depend, in many respects, on decisions made at this summit.

The Millennium Declaration is a vitally important document, directed towards the future and raising hopes for billions of vulnerable people. Yet if we consider it from a different perspective, the very fact of this Declaration, which stressed today's most pressing problems at the level of the UN General Assembly, is clear evidence of the catastrophic situation that our civilisation has brought upon itself. The Millennium Declaration is not just a document; it is an SOS call and a desperate cry for help on behalf of that immense part of humankind that lives in subhuman conditions. But the question remains, will this cry be heeded or will it still be considered a mere voice in the wilderness?

I am not a panic-monger; on the contrary, I am a convinced optimist. But working with Green Cross International I come across statistics that are hard to bear. More than 1 billion people live below the poverty line, meaning on one dollar a day or less. Of these, about 798 million suffer from chronic hunger, and thus cannot lead active, healthy lives.

In the last two years the number of people living in slums, which are a breeding ground for HIV-AIDS and other diseases, has grown by 50 million. In some poor countries every eleventh child dies before reaching the age of five.

Eight hundred and eighty million people, or one out of every five adults on the planet, are illiterate; two thirds of them are women.

And what is happening to the environment? According to a recent study, carried out under the aegis of the UN by 1300 experts in 95 countries, 60 per cent of the ecosystems that maintain life on the Earth are in such a state of decay that they can hardly be restored. And this is not the only problem. Scientists believe that the destructive consequences of this degradation will become even stronger in the next 50 years.

Civil society, which in the last few years has turned from an abstract notion into a real force that has to be taken into consideration both by politicians and businessmen, must play an important role in solving the mounting problems, but governments still have the primary responsi-

These were among the official recommendations of Green Cross International, as was the request to institute international support for the creation of a Water Cooperation Facility, to work with basin authorities, governments and stakeholders to resolve intractable water disagreements.

There are many disputes within the water sector: about how much it will cost to provide water and sanitation to those in need (compare the estimates of the Camdessus Report to those made by the Water Supply and Sanitation Collaborative Council (WSSCC), WaterAid and others); about the role of the private sector and the issue of cost-recovery; about the appropriate techniques to be applied and the scale at which projects should be designed and implemented; and, particularly relevant after the Cancún WTO Ministerial, the debate about GATS.

From a practical point of view it is the lack of a suitable legal framework for resolving international water resource disputes that presents such a huge stumbling block to the solution of the global water crisis.

Providing essential services such as energy, water and sanitation usually falls under the responsibility and the competence of local and regional governments. Without rules and regulations formulated and guaranteed by national governments and supported by international backing, it is impossible for many local governments in developing countries, especially in their larger cities, to ensure these basic services to everyone.

Supporting the ongoing work of United Nations institutions, like the UN-HABITAT, which promote the adoption of a universal declaration on access to essential services, Green Cross and its partners believe that an urgent and radical effort must be made towards international regulation of water supply and sanitation. One could wonder how it is possible that such an important component of an individual's life is not guaranteed by international law. Surprising as it may be, it is not.

An international document guaranteeing that everyone has a right to safe and affordable water, which would be binding for national governments and that, most importantly, would provide a schematic for the implementation of this right, does not exist. In spite of this being a critical situation, governments, with few exceptions, are reluctant to open complicated and time-consuming negotiations for a new international law.

An important step in the right direction was made in November 2002, when the UN Committee on Economic, Social and Cultural Rights (CESCR) recognised the right to water as a fundamental human right.

This should, in theory, commit the 145 states that have ratified the International Covenant on Economic, Social and Cultural Rights to gradually ensure fair and non-discriminatory access to safe drinking water. Unfortunately, however, the status of the interpretation by CESCR does not confer a legally binding governmental obligation.

Green Cross and its partners are proposing the negotiation and adoption of a Global Treaty on the Right to Water, which, when ratified by the member states of the United Nations, will give all people a tool through which to assert their right to safe water and sanitation and would oblige national governments to make sure that this right is respected. The rights-based approach to the management of water resources will open the road to access to water for all.

The fundamental principles of this Treaty have been discussed over the past four years, and were agreed to by more than 1100 representatives of one hundred non-governmental organisations from around the world during the Water for Life Dialogue, hosted by the Universal Forum of Cultures in Barcelona, in June 2004.

In order to recognise the importance of this issue so that governments acquiesce to a new international treaty, their respective electorates must give them clear indications and sufficient pressure. To realise this, a worldwide public awareness campaign is necessary.

This is why Green Cross International, together with other international, national and local organisations, has launched an international public campaign to convince national governments to start the negotiation of this Treaty.

I encourage and invite all readers of *The Optimist* to become ambassadors for this global citizens' initiative in your countries, your communities, and your institutions. The Right to Water is our common cause, and in order for it to succeed we need every voice to make itself heard.

During this period, the Green Cross campaign for the recognition of the human right to water gained momentum, thanks to a large degree to Gorbachev's personal support and active engagement. Many important governments and organisations recognised the right to water for the first time, and the groundswell of public support led to the issue being placed firmly on the table. Mikhail Gorbachev wrote to dozens of heads of state and other influential people, stressing that only a rights-based approach would give 'water for all' the priority it deserved in development strategies and budgets. It began to be clear that opinions on this question, including at the highest level, were beginning to shift – in the right direction.

All of Us Should Be Ashamed

By Mikhail Gorbachev and Jan Kulczyk
Financial Times, 21 March 2007

Two years ago at the United Nations headquarters in New York, Green Cross International (GCI) appealed to the Commission on Sustainable Development.

Addressing the 123 ministers gathered, we stressed the urgent need to meet the Millennium Development Goals (MDG), commitments pledged by world leaders at the UN in 2000.

We focused on providing safe drinking water and basic sanitation to all people, because more than five million die every year for want of these most critical of services.

If we could speak to the same audience today, we would simply say that all of us should be ashamed.

The 2006 Human Development Report stated that – if we continued with business as usual – the MDG safe water target would be missed by 234 million people, and the sanitation target would be missed by 430 million people. Behind these figures are the faces of sick children, desperate mothers, and men looking for a minimum of subsistence, of dignity. Their suffering shines a spotlight on our humanity, or indeed inhumanity.

Is it justifiable for humankind to accept this *état de fait*? Certainly not. Failure to achieve the MDGs would damage the credibility of the UN, the entire system of global governance, and governments of rich and poor countries alike.

Although access to safe drinking water has been recognised as a universal human right since 2002, as established by the UN Committee on Economic, Social and Cultural Rights, it is far from being realised.

Appropriate ways and means to extend this basic human right to all people are yet to be clearly defined and deployed, and the majority of countries are yet to confirm this right in their legislation.

It is not too late to act. Achieving the water and sanitation MDG is eminently doable, and at a reasonable price: it will cost only around £10bn per year over the next 10 years. This is less than half of what rich countries spend each year on mineral water. It is not charity, but an investment in humanity that will reap global economic benefits of at least £20bn annually and unleash massive increases in productivity.

The UK Government has recently formally recognised for the first time that access to safe drinking water is a human right. Its international development secretary, Hilary Benn, has called for a global action plan to solve the water crisis, and pledged to double UK support to water and sanitation in Africa by 2008.

Doubling international aid to water is absolutely essential, but to secure the flow of finance for water and sanitation infrastructure in poor countries it is important to improve local governance, to train local decision-makers.

Anna Tibaijuka, Executive Director of UN Habitat, once said that even if enough funding was channelled to Africa, it would be impossible to use it effectively. Capacity building to improve governance and management must therefore be a priority.

During the 4th World Water Forum in 2006, Antoine Frérot, Chief Executive of Veolia Water, proposed the creation of an International Observatory of Good Water Practices, which would be available to water managers and decision-makers everywhere. This is an excellent idea and GCI encourages the business community to support this with resources and experience.

In rich countries, the state has invested in water infrastructure over the centuries and asked consumers to cover the cost of water services. Many developing countries are so indebted that the state is unable to invest in infrastructure without the support of the international community. We cannot expect poor people to pay for water infrastructure; eventually, people could pay a reasonable, affordable charge for their water – but only once the services actually exist. New financial mechanisms urgently need to be put in place. Decentralised financing and cooperation must be enhanced, including targeted development loans guaranteed by local authorities from the north.

GCI strongly commends the stance being taken by Stavros Dimos, the European environment commissioner, on the recently proposed directive that obliges EU states to treat serious offences against the environment as criminal acts.

To repeat: there is still time to act. The battle for clean and safe water for all must not be lost.

Jan Kulczyk is the Chair of Green Cross International.

© *Financial Times*

This article again implores governments and the private sector to invest in humanity, stressing that allocating a relative pittance – in global financial terms – to securing basic water services for all people is not charity, but will stimulate productivity in the future. Written on the eve of the global financial crisis that so starkly highlighted the misuse of the vast wealth generated during the 'boom' years, and pushed international development even further down many government priority lists, in retrospect these words appear even more poignant.

Climate Change and Water Security: Solving the Equation

By Mikhail Gorbachev and Jean-Michel Severino
Project Syndicate, 6 June 2007

The Intergovernmental Panel on Climate Change recently released alarming data on the consequences of global warming in some of the world's poorest regions. By 2100, one to three billion people worldwide are expected to suffer from water scarcity. Global warming will increase evaporation and severely reduce rainfalls – by up to 20 per cent in the Middle East and North Africa – such that the amount of water available per person could be halved by mid-century in these regions.

This sudden rarefaction of an element whose symbolic and spiritual importance matches its centrality to human life will exert considerable stress on nations and their inhabitants, and exacerbate conflicts worldwide. Africa, the Middle East and central Asia will be the first exposed. The repercussions, however, will be global.

Yet this bleak picture is no excuse for cynicism, no legitimate ground for pessimism. Conflicts may be inevitable; wars are not. Our ability to prevent water wars will depend on our collective capacity to anticipate tensions, and to find the technical and institutional solutions to manage emerging conflicts. The good news is that such solutions exist, and are every day proving their efficiency.

Dams – provided they are adequately sized and designed – can contribute to human development by fighting climate change and regulating water supply. Yet in a new context of scarcity, upstream infrastructure projects on international rivers may impact water quality or availability for neighbouring states and cause tensions. River basin organisations such as that established for the Nile, Niger or Senegal rivers help facilitate dialogue between states that share hydraulic resources. By developing a joint vision for the development of international waterways, these regional cooperation initiatives work towards a common ownership of the resource, thus reducing the risk of disputes over water use escalating into violence.

Most international waterways have such dedicated frameworks for dialogue, albeit at very different stages of advancement and levels of achievement. Will they be robust enough to cope with the strains that will inevitably arise from increscent water scarcity? If we are to take climate change predictions seriously, the international community

Water for Peace — Peace for Water

Foreword to the Green Cross co-publication for the Expo Zaragoza 2008

Water for Peace is both a very ancient and very modern concept. Since the beginning of human civilisation water has brought people together, allowing them to trade, travel and communicate. But water has also divided people. The blue lines on the map are much older than the ones drawn and redrawn by us over the centuries, and access to watercourses for domestic uses, irrigation and navigation has always been central to political and military strategies. But it is only relatively recently that water has been acknowledged as a global security issue.

According to the 2006 Human Development Report (UNDP, 2006), at least 700 million people in 43 countries currently live in countries facing water stress. This figure will reach 3 billion by 2025 as populations grow. At the same time, demand for water is rapidly rising. By 2050, an additional 2.7 billion people will need to be fed worldwide. Meeting this challenge will increasingly fall on irrigated agriculture, which alone currently accounts for more than 80 per cent of water use in developing countries. Industrialisation will drive demand up even further. Symptoms of water stress seen today, such as sinking groundwater and rivers that no longer reach the sea, are set to worsen acutely, and the effects of climate change on water resources will exacerbate this crisis enormously. Meeting future global water security needs is thus a major challenge demanding concerted global action.

Unfortunately, politics has been lagging in its reaction to the world water emergency. As a result we are now engaged in a global game of catch-up, decades behind where we should be in terms of dealing with today's water challenges, in which the number of victims runs into the millions.

Today we are already witnessing deadly conflicts with access to water resources at their root, and we are completely unprepared to deal with the onslaught of resource-related conflicts which climate change is threatening to unleash.

I am therefore honoured to introduce this unique collection of essays on *Water for Peace* by some of the world's leading voices in the fields of water, peace and development, which is intended to raise awareness of the connection between water, poverty and security and inspire action at both the global and local levels. In 2000 I co-wrote a report, *National*

Sovereignty and International Watercourses, with three other former heads of state or government, Ingvar Carlsson (Sweden), Sir Ketumile Masire (Botswana) and Fidel Ramos (the Philippines). The 2000 report was well received by water professionals, but eight years later many of the practical recommendations we made remain recommendations. The *Water for Peace* message must reach political decision-makers at the highest level, and world citizens must demand that action is taken urgently to address the appalling consequences of the water crisis and harness the power of water for sustainable peace.

We may not be seeing national armies fighting battles over water, but this does not mean that people are not dying or that the security of whole regions is not in peril.

Green Cross International has been a leading organisation in the field of water conflict prevention for 15 years, and even in this short space of time the level of urgency has risen dramatically. What was a threat has become a reality. Today we are already witnessing deadly conflicts with access to water resources at their root, and we are completely unprepared to deal with the onslaught of resource-related conflicts which climate change is threatening to unleash. The horrific conflict in Darfur, civil violence in northern Uganda and continued instability in Somalia, must be wake-up calls for us all.

The very nature of security has changed remarkably in the two decades since the end of the cold war. Unlike traditional threats emanating from an adversary, however, new challenges are better understood as shared risks and vulnerabilities. Raising military expenditures or dispatching troops cannot resolve them. Nor can sealing borders or maintaining the status quo in a highly unequal world contain them. The Intergovernmental Panel on Climate Change recently released alarming data on the consequences of global warming in some of the world's poorest regions. Increased rates of evaporation will severely reduce rainfall – by up to 20 per cent in the Middle East and North Africa – such that the amount of water available per person could be halved by mid-century in these regions.

I believe that Water for Peace has three main manifestations.

First, we must consider the planet's 263 international watercourses, in the basins of which nearly half the world lives, which absolutely require cooperative, equitable management based on individual basin treaties and international law. The environment, and rivers in particular, pay no heed to our political borders and these shared natural waterways have the potential to be invaluable pathways to peace even among nations with serious political, religious or territorial disputes. But, sadly, at the moment many opportunities for stronger cooperation are being lost in endless negotiations and stalemates over water allocation and failure to take a holistic view of the whole basket of benefits from the shared resource that should be put on the negotiation table. As pressures mount it will be essential that states sharing trans-boundary basins have recourse to international and regional legal instruments — specifically river basin treaties — to guide them through inevitable tensions and disputes peacefully.

Second, we must understand the multi-faceted relationship between water and war itself. Whether in times of political or ethnic tension, civil or regional conflicts, or post-war rehabilitation, having a strong and well-executed water strategy which takes into account both the natural resource and its management and distribution is absolutely critical to preventing violence and allowing people to build peaceful, stable communities. The best means of fighting the spread or re-ignition of violent conflict, and creating the conditions for long-term peace, is to combat poverty, hunger and disease. Water is the key to achieving this. But, while military budgets swell into the trillions — often in the name of 'peacekeeping', water and sanitation receives just five per cent of relatively tiny international development aid budgets. Recent studies have shown that two of the strongest indicators of high-intensity conflict are prolonged drought and high infant mortality — which make a particularly deadly cocktail when coupled with the proliferation of small arms. But failure to realise the importance of water in volatile arid regions, particularly following conflicts, has resulted in large swathes of the world being trapped in decades-long vicious cycles of violence and poverty.

Third, the reliable, equitable provision of safe water and basic sanitation is the bedrock of citizens' relationship with their local public authorities. Whether in the developed or developing world, all of our daily lives are punctuated with the constant need for water for drinking, washing, cooking and hygiene. Since the provision of water creates a relationship of total dependence between people and their service providers, failure in this provision can very quickly undermine a state or local government's moral authority and lead to civil unrest. In recent years there majority of 122 states, developing and industrialised, officially recognised it – among which were European countries, China, Brazil and the Russian Federation. None will, from now on, be entitled to say that the right to water and sanitation is not a recognised human right. It paves the way for further clarification of these rights and will strengthen the framework for actual implementation and international cooperation. That is a major breakthrough.

CSA: Green Cross is part of the Climate Change Task Force, which has been helping to maximise the outcome of Copenhagen. What do you see leading up to and coming out of the COP 16 meeting in Cancún?

MG: On the road to Cancún, I firstly note that climate science tells us we need to act urgently if we are to avoid catastrophic consequences. As all the attacks against climate science, the UNFCC and the climate-gate scandal have been rebuked, there is more than even a consensus on the scientific front. On the policy front, little progress has been made towards a global agreement. Still commitments are taking shape in different parts of the world that seem ready to go further than ever before. Europe is now talking of a 30 per cent reduction by 2020 to ensure its industry will not fall behind in the race to a low carbon economy. China is also pushing ahead in promoting energy efficiency and lowering its carbon intensity. While many have already voiced pessimism as to the outcome of the Cancún talks, I am most impressed by calls from industry groups that are for the first time raising their voices forcefully in favour of more ambition CO_2 reductions – I am referring here to a letter from major European corporate groups stating that the 'EU's future competitive advantage lies in encouraging and enabling its businesses to help drive the transformational change that will occur in the world economy within the next couple of decades, not to hide from it.' To me, this may just be the beginning of a trend that has the potential to overcome the status quo imposed by the fossil fuel and other vested interest groups.

CSA: Back at the UNESCO 5th Global Conference on the Oceans, in Paris, you described the BP oil spill as an 'ecosystem massacre'. How do you think the clean-up effort has been handled by both BP and their subsequent partners from the New Horizon Well, as well as the US Government?

MG: The apparently successful plugging of BP's oil gusher is a huge relief. But it is not the end of a nightmare. The spilled oil in the Gulf of movement to formally declare safe water and sanitation as human rights. We must seize this moment and translate our enthusiasm into solid, binding legislation and action at the national and international levels – starting with the expected UN vote this month.

I was pleased a few weeks ago to hear President Nicolas Sarkozy call for the 2012 World Water Forum – to be held in the French city of Marseille – to be the venue for the international recognition of the universal right to safe water and sanitation. This cause needs more 'champions' – respected public figures and opinion leaders who act as its ambassadors around the world.

The actions and voices of millions of citizens have brought the global movement for the right to water this far. I hope that more people will join us to help bring us closer to the ultimate goal – a world where everyone's right to safe water and sanitation is not just recognised but is also fulfilled.

On 28 July 2010, less than two weeks after this article and in no small measure owing to years of work of Gorbachev, GCI and other civil society activists around the world, the UN General Assembly declared that 'Safe and clean drinking water and sanitation is a human right essential to the full enjoyment of life and all other human rights.' The resolution was carried by 122 votes in favour, with 41 abstentions and no votes against – an unprecedented result showing that no nation will today stand up and deny the right to water and sanitation. A triumph for deprived people everywhere. The GA also called on Member States and international organisations to offer funding, technology and other resources to help poorer countries scale up their efforts to provide clean, accessible and affordable drinking water and sanitation for everyone. Making sure that this happens – that the right becomes a reality – is the next challenge.

essential. The reluctance of a handful of countries cannot derail this vitally important trend.

Recognising water as a human right is a critical step, but it is not an instant 'silver bullet' solution. This right must be enshrined in national laws, and upholding it must be a top priority.

Failures to provide water and sanitation are failures of governance. Recognising that water is a human right is not merely a conceptual point; it is about getting the job done and actually making clean water widely available. We must clarify the obligation of governments to finance and carry out projects that bring these services to those who need them most.

Developing countries that have incorporated the right to water in their legislation, like Senegal and South Africa, have been more effective in providing safe water than many of their neighbours.

Recent UN statistics show that the world is on track to meet, or even exceed, the Millennium Development Goal to halve the number of people without safe drinking water by 2015. This should be applauded. But the goal for sanitation will be missed by one billion people. At current rates, some parts of Africa are at least a century away from providing safe water and sanitation to all. A 'water apartheid' has descended across the world – dividing rich from poor, included from excluded. Efforts to redress this disparity are failing.

Expanding access to water and sanitation will open many other development bottlenecks. Water and sanitation are vital to everything from education to health and to population control. As population growth and climate change increase the pressure for adequate water and food, water will increasingly become a security issue. As global temperatures rise, 'water refugees' will increase. Water touches everything, and strong collaboration among all sectors of society – governments, activists, farmers and the business and science communities – is needed to increase its availability.

Making access to water and sanitation a daily reality is good business, and good for the world economy. According to the UN Environment Programme, a 20 million dollars investment in low-cost water technologies could help 100 million farming families escape extreme poverty. Dedicating 15 billion dollars a year to the water and sanitation millennium goals could bring 38 billion dollars a year in global economic benefits. That's a pretty good rate of return in today's financial climate. It is within our grasp for the first time.

There is tremendous political will and popular momentum behind the

The Right to Water

New York Times, 16 July 2010

The right of every human being to safe drinking water and basic sanitation should be recognised and realised.

The United Nations estimates that nearly 900 million people live without clean water and 2.6 billion without proper sanitation. Water, the basic ingredient of life, is among the world's most prolific killers. At least 4000 children die every day from water-related diseases. In fact, more lives have been lost after World War II due to contaminated water than from all forms of violence and war.

This humanitarian catastrophe has been allowed to fester for generations. We must stop it.

Acknowledging that access to safe water and sanitation is a human right is crucial to the ongoing struggle to save these lives; it is an idea that has come of age. It was first proposed a decade ago by civil society organisations, like Green Cross International, which I helped establish in 1992. Today, it is a mainstream demand that many governments and business leaders support. That is a great achievement.

This month, for the first time, the UN General Assembly is preparing to vote on a historic resolution declaring the human right to 'safe and clean drinking water and sanitation'. It is a pivotal opportunity. So far, 190 states have acknowledged – directly or indirectly – the human right to safe water and sanitation. In 2007, leaders from the Asia-Pacific region recognised safe drinking water and basic sanitation as human rights and fundamental aspects of security. In March, the European Union affirmed that all states must adhere to their human rights commitments in regard to safe drinking water.

Not all nations are on board, however. The United States and Canada are among the very few that have not formally embraced the right to safe water. Their continued reluctance to officially recognise the right to water should be questioned, not least by their own citizens. President Barack Obama's national security strategy calls for furthering human rights and sustainable development around the world; that goal should be translated into support for access to water as a human right.

A few other states, like Turkey and Egypt, have also hesitated to formally acknowledge the right to water, mainly because of boundary-related water issues. However, an absolute global consensus is not

Tomorrow May Be Too Late to Address the Water Crisis

Speech at the 'Peace with Water' conference at the European Parliament, Brussels, Belgium, 12 February 2009

I am happy to see here among us, and to welcome them personally, Prince Albert of Monaco, Danielle Mitterrand, Federico Mayor, and Mercedes Bresso, my co-chairman in the World Political Forum. Unfortunately, for health reasons, my friend Mario Soares was not able to come. What has brought us together — scientists, environmentalists and politicians — is the problem of water, which is today, without a doubt, a political problem.

We are meeting at a time when the world is going through an unprecedented global crisis, a crisis of the model of development that is unsustainable. The unsustainability of this model is reflected in the water problem, which is a microcosm of this model. The water crisis is part of the global crisis, part of the crisis of world politics as it brings together social, economic, environmental and political factors.

According to a report by the United Nations Development Programme (UNDP), currently at least 700 million people (an estimated one billion people until recently) face a shortage of water. At the same time the demand for water is constantly growing and will continue to grow. We will have to feed the growing world population. Eighty per cent of the water usage in developing countries is for irrigation.

The problem is being made more acute as a result of global climate change. The access to water is becoming a source of international conflicts. Recently Ban Ki-moon, the United Nations Secretary-General, really sounded the alarm when he said that the hour of danger is very near.

As far as conflicts are concerned, we already see an armed conflict in Sudan and we also see even more casualties or losses as a result of the health consequences of the water crisis. According to a WHO study conducted in five continents, 80 per cent of infectious diseases in the world are the result of the use of contaminated water. In the developing countries, about 95 per cent of all surface waters are polluted.

The prospect of a water crisis is looming over countries that are very important to the world economy and world politics — such as China and India. Even in the wealthier countries, the picture is far from perfect. In Eastern Europe, adequate water and sanitation is not available to 16 per tical remedies to help tackle them. Each author is a genuine world leader in this field and I am delighted that Green Cross International has had the opportunity to gather such a wealth of wisdom, experience and inspiration into this unprecedented volume. It is no accident that the contributors include Nobel Peace Prize laureates, past and present heads of state and government, leaders of UN agencies and a European Commissioner; this is a reflection of the huge importance of water security for the peaceful and sustainable development of our planet. I am confident that this publication will serve to open more eyes and encourage progress.

We live in volatile and changing times, faced with the awe-inspiring global challenge of climate change, the devastation of civil wars, and the hope-crushing scourge of extreme poverty, but one thing is constant: no region or community can enjoy genuine long-term peace without water security. Whole regions are languishing in poverty and conflict, effectively held hostage by their hydrology; we must break this cycle and give people a chance for peace. Benjamin Franklin said that 'when the well's dry, we know the worth of water'. The alarm clock has been ringing on deaf ears for far too long – it is time to wake up to the water security crisis before it is too late, before the wells of the world have run dry.

'Water for Peace – Peace for Water' has been a rallying cry of GCI, and a strongly felt priority of Gorbachev for over a decade. This publication for the International Expo in Spain was an opportunity to reach a large new audience, and update the message for modern times – telling the world to wake up to the water threat and embrace the many ways that water, properly managed, can unite people. The year 2008 was a turning point, with the election of President Barack Obama and further unfolding of the global financial crisis – Gorbachev took every opportunity to remind leaders and citizens alike not to forget the world's poorest people or lose sight of development and security goals.

have been numerous cases of conflicts breaking out as a result of problems related to water supply – from violent riots over privatisation in Bolivia and South Africa to protests against the use and pollution of water by private companies in India and Peru – as well as countless instances of corruption, mismanagement and abject failure on the part of public and private water service providers alike. Alternatively, where water services are perceived to be efficient and fair this can contribute greatly towards building wider trust and stability. In this respect, peace can be strengthened by respecting the universal human right of all people to basic water and sanitation services, and their right to be informed of and engaged in the related decision-making processes.

In response to these three primary Water for Peace challenges, Green Cross International has long been actively promoting three essential actions:

1. The entry into force of the UN Convention on the Non-Navigational Uses of International Watercourses which promotes cooperation and peaceful relations between riparian states, and the peaceful resolution of water conflicts. This Convention was adopted by the General Assembly in 1997 but still has not been ratified by enough states to enter into force.
2. The protection of watercourses, resources and facilities during times of war and conflict, and the inclusion of water strategy in post-conflict rehabilitation plans from the outset.
3. The negotiation and adoption of a Global Framework Convention on Water, which, when ratified by the member states of the United Nations, will give all citizens a tool through which to assert their right to safe water and sanitation, and would oblige national governments to make sure that water provision and protection is prioritised. Other crucial environmental challenges – including climate change and biodiversity – benefit from an international convention, so considering that eight million people die each year due to dirty or insufficient water this issue clearly deserves no less.

Tackling the water crisis requires that we make tough decisions and deal with very contentious subjects. The international community and national governments must end the habit of following strongly worded promises at conferences with business as usual in practice.

The seven essays contributed to this book by my esteemed colleagues address the interrelated Water for Peace challenges and propose prac-

Mexico now enters a phase where its impact on wildlife, ecosystems, people, jobs and tourism could be as bad as ever – just more difficult to see amid a cloud of complexity.

The spills have been happening for a long time and in many places around the world. Consequences from the *Exxon Valdez* spill in Alaska in 1989 and from the *Prestige* in Spain are still impacting the environment despite the clean-up efforts. There are also many other spills occurring on the shores of Ghana or Nigeria that are less publicised but no less disastrous to the local environment and communities. The Mexican Gulf disaster is a deafening alarm that we should stop trying to artificially extend the carbon era by technological innovations that are beyond our control when things go wrong.

CSA: Did they do enough? More importantly, what lessons can oil companies, as well as we as a society, take from this to prevent future 'ecosystem massacres' such as this one?

MG: What we need to realise is that to some extent we are all responsible for what happened because we all participate in the fossil fuel economy through the consumption decisions that we make every day. Moving to a clean energy society is a first step in the right direction and as consumers we can have a major impact. As voters we can also impact government policy – that is the foundation of democracy. This makes sense not only for environmental reasons but also to make our world more secure and our economies more resilient. Civil society also has a role to play not only in clean-up efforts but also in helping us move towards a more sustainable world. Green Cross has many initiatives in this area like the organisation of the 'Earth Dialogues' conference-events that promote sustainability across all sectors of modern society, 'Environmental Diaries' for schoolchildren around the world to positively impact their communities, or the 'Eco-Office' programme that helps businesses increase their bottom line by implementing actions that help protect the environment.

CSA: Much has changed in the world since you served as President of the Soviet Union, both politically and socially. Using what you have witnessed and learned in the past 20 years, what lies ahead for us as a civilisation?

MG: Winston Churchill was right in saying, 'It is a mistake to try to look too far ahead. The chain of destiny can only be grasped one link at a time.'

The end of the cold war gave the world a unique historic opportunity. I was convinced of it then. I still believe it today — how these opportunities were used is a different story... Anyway it has cleared the way for new powers to rise — China and India in particular — and removed ideological obstacles to globalisation. Cross-border migration has surged. The technological revolution has transformed international communications, the flow of information, financial trading and political awareness. After 20 years lost to capitalism 'alleluia chanting' it took a crisis almost as massive as that of 1929, with a global impact on employment and growth, to induce the preachers of neo-liberal globalism towards cautious silence. A new world order is replacing the old — 20 years later, we are closer to this goal but there is still a long way to go and the road, as we can already feel, will be bumpy.

The multi-faceted crisis that has hit the world shows with a renewed sense of urgency how tightly the key challenges of environment, development and security are intertwined.

Climate change, being but a tip of this crisis, gives global stability and security threats existential proportions that can shock the foundations of modern civilisation. It threatens to unleash multi-million migrations and exacerbates the problems of growing poverty, social inequality, water, energy and food crises.

Therefore the biggest challenge in the next ten years will be our ability to offset this systemic crisis with comprehensive solutions based on scientific knowledge, focusing on the problem itself and not on conventional political 'priorities'.

Outcomes are not predetermined. They depend on both events and purposeful actions. To meet new challenges, we need to change our mentality just as we did to end the cold war; we need to take down the wall that separates us from our future.

Part Two

TRIBUTES TO GORBACHEV

*Gorbachev and Ruud
Lubbers sign the
agreement launching
Green Cross in the Hague
in 1993*

about globalisation with a human face – you urged us to include in our efforts religions and spiritual movements. And we did – from the very beginning of the Earth Charter, where we wrote in the preamble, 'To move forward we must recognise that in the midst of a magnificent diversity of cultures and life forms we are one human family and one earth community with a common destiny,' till the very end where we concluded: 'Let ours be a time remembered for the awakening of a new reverence for life, the firm resolve to achieve sustainability, the quickening of the struggle for justice and peace and the joyful celebration of life.' We mapped the way forward as the ultimate of practising harmony and living in such a way that our children, grandchildren and great-grandchildren will not have to face an exhausted nature, but a world where we practise multi-polarity and diversity, by paying respect.

Mikhail, you are blessed. Not only with 80 years, but also as a great-grandfather and by your great-granddaughter.

Mikhail, by your reforms you did not give shape to the end of history, as Francis Fukiyama said in those days, but to the beginning of a new chapter in history outlined in the Earth Charter. You were instrumental in that.

Mikhail, long before that memorable meeting in the Catshuis you played an important role in my life. When I became Prime Minister in 1982, I was confronted with the dilemma of more and more SS-20s in your Soviet Union and with growing intermediate nuclear forces in West Europe. Ronald Reagan and you were seen as confronting each other. But I was blessed knowing that Ronald Reagan at the end of the day truly wanted a zero-zero agreement, as did you; and so it happened in Reykjavik. In my country those systems were never deployed. But my decision to be prepared to deploy them was instrumental to reaching the zero-zero agreement. In those days you conveyed to me via our mutual friend Rajiv Gandhi, then the Prime Minister of India, the message: 'I will criticise loud and clear your decision to deploy, even when I do not blame you on a personal level, but my advice is not to hurry with implementation. In a year from now I expect zero-zero.' That is what you conveyed through Rajiv to me. And so it happened.

And when the cold war was over and I was confronted with the controversy between Kohl, Mitterrand and Thatcher, I went for the Energy Charter to find a way for a new European way forward together. After the zero-zero success, the Energy Charter proved to be a new way to share our enthusiasm; and that very Energy Charter together with your constitutional generosity gave oxygen to the concept of the Commonwealth of Independent States; and that again proved to be the way to a nuclear-free central Asia.

Here I touch on another area you worked so hard on: a genuine implementation of the Nuclear Non-Proliferation Treaty on the way to a Global Zero.

Mikhail, we have travelled a long journey; and it was so gratifying for me to be blessed by walking with you. I could speak now at length about the actual global challenge 'Climate Change' and – maybe even more important – overcoming the division between the world of Islam and the rest of the world. But I will not do that and limit myself to what really connects us: the Earth Charter and its last words 'the joyful celebration of life'. You and I, we were practical no-nonsense politicians, but we know as well that the world needs not only efficiency and modern life, but also even more compassion and compassionate leadership.

Indeed, the most important thing is to learn to practise the joyful celebration of life.

Rudolphus 'Ruud' Lubbers was Prime Minister of the Netherlands from 1982 to 1994, the longest serving Prime Minister in Dutch history. He was also the United Nations High Commissioner for Refugees from 2001 to 2005. Dr Lubbers has been actively involved in Green Cross International from the very beginning, both as an Honorary Board Member and through his role in the establishment and continuing work of the Earth Charter. The Earth Charter was presented at the Peace Palace in The Hague in June 2000 and Dr Lubbers continues to be a member of the Earth Charter Commission.

Mario Soares

A Tribute

I personally met Mikhail Gorbachev in Moscow, when he was General Secretary of the Communist Party and had already launched perestroika and glasnost. It was during an official visit I made to the USSR, as President of the Republic of Portugal, in which I had the pleasure to offer him a copy, in Portuguese, of his book *Perestroika*, published by the editor Lyon de Castro, an old friend of mine and a former communist dissident.

The impression Gorbachev made on me was an instantaneous and excellent one. He did not speak *la langue de bois*, as the French say, to designate the ideological speech used by the Soviets of that time, even at the highest level. He answered my questions with a straightforwardness, clearness and sincerity that touched me. It represented something genuinely new to a Western man, like me, with some experience of communism through previous trips to the Soviet Union, to Czechoslovakia, to East Germany and to Cuba.

Gorbachev was a highly original and surprising phenomenon, as history would later prove. A humanist with great experience and culture, a humanised politician, curious about others and of what was different. A strong supporter of peaceful coexistence and of peace, and absolutely determined to change the Soviet Union, fighting for freedom, for the respect of human rights and for environmental values. At that time, all this represented a huge novelty, especially in the Soviet Union. Since the first conversation I had with him I realised — allow me to say it — that I was in front of an exceptional politician of an extremely rare breed, one which appears only from time to time, with the political and moral dimension of a man like Mandela or, moving back in time, Churchill or Gandhi — a politician willing, in conscience, to change not only his own country, but also the world.

On that visit, I had the opportunity to meet Andrei Sakharov, a scholar, a humanist and a dissident, at the Portuguese Embassy in Moscow, which was not easy at all. I was only able to do it thanks to Gorbachev's intervention. Sakharov was also a very exceptional man, who has left a deep impression on me. I refer to this meeting because it is related to another visit I made to Moscow, when the Soviet Union was in full change, under Gorbachev's presidency. After Sakharov's death, his widow Elena Bonner and the great cellist Mstislav Rostropovich invited me to attend a tribute to him at a Moscow theatre in May 1991. I went on a non-official journey but nevertheless thought I should inform Gorbachev about it. He was extremely kind, invited me to lunch with him and, on the way out, he told me that we would meet again for sure, at the theatre where the ceremony was going to take place in honour of Sakharov. I remember what happened there as if it were today. I arrived just in time and I was invited, together with my wife, to go to the box next to the stage. The room was full and Yeltsin was in the audience, receiving great applause by all present.

The ceremony began with Mstislav Rostropovich playing his cello with his back turned to the box where Gorbachev was. There was an obvious feeling of hostility in the room. When the speeches began, it was not only an opportunity to honour Sakharov but also to criticise Gorbachev. Because I do not understand Russian, I had an interpreter – who sometimes remained silent. Gorbachev told him to translate everything, even the injuries addressed to him. I was really surprised with Gorbachev's presence of mind – and self-confidence – that remained calm despite the shouting, the insults and the threats.

At the break, a little snack had been prepared at a room next to our box. Gorbachev invited Sakharov's widow and other distinguished guests to it. Rostropovich and Yeltsin did not attend. But Elena Bonner came, together with two or three people, who immediately began to criticise Gorbachev and his wife for being there. They did not consider him worthy to attend a tribute to the memory of Sakharov. But they were doing it in a tremendously aggressive tone. With extraordinary self-restraint, Gorbachev never raised his voice. Besides my wife, also present were an American atomic scientist and the former Slovak President, Alexander Dubček, who also understood Russian. They were both as amazed as I was. Dubček made many comments to me in French about what was happening, and we all sat there admiring Gorbachev's presence of mind.

I met Gorbachev once again in Lisbon, after he left power and after his wife's death, which was a big setback for him. He was the same self-confident man, aware of the general revolution he had provoked in Russia and worldwide. He had then a very broad view of what he should do: to work for peace, for the protection of the threatened planet, for the respect of human rights and peoples' dignity.

I spoke with him for a long time, and showed him around Lisbon. He has since invited me to participate in some of the organisations he had created in the meantime, like Green Cross and The New Policy Forum. I have accepted with great honour. The Portuguese communists, once so reverent towards him, have never forgiven him for having shown the world the colossal lie that communism was from the time of Lenin, Stalin, Khrushchev and Brezhnev, until Gorbachev arrived. He is someone who has changed everything like magic, without violence or bloodshed. We must pay honour to him.

He is one of the most extraordinary and complex political figures of the mid-twentieth century and of our twenty-first century. He is a Nobel Peace Prize laureate, a man who has contributed – perhaps more than anyone else – to changing the world, bringing it more freedom and showing an absolute respect for peoples' dignity. Since then I have met him in several countries. I have been following his career closely and I continue to admire his magnificent work.

Mario Soares served as Prime Minster of Portugal from 1976 to 1978 and from 1983 to 1985, and as President from 1986 to 1996. He is a co-founder of the Portuguese Socialist Party and was its Secretary-General for 13 years after its inception. Currently he is President of the Mario Soares Foundation and is a member of the Green Cross International Board of Directors.

George H.W. Bush

I am pleased to salute my friend and esteemed former colleague, President Gorbachev, as he and his friends — including the Bush family — celebrate his 80th birthday.

We worked together for nearly three years during a period of remarkable change in our world; and when Mikhail left office on Christmas Day 1991, I felt the same way toward him that President Eisenhower felt toward Winston Churchill when he wrote: 'When finally he laid down the mantle of his high office, I could not help feeling that, for me, a treasured partnership had been broken; but never will I lose any of the affection and admiration I hold for him personally . . .'

I still feel this way towards my friend Mikhail, and was deeply touched when he came to my 80th birthday in Texas. Some of you may have heard about this, but I made a parachute jump to try and prove that advancing age does not mean you cannot achieve certain goals. When I landed, my friend Mikhail was standing there with Barbara, flowers and fine vodka in hand.

Friendship aside, however, I am confident that history will be kind to Mikhail Gorbachev as the architect of glasnost and perestroika — because these policies helped build the 'common European home' of which he so frequently and eloquently spoke. It was just over 25 years ago that he assumed his post of leadership; and a quarter century later, there is no doubt that the hopeful, peaceful world in which we live today is thanks in large measure to Mikhail Gorbachev.

Happy birthday, my dear friend!

George Herbert Walker Bush is the 41st President of the United States, holding the office from 1989 to 1993, and also served as the 43rd Vice President of the United States from 1981 to 1989. As President, he first met with President Gorbachev just after the fall of the Berlin Wall on 2 December 1989 in Malta. At this summit they formally declared the cold war over. During his presidency, George H.W. Bush and Mikhail Gorbachev met several more times, including in Moscow in July 1991 to sign the Strategic Arms Reduction Treaty (START I).

stage came when the results of that research were translated into the production of weapons on a large scale.

As the discussion wore on it was clear that the Soviets were indeed very concerned about SDI. They wanted it stopped at almost any price. I knew that to some degree I was being used as a stalking horse for President Reagan. I was also aware that I was dealing with a wily opponent who would ruthlessly exploit any divisions between me and the Americans. So I bluntly stated – and then repeated at the end of the meeting – that he should understand that there was no question of dividing us: we would remain staunch allies of the United States. My frankness on this was particularly important because of my equal frankness about what I saw as the President's unrealistic dream of a nuclear-free world.

The talks were due to end at 4.30 to allow Mr Gorbachev to be back for an early evening reception at the Soviet Embassy, but he said that he wanted to continue. It was 5.50 when he left, having introduced me to another pearl of Russian popular wisdom to the effect that, 'Mountain folk cannot live without guests any more than they can live without air. But if the guests stay longer than necessary, they choke.' As he took his leave, I hoped that I had been talking to the next Soviet leader. For, as I subsequently told the press, this was a man with whom I could do business.

––––––

'Happy Birthday Mikhail!' Margaret Thatcher

The Rt Hon. The Baroness Thatcher *served as the British Prime Minister from 1979 to 1990, winning three general elections and holding the position longer than anyone in modern times. In 1992, she was made a life peer as Baroness Thatcher of Kesteven, giving her a seat in the House of Lords. In 1995, Baroness Thatcher was appointed a Lady Companion of the Order of the Garter, the United Kingdom's highest order of chivalry. She has also been awarded the Presidential Medal of Freedom, the highest civilian honour awarded by the United States. Already a strong ally of President Reagan, Margaret Thatcher developed a constructive relationship with Mikhail Gorbachev following their meeting in 1984, and played a key role in the diplomacy that brought the cold war to an end.*

Frederik Willem de Klerk

A Message to Mark the 80th Birthday of President Mikhail Gorbachev

There can be little doubt that the processes that President Gorbachev initiated in the Soviet Union during his presidency will be viewed by historians as one of the turning points of modern history. In effect, the decisions that he took changed the world forever – and overwhelmingly for the better.

More than any other individual, he was responsible for breaking the log jam of bipolar nuclear confrontation that had dominated international relations since the end of the Second World War. The new Europe would not have developed in its present form without the reforms that he initiated.

His actions in bringing an end to global bipolar confrontation also had a profound impact on developments in southern Africa. Under his leadership, the Soviet Union played a constructive role in the negotiations between South Africa, Angola and Cuba, which resulted in the withdrawal of Cuban forces from Angola and the successful implementation of the United Nations independence process in Namibia.

These developments also had a seminal impact on the evolution of the political situation in South Africa as well. Without the reforms initiated by President Gorbachev our own transformation process in South Africa would have been much more difficult and might have been delayed by several years. As it was, the developments in the Soviet Union and central Europe that he initiated helped to open a window of opportunity for South Africa as well. It was my – and President Mandela's – privilege

Gorbachev with Lech Walesa and Fredrik Willem De Klerk at the 10th Nobel Peace Laureates Summit in Berlin in November 2009

to lead South Africa through this window of opportunity to the non-racial constitutional democracy that we established in 1994.

For all these services to mankind President Gorbachev was awarded the Nobel Peace Prize in 1990. Having achieved so much, many other leaders would have rested on their laurels and disappeared into well-deserved retirement. Instead, Mikhail Gorbachev sought new causes for which to fight and new goals for which to strive.

Long before the rest of the world became aware of the unsustainability of mankind's current exploitation of the Earth's natural resources, Mikhail Gorbachev identified the need to mobilise opinion and resources to protect our environment. In 1993 he established Green Cross International to build on the work of the Earth Summit in Rio de Janeiro in 1992. He chose the theme of the Green Cross to replicate in the sphere of the environment the emergency remedial work of the Red Cross in the sphere of human crises. Since then Green Cross has become a prominent voice in the campaign to ensure sustainable development and to combat the threat of global warming. Green Cross is now represented in over 30 countries around the world.

President Gorbachev and the Gorbachev Foundation have also played the leading role in establishing the Secretariat of Nobel Peace Summits and in organising annual summits of Nobel peace laureates. The annual summits provide peace laureates with the opportunity of focusing their collective wisdom and experience on continuing threats to international peace.

For all these enormous contributions to international peace and to the well-being of mankind it is an honour for me to be able to congratulate President Gorbachev on his 80th birthday and to wish him every happiness and success in the future.

Frederik Willem de Klerk *served as the seventh President of South Africa from 1989 to 1994. It was during his watch that apartheid was dismantled in South Africa. He then served as Deputy President until 1996, under the presidency of Nelson Mandela. He was awarded the Nobel Peace Prize, with Nelson Mandela, in 1993 for his contribution to the end of apartheid and continues to be an active member of the Nobel Peace Laureates Summit alongside Mikhail Gorbachev.*

Shimon Peres

The Honourable Mikhail Gorbachev

Dear Mikhail, Dear Friend,

It is my personal pleasure to extend my heartfelt congratulations on the occasion of your 80th birthday, wishing you much success in your notable endeavours, good health, continued productive activity, and a future filled with much happiness among your family and friends – until 120 and beyond!

From this milestone in your life, you can look back with pride and a great deal of satisfaction on your tremendous achievements, that have had a significant impact on the course of history. You played your role in history with courage and wisdom, becoming one of its truly towering personalities who changed the world. You generated light and hope, and the world is enlightened and hopeful again. At the same time, you can look towards a tomorrow in which democracy across the world is in the ascendancy, in keeping with your vision and which you seek to promote.

Gorbachev with Shimon Peres

Dear Mikhail, ours has been a friendship of many years, a friendship that I value, and from one friend to the other, I wish you a warm *Mazal Tov*, and everything that your heart desires.

Shimon Peres

Shimon Peres *is the ninth and current President of Israel. He was elected in 2007 and previously served as Prime Minister from 1995 to 1996 and from 1984 to 1986. He was awarded the Nobel Peace Prize in 1994, together with Yitzhak Rabin and Yasser Arafat, for his role as Israel's Foreign Minister during the Peace Talks that resulted in the Oslo Accords. He has also served on the Green Cross International Board of Directors. The Peres Centre for Peace, which he founded, works closely with Green Cross International on projects in the Middle East.*

Ricardo Lagos

Mikhail Gorbachev and the Twentieth Century

Mikhail Gorbachev is one of the great personalities of the twentieth century. In March 1985, he reached the pinnacle of his political career after being elected Secretary-General of the Communist Party of the Soviet Union – which, at the time concentrated all the power in one of the two superpowers confronting each other during the cold war. Gorbachev had powerful influence in the neighbouring countries over which the USSR exerted its hegemony and authority, and this influence was also felt in those countries of Asia, Africa and Latin America that received the economic, political and military support of the Soviets.

From this position of power and influence, Gorbachev centred his efforts on reforming Soviet communism with a democratic sense, aiming to restore total sovereignty to allies in central and Eastern Europe, to peacefully resolve the various and different wars that were affecting the Third World and, what seemed even more incredible at that time, to negotiate with the United States and its allies a new world order based on multilateral cooperation that would leave the cold war and nuclear apocalypse behind us.

The fact that a man, trained and educated in the Soviet system, would have these objectives upon reaching office naturally led to confusion amongst both communist orthodoxy and headstrong anti-communists. They were all convinced that the Soviet system was unalterable. No one had perceived that, since the mid-1950s, tension had been building up between an emerging modern society and the very rigid ideological superstructure of power established in the times of Lenin and Stalin. The blows inflicted during Khrushchev's Thaw had not been not been enough. Like Nagy in Hungary in 1956, and Dubček in the Prague Spring of 1968, Gorbachev was a leader who had arisen from communism and now wanted to democratise the system.

In March 1990, five years after becoming Secretary-General of the Communist Party of the Soviet Union, Gorbachev was elected President of the Soviet Union by the Congress of People's Deputies in the first free elections in Soviet history. The objective was to move towards a mixed economy. A year earlier, in 1989, and through diverse means, the European states under Soviet domination had freely started a process of transition towards democracy and the recovery of full sovereignty for their people. The Berlin Wall was already history, as was the division of

Europe. In Africa, Asia, as well as in Latin America, people were looking for a peaceful end to long and painful conflicts. There we find Nelson Mandela's liberation and the consolidation of democracy in Latin America after the lost decade of the 1980s and its dictatorships.

It is because of these contributions that Mikhail Gorbachev was awarded the Nobel Peace Prize in 1990, in recognition of the action of one man who, like few in history, used the enormous power he held to bring about profound changes that, in fact, entailed a huge abatement in his own power. Gorbachev initiated the political democratisation that became known as *glasnost* and, through *perestroika*, sought the economic and social restructuring of the Soviet system. Introducing these changes placed him the middle of intense crossfire – he was equally attacked by both conservatives from the former regime and by those who were impatient and eager to accelerate its demise.

The *coup d'état* attempt against him aimed to re-establish the former system, and even though it failed in August 1991 it hindered the reform process he had laboriously been implementing and which eventually led to the collapse of the Soviet Union. This is how a new Russia was born – a community of states that would, through different means and with different degrees of success, seek their own path towards democracy

Gorbachev and his translator Pavel Palajchenko with Ricardo Lagos and Ruud Lubbers

and integration into the world economic and political order. Gorbachev shares the fate of history's greatest reformists and revolutionaries. He did not manage to exactly reach the goals he had set for himself. Nevertheless, he was able to remove enormous obstacles and, in this sense, pave the way for a world that is undoubtedly better than the one that existed before he changed his way of thinking.

Conscious of this, he understood that his role would be that of a light showing the way into the twenty-first century, and he took up new challenges, like the International Green Cross, through which he became a harbinger of what would become one of the major issues of the twenty-first century: global warming. He saw the need to ensure development that was sustainable in order to guarantee that this planet on which we all live can also be the one of our children and grandchildren.

Through the very profound reforms he was able to introduce in the Union of Soviet Socialist Republics, Gorbachev emerges as a leader in his own class, with the authority to call his peers – the leaders of the twenty-first century – to action and to face the challenges that must be addressed on a global scale. Today, his actions continue to remove barriers, exactly as they did 25 years ago, so that the world can reach a consensus that will allow us to save the planet.

Congratulations for these 80 years, Gorbachev! Mikhail, you can look back with pride at what you have accomplished and forward to the challenge of all that is still to be achieved in your long life. Congratulations!

Ricardo Lagos served as President of Chile from 2000 to 2006. Prior to this, in the 1970s and 1980s, he was one of the most prominent and outspoken opponents of Augusto Pinochet's military regime. In 1978, he became President of the Democratic Alliance, a coalition of opposition parties. After the departure of Pinochet, Ricardo Lagos served as Minister of Education and as Minister of Public Works during the 1990s. Ricardo Lagos founded the Fundación Democracia y Desarrollo (Foundation for Democracy and Development) in 2006. He is also co-Chair of the Inter-American Dialogue, a member of the Club of Madrid and a Special Envoy for Climate Change for the United Nations Secretary-General. Ricardo Lagos is a member of the Climate Change Task Force along with Mikhail Gorbachev. He is also an economist and academic, currently holding the position of University Professor at Large at Brown University in the USA.

Achim Steiner

No 80th birthday celebration for Mikhail Gorbachev would be complete if his significant contribution to the environment was not acknowledged on this special day.

Many will quite rightly point to his achievements as a key architect behind the reforms that swept the Soviet Union in the later half of the twentieth century and which led to the collapse of the Berlin Wall.

But none should ignore Mr Gorbachev's campaigning on the links between environment and peace – and on the challenges to humanity of breaching ecological limits: these rank alongside the end of the cold war as one of his outstanding accomplishments and legacies.

Green Cross International, which he founded one year after the Rio Earth Summit of 1992, has played a pivotal role in catalysing action on the safe decommissioning of conventional and chemical weapons in Russia while bringing former military bases back into civilian use.

But this work has expanded geographically and in cooperation with many partners including the United Nations. In many ways this has helped lay the groundwork and direction for various other transformative initiatives operating in the world.

These include the Environment and Security Initiative in which UNEP, the UN Development Programme and many others including the Organisation for Security and Cooperation in Europe are members.

The focus has been in part on the pollution hot spots that have been left by the Soviet Union, many of which are trans-boundary in terms of their potential to cause environmental damage and disasters and thus trigger tensions between communities and countries.

The work that Green Cross has undertaken and which has been complemented by other organisations is also premised on the way environmental cooperation can act as an important catalyst for preventing conflicts, building trust and promoting peace.

These are the same principles underpinning the work of UNEP's post-conflict and disaster management branch, created after the war in the Balkans, which has carried out assessments and cooperated in clean-ups in countries ranging from Afghanistan and Iraq to Liberia and Lebanon.

Mr Gorbachev's central role, along with former UNEP Executive Director Maurice Strong, in the 2000 Earth Charter must also go down as an inspiring attempt to crystallise the principles of sustainability alongside concepts of ecological integrity and social and economic justice.

The Earth Charter has since achieved resonance across the world and has been endorsed by organisations from UNESCO and IUCN to cities, religious groups and non-governmental organisations.

The Charter has had its critics too, but such is the nature of an idea which is essentially disruptive in terms of challenging the status quo.

Indeed Mr Gorbachev stands out as one among a few who grasped early on the kind of wide-ranging ideas that have now evolved into the concept of the Green Economy – an initiative that underlines that the future sustainability of the human race and of the global economy will hinge on a transition to a far more low carbon, resource-efficient path.

This is also a path that factors in the economic importance of the Earth's natural and nature-based assets, particularly in respect to the poor, and understands that there are limits to the extent to which these assets can be mined before fundamental 'tipping' points are reached that may turn nature into a wasted rather than a productive resource.

'Man has exceeded nature's allowable limits. Civilisation must adjust to the laws of the biosphere. We have little room for manoeuvre – and little time,' he argued in an essay in *Time* magazine in 1998.

And he added, well before the financial and economic crisis of 2008, 'Our main goal is to help set in motion a value shift in people's minds. Our environmental education programmes … aim at helping people understand a simple truth: man is not the master of nature but just a part of it.'

Like many environmentalists, who have grasped that fundamental truth concerning humanity's place in the wider, natural world, Mr Gorbachev's ecological perspective grew from working on the land and later through trying to manage human-made natural disasters.

It was when working on a farm in a Soviet collective that he witnessed first hand how unsustainable management can trigger erosion of soils and pollution of water and air.

And later, while working as a Communist Party official for a natural resources commission, he saw how poor construction and unsustainable operations of irrigation and hydroelectric plants can turn fertile into barren land while harming both the freshwater and marine environments.

He further witnessed first hand the critical environmental, strategic and social importance of water resources as State Secretary for Agriculture when he was faced with the terrible calamity of the Aral Sea while personally intervening to prevent projects that would have diverted rivers in Siberia.

The 1986 Chernobyl nuclear accident was also a formative 'watershed' experience that triggered a widespread rethink of nuclear power and the closure of old and polluting industrial facilities across the Soviet Union.

Mr Gorbachev has quite rightly won many awards for his environmental work including the 2008 Energy Globe Award and a special prize under the 2010 German Environmental Awards for his work on environmental protection and – his twin passion – campaigning to avert climate change.

German President Christian Wulff called his work 'ecological perestroika', drawing a green analogy to Mr Gorbachev's political reforms and restructuring during his time as Soviet President.

In 2006, UNEP honoured him as one of our Champions of the Earth, describing Mr Gorbachev as an individual who has striven to prevent conflict over shared water resources including mediating between Israelis and Palestinians in the Middle East.

'He has personally supported through Green Cross water conflict prevention initiatives in Africa, South America, Central Europe, and in his own native river basin, the Volga. His involvement has been critical to breaking deadlocks and encouraging parties to negotiate,' said the Champions of the Earth laudation.

'In 2003, he launched a Local and Regional Authorities Water Initiative aimed at strengthening decentralised cooperation and North-South solidarity to provide drinking water for the world's most desperate people while respecting local cultures and ecosystems,' it added.

In terms of awards, there can be few, if any, higher accolades than winning the Nobel Peace Prize, which Mikhail Gorbachev did in 1990 for his achievements in terms of nuclear disarmament and for his part in ending the cold war while ushering in a new chapter of freedom for the peoples of Central and Eastern Europe.

If the Nobel Peace Prize committee were awarding Mr Gorbachev the same prize in the year of his 80th birthday, the citation might carry some additional and poignant remarks.

Ones that underline that peace in the twenty-first century will depend on keeping the missiles firmly in their silos and eventually eradicating them from the planet, but also on better managing the planet itself in ways that allow resources to be shared and to be shared sustainably.

Mr Gorbachev's role in cementing within the global consciousness these essential realities, ones that become ever more central on a planet growing from over six billion to over nine billion people by 2050, is an achievement many have striven to emulate.

Indeed, as we celebrate his 80th year, history may prove that Mr Gorbachev's work on the environment will eventually become the most enduring legacy and real peace dividend of the writings, speeches, actions and campaigns of this quite remarkable man.

Achim Steiner, a UN Under-Secretary General, has been the Executive Director of the UN Environment Programme (UNEP) since 2006 and the Director-General of the UN Offices at Nairobi since 2009. Prior to joining the UN he served as Director-General of the International Union for Conservation of Nature (IUCN) from 2001 to 2006. UNEP and Green Cross International work together on a variety of issues and initiatives, including the Green Star Awards.

Federico Mayor Zaragoza

Vision, Willingness, Leadership

After the meeting of the Issyk-Kul Forum in the mountains of Kirgyzia, we were received by the General Secretary of the USSR Communist Party in Moscow: 'Perestroika and glasnost are an aim and a way. I know the reality of this country in depth; we can, we must transform it in depth.'

This gathering took place on 20 October 1986, one week after the very important encounter with President Reagan in Reykjavik.

I had just presented, as Chair of the Forum, the conclusions of our meeting, convened by the dissident writer Chingiz Aitmatov, a man with freedom in his veins. Arthur Miller, Alexander King, Alvin Toffler, Claude Simon, Zülfu Livanelli, Augusto Forti, Rustem Khairov ... were among the group ready to support the radical changes that were about to be undertaken.

We were surprised and progressively attracted by the strong personality – with vision, willingness and leadership – of the General Secretary, Gorbachev.

A week before, at the opening of the encounter in the Issyk-Kul Lake, Chingiz Aitmatov declared that, 'if we dare to act according to our consciences, if we are awakened enough ... we could tell our children that we did all we could until the last moment. Only if mankind designs and builds its future will it be at the height of its greatness.'

At the meeting with the General Secretary, he repeated that 'a new thinking' was needed. A new reality was emerging and the best solution is always to foresee in order to prevent. 'It must be very clear to all of us that the most important point of reference is always each human being.' And he concluded: 'Those who do not dare do not achieve anything.'

You can imagine how impressed we were when we left Moscow and how hard we were working afterwards in order to better fulfil, in our modest capacity, the mobilisation of intellectuals that he was looking for.

After some days I wrote this poem for Mikhail Gorbachev:

To copy
such a rift,
to narrow
this gap,
to make fertile
this desert

when harsh memory
stalks
our progress,
memory
both lush
yet desolate,
we must go forward
knowing that only the future
has not died.

While in Frunze, today Bishkek, the capital of the Kyrgyz Republic, I
wrote:

I will raise my voice
each morning,
each evening,
each night.

Non-stop
my cry will resound
in the ears
of the elite
until the whole
world is filled
with love.

While I still live
and still have the power
of speech
I will shout to the winds
of each new day
that there should be no truce
until every yoke
has been lifted.

Some years later, in August 1991, I wrote the following poem for
Mikhail Gorbachev, when the big changes were already accomplished
and regretfully his vision was not matched by other big powers of that
moment:

Let them count the cost.
Interest. Yields
Those who came from the ice

dreaming of arms open wide,
they only found
merchants.
And now, what are we
to do now?
Wealthy Europe
wanted to float and keep clothed.
When the spurring faltered
all over the world
with the takers of risks
and the givers of generosity,
where were those who heard
the voices of the vigils
and the warnings of the wind?
And, as ever, when the spurring falters,
those remaining
in all walks of life
were the most cunning.

It was Chingiz Aitmatov who declared of Gorbachev on his 70th birthday that: 'He is heralding a new age on Earth.' What was the secret of Mikhail Gorbachev, enabling him to produce so many rapid and profound changes? One of them was his ability to show a 'new Kremlin' to the whole USSR 'empire'. He was a 'magician of the media', able to disseminate his message, particularly through the TV. And not just with leaders, statesmen or Nobel laureates, but through world-famous artists and cinema stars. I remember vividly the immense impact of the Moscow Forum, with Gregory Peck, Claudia Cardinale, and many renowned personalities, to accelerate the evolution – and even revolution! – of consciousness in the Soviet Union, bottom-up.

Let me now give some examples of his words and messages that showed the way to a new era:

- In Paris, at the Sorbonne, on 5 July 1999, Gorbachev said that 'perestroika has been a breakthrough towards freedom and an attempt to combine socialist values and democracy.'
- So early, at the same time, he was able to predict important events, such as those relating to China: 'The progress at the worldwide level will depend to a great extent of the direction followed by China ... I hope that the problems that were debated in Tiananmen Square could be addressed again before long.'

- In the Council of Europe, during the same month of 1999, he said: 'Europe could only adequately face the challenge of the next century if it is able to join many efforts... The European citizens need one united Europe, a Europe in peace and democracy, keeping its diversity ... and helping with solidarity the rest of the world.'
- Later, after the experience of the last decade of the twentieth century, with 'globalisation' (that meant the weakness of the United Nations system and market laws substituting for democratic principles and values) Gorbachev, in an interview at the end of the year 2000, said in relation to the Western policy of the last decade: '... how inhuman and, forgive me for being straightforward, stupid [it] has been'. He was crystal clear in expressing that these were the policy changes expected to be followed by the 'great domain' (military, energy, financial and media powers).

Now I wish to briefly refer to the immense task accomplished by President Gorbachev in trying to promote everywhere – especially through the Green Cross – a better understanding of ecology in order that *all citizens could help to reduce environmental damage*. To highlight his activities and far-sightedness in relation to the environment, I have chosen to quote the following: 'The real problem is this: how to save the world, how to keep it intact ... mankind needs to make a choice ... and the only way we have to save ourselves is to work together.'

President Obama urged a 'new beginning' in his speech in Cairo on 2 June 2009. Yes – this is what the immense majority of humankind requests: a 'new beginning', an expression that Mikhail Gorbachev, as one of the Commissioners of the splendid text of the Earth Charter (2000), wrote in *The Way Forward*. I remember his precious booklet *In search of a new beginning, developing a new civilisation*, which has, in its excellent translation made in Mexico, been one of my guides.

'It is my firm conviction that the infinite and out of control power of nuclear armament must never be in the hands of any human being... Never more, for any reason.' His confidence in human capacity represents a great hope: 'Humanity is able to overcome the challenge: all united, with the responsibility of each one of us, we can ensure life on Earth ... We must develop environmental policies in which the human race understands that it is a part of nature.'

A new thinking for a new era, for a new beginning

Concerning the necessity of an efficient multilateral system, he wrote: 'I believe we could move towards a new world order through international organisations. But to do so we need to revise their functions.'

Recently, in the meeting 'Europe looks East', organised by the New Policy Forum in Sofia on 7–8 October 2010, the results of a Europe lacking in autonomy and a clear role in the world scenario were shown as being particularly worrying after the 'rescue' of the financial institutions and the recovery of the market prevailing again over political action. It was concluded that in the past Europe looked to the East with too much greed, delocalising to China most of the production, as the 'world factory'. Recently, President Gorbachev said that 'the present global economic crisis was necessary to solve the organic defects of the Western model of development that was imposed on the rest of the world as the only possible one. It has also been shown that not only bureaucratic socialism but also ultra-liberal capitalism urgently need a profound democratic reform.'

The main challenges of the globalisation of poverty and exclusion, the environment with potentially irreversible damage, and the danger of progressive uniformity are to be counteracted with better sharing, value-driven as opposed to market-driven actions, knowledge of the reality in depth and preventative action. These criteria should be applied to the effectiveness of two main solutions: citizens able to build a participatory democracy, and the foundation of an efficient UN system.

He changed the trends of the world. Regretfully, the 'powers' were too short-sighted and irresponsible to take advantage of these unexpected turning points.

My feelings of friendship and admiration for the man who, without the shedding of a single drop of blood, was able to suddenly build the pillars and bridges of a new era are profound. In 1991 I wrote: 'The Wall of Berlin collapsed because a system based on equality forgot freedom. Now, the alternate system will fall as well because, based on freedom, it has forgotten equality. And both forgot justice.'

Mikhail S. Gorbachev is a giant star of reference to guide the paths of succeeding generations. He is now 80 years old. His legacy will remain for ever.

At the end of our first meeting, in 1986, I asked him, as a scientist, to free Andrei Dimitrievich Sakharov who was 'prisoner-in-residence' in Gorky. He told me: 'I will do my best in the context of the present legal framework.' A few months later, the first private Foundation of the USSR was set up in Moscow. Around the table were members of the Issyk-Kul Forum, the granddaughter of General Eisenhower, and Andrei

Sakharov! At the beginning of the founding meeting, Prof. Sakharov expressed his gratitude to President Gorbachev: 'Now I am free, and I am thankful to you … but − he added while showing a list of other prisoners − there are still many in undue captivity.' And Gorbachev rapidly replied: 'I know. But now we are two to work for their freedom!'

I vividly remember when he went to Paris with his wife Raisa Maximovna. He was astonished with the way the 'Westerners' were reacting at the fantastic and unexpected changes in the Soviet Union. The former submitted states were now on the long road to democracy and the Commonwealth of Independent States was emerging. What a wonder! − except for those who were prepared for a solution of force instead of a solution of word.

When he told me that he was going to be a candidate for the presidency of the Russian Federation, I passed to him a note: 'You cannot pretend to be in the history and in power at the same time.'

He is a peacemaker, a bridge-builder. Mikhail S. Gorbachev is history alive. Let us learn from him. He has paved new ways that − leaving the market aside and putting universal ethical values at the centre of our everyday behaviour − can lead before long to the world we dream of.

Perestroika and glasnost are two key words of the past and of the future alike.

Federico Mayor Zaragoza was the Director-General of UNESCO from 1987 to 1999. Upon his return to Spain in 1999, he created the Foundation for a Culture of Peace. In 2001, Federico Mayor founded the UBUNTU World Forum of Civil Society Networks, which in turn launched the Campaign for the In-Depth Reform of the System of International Institutions. In 2002, he was selected to chair the European Research Council Expert Group (ERCEG) and, in 2005, UN Secretary-General Kofi Annan appointed him co-President for the High Level Group for the Alliance of Civilisations. Federico Mayor has also published several volumes of poetry. He first met President Gorbachev in 1986 and has worked closely with him and Green Cross International ever since.

Maurice Strong

My Tribute to Mikhail Gorbachev on his 80th Birthday

On this important milestone in his remarkable life I am pleased to have the opportunity of joining with countless others around the world in paying tribute to Mikhail Gorbachev. I admire him as the leader who has had the greatest impact of any in reshaping the history of our times and I am privileged to know him as a valued friend. In championing the enlightened policies of glasnost and perestroika he set the Soviet Union on the pathway to greater freedom and democracy for its people and in bringing the cold war to an end he led the way to a reunited Europe and a more secure and peaceful world. Despite the difficulties to which these dramatic changes gave rise within his own country, history will remember him as the person who took the courageous decisions that made a new era of progress for his country and its place in the world.

On the personal level he is an engaging, charismatic and caring friend with whom I have shared some of the most important interests and experiences of my life, notably in the field of the environment. Especially noteworthy were his initiatives in establishing the Green Cross and joining with me in the Earth Council to launch the Earth Charter through the good offices of the Netherlands Prime Minister Ruud

Gorbachev with Maurice Strong

Lubbers and the guidance of Canada's leading environmentalist, James MacNeill.

I particularly recall the weekend we spent together in The Hague with Prime Minister Lubbers and the long walk we had on the Sunday afternoon as Mikhail Gorbachev and Ruud Lubbers walked together and I walked hand in hand with Gorbachev's intelligent and accomplished wife, Raisa, a great influence on him. We shared and continue to share our interests in promoting the Earth Charter movement, which is now being widely accepted as a set of principles to guide the conduct of people and nations towards the Earth and each other.

I treasure his friendship and continue to be inspired by his leadership as one of the truly great people of our times. May he have many more years to make his unique contribution to our troubled world, which was never more in need of his influence and example.

Maurice Strong *served as Secretary-General of the 1972 UN Conference on the Human Environment, the first major world conference on environmental issues, and then became the first Executive Director of the United Nations Environment Programme, serving from 1972 to 1975. He was also a commissioner of the World Commission on Environment and Development in 1987, where the idea for the Earth Charter was born. He was Secretary-General of the 1992 Earth Summit in Rio de Janeiro, where President Gorbachev was given the mandate to create GCI. Following this, he founded the Earth Council, which together with GCI launched the Earth Charter initiative in 1994, and formally presented the Earth Charter in 2000. Today, Strong is the President of the Council of the UN University of Peace and Chairman of the Advisory Board for the Institute for Research on Security and Sustainability for north-east Asia.*

Ismail Serageldin

Practising Optimism by Action

Mikhail Gorbachev is a man with a vision, a true leader who has altered the course of history and continues to work towards creating a world based on the respect of mankind and Mother Earth. He is an optimist and a man of action rather than words, as he declares:

> Being an optimist, as I see it, means to refuse to make do with the status quo, and instead to consciously look for ways to make the world a better place and help address the practical challenges faced by people here and now.
>
> I call this 'optimism by action', and I believe that such a philosophy of life can provide the catalyst for our much-needed transformation to sustainable development.

> (From *The Art of Living: A Practical Guide to Being Alive*,
> Claire Elizabeth Terry, ed., 2008)

This 'optimism by action' has given hope to many people around the globe who worry about the future of our planet and of mankind in general. President Gorbachev's work has helped restore the confidence of many of us in the possibility of working together to secure a better future for our children.

His enthusiasm and sincerity in serving peace, development and the environment continue to impress us today as they first did when he played an instrumental role in ending the cold war and finding a peaceful alterative to decades of international tension and strife. Surely one cannot but respect and admire the Nobel Peace laureate whose acceptance speech in 1990 unravelled his profound commitment to peace and human security when he said: 'Immanuel Kant prophesied that mankind would one day be faced with a dilemma: either to be joined in a true union of nations or to perish in a war of annihilation ending in the extinction of the human race. Now, as we move from the second to the third millennium, the clock has struck the moment of truth.' Sure enough, he began his journey to realise his dream of a world of 'a true union of nations' through his endless endeavours to propagate peace, sustainable development and environmental consciousness.

Recognised as the man who succeeded in bridging the gap between two warring ideologies, he has been a sincere advocate of peace and democracy; for he believes that 'it is better to discuss things, to argue and engage in polemics than make perfidious plans of mutual destruction.' Thus, he has always urged the international community to stop the arms race, focus on development and rescue the environment from degradation. To President Gorbachev, these are the true routes to peace and security. In his October 2009 Geneva Lecture at the UN he speaks against nuclear weapons proliferation and states that, 'Our goal should certainly be the movement towards a nuclear-free, non-violent and demilitarised world where everyone is secure. I believe that this is exactly the goal that is in the interest of all countries and all people.'

President Gorbachev has always linked peace and human security to development and preserving the environment. His active involvement in Agenda 21, which was first adopted during the Rio de Janeiro United Nations Conference on Environment and Development in 1992, is only one example of his efforts to create an international coalition to face future global challenges. Similarly, his founding of Green Cross International in 1993 to address issues related to poverty, security and environmental degradation and his launching of the Earth Charter Initiative in 1994 bear witness to his dedication to the cause of a better future for humanity.

He underscores the vital importance of saving our planet as a security priority, urging peoples and governments worldwide to act wisely and work for a better future for mankind. Climate change and peoples' right to clean water and sanitation are issues that he advocates vehemently. In February 2009, he launched a water initiative in the European Parliament, and clearly stated that 'water is without a doubt a political problem, and a crisis of development that is unsustainable. It is part of a global political crisis.' He also adds that 'water will increasingly become a security issue', and that it is imperative that governments and civil society endorse the right to clean water as a legitimate human right.

At the heart of his philosophy are perestroika and glasnost, two concepts that have altered the direction of the former USSR and currently underline his global welfare agenda and prompt his sincere endeavours to create a better world for future generations. The ambitious and challenging goals of restructuring world politics and economy to cater for the real stakeholders and promote openness to formulate a cooperative, harmonious international community will forever put him at the forefront of history's most influential figures.

Judging by his personal history, President Gorbachev has proven to be a successful politician and a great president who brought freedom and democracy to his country after decades of authoritarianism. Now, in his position as a citizen of the world, he has also succeeded in mobilising a multitude of NGOs, statesmen, public figures and people to carry on the good work he began.

Mikhail Gorbachev is a man who has a clear global welfare agenda, which has driven him to pursue an active role in world affairs, a man who has never yielded or faltered and who stood firm for what he believes in. Here, I reiterate what the Italian journalist Giulietto Chiesa once wrote about President Gorbachev: 'I am grateful to him for his having stuck to his convictions over the years that followed, when almost everyone was stained and guilty of self-betrayal. Mikhail Gorbachev remained unstained. He is an example and proof of the fact that it is possible to keep one's dignity in politics and remain devoted to the ideals of true democracy.'

Ismail Serageldin *is the Director of the Library of Alexandria, Egypt. He is also Professor of the International Chair for Knowledge Against Poverty at Collège de France in Paris. He is former Chairman of the Consultative Group on International Agricultural Research (CGIAR, 1994–2000), and Founder and former Chairman of the Global Water Partnership (GWP, 1996–2000). Dr Serageldin also served as Vice-President for Environmentally and Socially Sustainable Development (1992–8), and for Special Programmes (1998– 2000) at the World Bank. Mikhail Gorbachev and Ismail Serageldin worked together on the World Commission for Water in the 21st Century in 1999– 2000.*

Sergei Kapitsa

For M.S. Gorbachev's 80th Birthday

Anyone who looks at the actions taken by Mikhail Sergeyevich Gorbachev and at his personality will have to overcome a difficulty, which is due to the fact that Gorbachev ushered in a chain of great and multiple events. Historical perspective is yet to be shaped and political passions have not yet yielded to balanced assessments of history. This is why a reporter will be acting instead of a historian. This also why the author wants to look at events, in which – as fate has willed – he was taking part. These episodes are not events of historic significance – not in the least. However, when taken as a special example, they can help understand the past and to feel the atmosphere in which events unfolded that were already out of control of the people who had boldly initiated them. This is the way an occurrence can become a rule in the unstable and non-linear world of today.

The root-cause of changes is associated with the fact that the world is living through the most significant revolution in the history of mankind – a time of demographic transition when the sweeping population boom is being suddenly and ubiquitously stopped, and now on Earth we have a permanent size of the population. The transition started some 50 years ago. It will end within the current century and bring about a change in the paradigm of mankind's evolution from quantitative growth to qualitative development. It is right here that we are facing the challenge brought about by the crisis of world history that has so sharply expressed itself in Russia, which is a global structure in terms of its dimension.

In the spring of 1984, soon after my father P.L. Kapitsa passed away, I was invited for dinner by Igor Sokolov who worked in the International Department of the CPSU Central Committee. His other guest was Academician Abel Gyozevich Aganbegyan. Being a prominent economist, he gave us a wonderful account of the situation in the Soviet economy. It was in for a collapse, and innovations and investments were the only means that could save it. That morning he reported the results of his analysis to Mikhail Sergeyevich, who had requested him to make this study. I suggested that Abel spoke about this in my TV science programme, in which he had already participated several times. The prospect interested Abel but he said that TV bosses would never allow such a programme on television. But we recorded it anyway. Actually we made two programmes, each lasting 55 minutes. We surmised a happy end after investments in the economy and innovations in industry took us out of the deadlock. Mindful of that difficult time, I took the initiative and sent the full text to the State Planning Committee and got the official permission of its Deputy Chairman who made no critical remarks.

In the autumn of that year the first part of the programme, which contained criticism, was shown on the main channels of Central Television three times. And we had a scandal on our hands right away: the Chairman of the State Planning Committee N.K. Baibakov accused us of having disclosed the state secret about the situation in the Soviet economy and of having grossly misinformed the Soviet people. As a result, the second part of the programme – the one with the happy ending – was banned, and two commissions were set up. One was a KGB commission that studied the fact of state secret disclosure. The other was a Central Committee commission that studied the fact of ideological subversion on Central Television. It was during the time when Chernenko was the General Secretary – the time of stagnation – and what saved us then was the text with an official approval of Gosplan, whose officials seemed to carry fire in one hand and water in the other. Several months passed, and Chernenko died. Gorbachev became General Secretary, and at the first Plenum after his election the problems of modernisation that had been raised in my programme were brought to light. Twenty-five years have passed since then, but exactly the same problems are still on the top priority agenda.

One summer day, Academician Ivan Frolov, who was an aide to Gorbachev, gave me a phone call and asked me to come to his country house. I did not know well the people who gathered at his veranda, but Ivan Timofeyevich invited me to take a walk with him in the garden. There he told me that the defence ministry officials had started to insist on drafting college and university students to the army. Gorbachev was against the idea but it was difficult for him to oppose generals. So Frolov asked me to write a letter to Gorbachev signed by outstanding scientists saying that drafting students to the army must never be done, mindful of the interests of the nation's security and the development of science and technology as the basis for the USSR's future economic power.

I did it, and everyone whom I asked signed the letter. Certainly, I did not tell anyone who had asked me to write the letter – I knew the rules of secrecy and I followed these rules when I handed the letter to Frolov. Later he told me about Gorbachev referring to this letter at a Politburo session, and at last they let the students be. But this was not yet the end of the story. Some time later, when Yeltsin and Khazbulatov opposed each other and when the federal government was weakened, generals raised the issue again. This time two officers of the General Staff came to me and asked me to write a similar letter. It turned out that they had known about my involvement and shared the stand that the scientists had taken. In other words, the army itself was not unanimous on this matter. At their initiative I had a meeting with Khazbulatov in the Government House, late in the night. We were walking down the corridors of power in semi-darkness and agreed that a letter be written to him and to Yeltsin. And this time, too, the letter worked. But even today this problem with the conscription of university students is still in abeyance ... I am recalling these situations because sometimes they can show how sluggish the mechanisms of power can be even when most of the time hidden behind the Byzantine screen of a seeming unity, and how slow is the execution of a political volte-face behind it. That is why I am so sceptical about all pundits and advice-givers who have the best answers to every question but neither possess information nor vision and experience, and, worst of all, who bear no responsibility at all for their advice or assertions.

When I am talking about Gorbachev's activity I want to recall things that got instilled in my memory. The first thing is his call for a 'new thinking'. I think this is a central issue of power because in our world, which is changing so fast, all potentialities open to us are far and away greater than our skill to control them. To employ phrases of the past, this is a result of a growing discrepancy between productive forces and relations of production. This circumstance became the chief impediment in the way of the new thinking and the settlement of mounting economic and social contradictions.

Due to this, it is impossible to solve political questions through military means following the maxim of Clausewitz that war is a continuation of political relations by other means. That is why the greatest credit that goes to Gorbachev is that there was no bloodshed accompanying far-reaching changes and, in particular, the end of the cold war and the disarmament steps connected with his initiatives. His main accomplishment is that he was able to change his country and the world without a civil war. The alternative would have been disastrous. Indeed, as we know now, he was compelled to take decisions under time pressure, when information available to him was inconclusive, if not controversial. Far too often he had to act when there was no unity between people who surrounded him or when the Communist Party resisted his actions.

Borders were opened when Gorbachev was in power. For some people this may have been the most tangible result of perestroika and, perhaps, certain consequences of this bold move are yet to be appreciated. Many people have well-grounded regrets that our artists, actors and, first and foremost, scientists are now working abroad because science is no longer in demand in their home country. But this phenomenon has a trait that is little if at all spoken about: the increasing influence of our science and culture in the world. This intellectual asset is the major part of the capital with which we can enter the contemporary globalised world. Right now it is really difficult to appraise the significance of those events or understand their long-term effects for Russia and for the world in general. But Gorbachev needed that, too, when he was turning to the potential of science, culture and the traditions of our country and to those who embodied them when he was looking for support for his policy of mutual understanding and cooperation in contrast to the negativism that is so fashionable nowadays.

I first met Gorbachev at Stanford University in California where he went when B.N. Yeltsin came to power. I was in the USA at the time and had meetings with American economists. My last meeting was with Milton Friedman. The famous scholar and Nobel Prize winner gave us seven minutes of his time, as he had informed the State Department representative who was accompanying us. But in reality we talked for one hour and a half. During this time Friedman's main interest was the changes in Russia. His main idea that he kept repeating was this: do not make haste with your reforms. He made no mention whatever of monetarism. This was at the prime time of Gaidar's shock therapy.

The TV recording was a very important and tiring experience. When I walked out of the TV studio I suddenly came across Gorbachev who promptly asked me: 'Sergei, what are you doing here? I saw you only on TV.' I remarked in the tone of his question: 'That goes for me too. I saw you only on TV.' Having made such an opening, I explained our programme to him and proposed that he gave us an interview. This was our short discussion in which Gorbachev was absolutely exact and insightful. And this was the time when our journalists avoided him like the plague.

And now one last thing that I want to remind everyone of: the freedom of expression and thinking that we owe him. To my big regret, our intelligentsia in its overwhelming majority is proving incapable of facing the challenge of modern development. For the time being we are producing extremely questionable and perishable products instead of truly free and profound creative works. Sophisticated minds have failed to supply the critical thinking that was expected of them. Neither are they aware of the responsibility that inevitably accompanies freedom. And the 'lost generation' of perestroika is looking for answers either in the faith of bygone epochs or in the marginalities of modern being and drinking. But the questions of morality and moral principles require an urgent solution within a society that is increasingly ruled by money and demons. There are people who are falling back on the experience of the Church, but when society's ethical superstructure is falling down we are facing an increasing loss of trust both among people as well as between people and power that jeopardises the integrity of the nation and of society.

Let us sum up the results. Politicians, whether they like it or not, must bear the burden of responsibility, and neither time nor circumstances can ever relieve them of this burden. Not one of them. Never. And nowhere. These are some ideas that life brought me to at a drastic turn of world history. These are the thoughts that come to one's mind when judging a great man facing the challenge of fast changes in the quest for a constructive new thinking.

S.P. Kapitsa is a Senior Research Fellow at the Lebedev Physical Institute, Russian Academy of Sciences and Professor at the Moscow Institute of Physics and Technology. He was also the host of a popular Russian television science programme and is known for his contributions to physics and historical demography, including developing a number of mathematical models of the World System population hyperbolic growth and the global demographic transition.

Professor Sir David King

In Honour of the 80th Birthday of Mikhail Gorbachev

Mikhail Gorbachev is deservedly respected worldwide as the single political leader who had the greatest effect on global affairs in the second half of the twentieth century. With glasnost and perestroika he transformed the USSR from a secretive police state to an open society. This alone was a significant accomplishment, but the list of his achievements does not stop there; he was a major player in ending the cold war, initiating nuclear disarmament on a massive scale. He can also be credited with ensuring the fall of the Berlin Wall and putting an end to the Iron Curtain around Eastern Europe. Then, in a world open to change, his approach contributed to the end of apartheid in South Africa. Yet he has also played a key role in the containment of the impacts of industrial societies on the global ecology. He is much less well known for this latter achievement.

Gorbachev himself states that his appreciation of the environment as essential to human well-being stems from his childhood. This is evident in his actions throughout his life, both whilst in power in Russia and afterwards to the present day. Throughout all his achievements he has clearly been mindful of the precarious balance between environment and society.

As the Communist Party's General Secretary and leader of the Soviet Union, Gorbachev had access to information that was kept secret from the general population. He gained an awareness of the true damage that industry, and particularly the growth of the defence industry, was causing to the environment. In his own words he 'became conscious of the economic, social and ecological crisis for which the Soviet Union was heading'. It became clear that growth was occurring only at massive cost to the environment and that the damaging effect this was having on the population was being kept quiet. The realisation of the damaging effects that poor ecological management was having on the health and living conditions of the population was a strong incentive to act. The USSR was the only industrialised country where life expectancy rates had decreased over time.

Gorbachev's glasnost and perestroika reforms also had ecological implications. They acted to allow for the first time a much greater awareness of the impact of how the state was run at the expense of the environment and a new openness with ecological data. Furthermore, following his implementation of glasnost, the people of Russia were permitted to speak out about the issues affecting them; one of the main issues raised was that of environmental degradation. Gorbachev took radical action on this, closing 1300 factories for ecological reasons, despite them still producing useful goods. It is rare that such respect for the environment over the economy is shown and highlights the uniqueness of Mikhail Gorbachev as a leader. There were other experiences that would shape his outlook; the collapse of the Soviet agriculture system gave him the courage to act on advice given to him concerning, for example, the risks of pesticides. Other radical actions that he took include cancelling the potentially disastrous plans to reverse the flow of Russian rivers.

An incident that was significant globally and in shaping Gorbachev's thinking in both his international politics and in his environmental stance was the nuclear accident at Chernobyl. This event highlighted the perils of nuclear power and weaponry and was to be a factor in high-lighting the dangers of continuing a nuclear arms race. In addition, the long-term effects that would be felt from this event allowed Gorbachev to gain fresh perspective on the on-going impacts of ecological degrada-tion. The impacts of the radiation that was released at Chernobyl will affect many generations of people and is not constrained by national boundaries. The situation is reminiscent of the global warming chal-lenge today. This event would also emphasise the scale of damage that human beings could do to the environment.

During his presidency his work to protect the environment was overshadowed by the reforms he put in place to give the Russian people the greatest freedom they had experienced in generations, but on leav-ing government his attention became focused more heavily upon eco-logical issues.

Following his resignation from the presidency of the USSR, Gorba-chev used his experience and authority to set up Green Cross Inter-national at the request of delegates at the 1992 Earth Summit at Rio. Green Cross International was based on a package of ideas that Gor-bachev had put forward to the UN in 1988. It was formally set up in 1993. As a reflection of how forward-thinking Gorbachev was in taking these actions it should be noted that issues such as climate change were only just gaining momentum at this stage. The first IPCC report was published in 1990. Gorbachev clearly was a forerunner of environ-mental action.

Green Cross International has since, under the direction of Mikhail

Gorbachev, acted to address ecological issues as wide ranging as climate change and chemical contamination. Green Cross International has also kept up a constant dialogue on ecological issues in order to stimulate public engagement and political action. The charity acts in multiple countries, reflecting the global nature of the problems that it tackles. Green Cross International has developed into a worldwide environmental protection body with a wide influence.

Gorbachev has been an outspoken critic of inaction on the issue of ecological damage, particularly of the USA since 2000. He frequently speaks to advise and stimulate leaders to commit to action on climate change. He has aimed to recalibrate the international response to climate change and drive forward action in line with the substantial threat that it poses to human security and development – a much-needed role. His current efforts to change attitudes in the dialogue on environmental issues have been likened to those that he displayed in the 1980s with his perestroika and glasnost policies. This is likely to be because he insightfully views the ecological issues that are becoming ever more pressing today as being intrinsically linked to the ideals of freedom, equality and democracy. Gorbachev is one of a few leaders who appear to have a real appreciation of the dependence of humanity on the environment and the key role that sustainability has to play in creating a fairer world. This is highlighted by his oft-shared view that

European Commissioner for the Environment Janez Potočnik, US Secretary of State for Energy Dr Steven Chu, Gorbachev and Sir David King at the World Forum on Enterprise and the Environment in 2010

environmental issues are the most urgent task facing humanity today.

In a sense Gorbachev can be seen as an example of the potential of what can be achieved. When he became the General Secretary of the Communist Party in 1985 there were many factors that acted against his humanitarian actions; he had to walk a delicate balance between hardliners in the Party and the West. It is easy to uphold the ideals of democracy and freedom when living in a democracy; it is another thing altogether to strive towards these things when up against powerful opposition. This is analogous to our present ecological situation and the challenges that Gorbachev is currently tackling. If we had global leaders today who could act with courage, vision and ambition for the safe future of humanity, our environmental problems would be much closer to solution.

Professor Sir David King is the Director of the Smith School of Enterprise and Environment at the University of Oxford, as well as a member of the Climate Change Task Force. As the UN Government Chief Scientific Adviser and Head of the Government Office of Science from 2000 to 2007, he greatly raised public awareness of climate change, highlighting the need for government action worldwide; he also created the Foresight Programme to help deal with a range of important long-term issues. During this period, the UK Government published the very important scientific report 'Avoiding Dangerous Climate Change' in 2005. Sir David King also initiated the £1 billion Energy Technology Institute, and co-authored The Hot Topic, *a book on climate change, in 2008.*

Jean-Michel Cousteau

There Can Be No Peace Without a Healthy Environment

When there is a momentous shift in the direction of international affairs, it is often difficult to predict the scope of change that will result. In the case of the influence of Mikhail Gorbachev, it would have been impossible at the time to fully understand how his political decisions have resulted in profound and continuing changes, politically but also, importantly, on the world's natural environment.

Famous for his work with then-President Reagan in ending the cold war, which transformed international priorities and opened wider the hope for ultimate nuclear disarmament – the greatest gift to the environment – President Gorbachev has long understood a fundamental principle of world stability: that ultimately we depend on the natural environment, the free services of nature, for everything.

The environment of what was formerly the Soviet Union has paid an enormous price in environmental degradation and neglect, and President Gorbachev has worked tirelessly to reverse this. Importantly, in 1993 he extended his commitment to the global environment through his founding of Green Cross International, now active in 32 countries.

President Gorbachev also emphatically stressed the environmental devastation brought on by war and military conflicts. Following the first Gulf War, he called on me and my team to document the devastation left behind – a wasteland of burning oil wells and, at the time, the largest oil spill and still possibly second only to the recent Gulf of Mexico oil spill.

Gorbachev with Jean-Michel Cousteau

We now know that decades are necessary for recovery and that most ecosystems are irrevocably altered.

Oil is visual and dramatic, but there is another very important and publicly unknown issue relating to war. The cold war with its nuclear agenda resulted in the mining and processing of uranium. Both in the United States and in what was the Soviet Union, there were nuclear reactors and other sophisticated systems that produced nuclear arsenals. These sites have been contaminated by radioactive materials that will remain harmful to human beings and ecosystems for tens of thousands of years. Our cold war legacy is large and it is serious.

In the USA, the Department of Energy's Office of Legacy Management is cleaning up and restoring these sites, and when this effort is complete, around 2050, the price tag will be about one trillion dollars. It is doubtful that a comparable effort is under way in Russia and neighbouring countries. I hope lessons learned from these environmental disasters will affect national policy in all countries. I believe there is a shift coming and I know President Gorbachev's efforts will be part of it.

It was Mikhail Gorbachev who forced the world to look at the environmental consequences of political decisions on a global scale and who continues to fight for restoration and sanity. His efforts, of course, long before much of his good work was accomplished, resulted in the 1990 Nobel Peace Prize. When I asked him if he would like to go diving with me, he said: 'Once the ocean is clean will I go diving with you, Jean-Michel.'

I like to believe that the honours paid to him are, in part, recognition that there can be no peace without a healthy environment, and it is my hope and life's work, along with luminaries like Mikhail Gorbachev, to see this achieved in our lifetimes.

Jean-Michel Cousteau is the Founder, President and Chairman of the Ocean Futures Society, as well as an architect, explorer, environmentalist, educator and film producer. He is Chairman of Green Cross France and is a member of the Climate Change Task Force.

Steven Rockefeller

A Visionary Commitment to a Sustainable Future: Mikhail Gorbachev and the Earth Charter

Mikhail Gorbachev will always be remembered for his courageous leadership in transforming the Soviet Union and ending the cold war. Over the past two decades he has also played a unique leadership role internationally in the effort to promote universal ethical values and worldwide cooperation in support of environmental conservation and sustainable development. One prime example of his many contributions in this regard is his role in the drafting and promotion of the Earth Charter.

Raised in a peasant family in a farming community in the south of Russia, he became keenly aware of the interdependence of people and nature and developed early in life a deep sense of belonging to the natural world. 'I grew up in a village and perceived the dying of rivers and land erosion as personal pain,' he writes in *The Earth Charter in Action* (2005). As the problems of environmental degradation worsened in Russia and throughout the industrialised world during the cold war years, he came to firmly believe that environmental protection and restoration are a fundamental moral responsibility of all leaders and people everywhere. Fully aware of the increasing interdependence of all nations, he well understood that reversing ecological decline requires international cooperation as well as local action.

In addition, as the leader of the Soviet Union (1985–91), Gorbachev recognised that building a sustainable global community in an age of weapons of mass destruction means the eradication of poverty and the non-violent management of conflict leading to peace and security as well as safeguarding Earth's ecological integrity. Reflecting on these three major interrelated challenges facing the world, and drawing on his experience with radical political and socio-economic reform in the Soviet Union, he explained in his Nobel Peace Prize acceptance speech in 1990 that 'perestroika and innovative political thinking … is of vital significance for human destinies all over the world'. Appreciating the critical role of ethical values in human behaviour and social change, he also realised that forming an effective global partnership for a sustainable future requires agreement on and commitment to shared ethical principles, including new science-based principles.

After resigning as General Secretary of the Communist Party and

President of the Soviet Union in 1991, it was concerns and convictions such as these that led Gorbachev in 1993 to found Green Cross International and in 1994 to form a partnership with Maurice Strong, the Secretary General of the 1992 Rio Earth Summit, for the purpose of launching a global initiative to create an Earth Charter.

The Brundtland Commission (World Commission on Environment and Development) had recommended in its report, *A Common Future* (1987), the creation of a new universal declaration or charter that sets forth fundamental principles to guide nations in the transition to sustainable development. With this recommendation in mind, Strong had made the drafting of an Earth Charter part of the agenda of the Rio Earth Summit. However, the Summit failed to reach agreement on the principles for the Earth Charter. With the support of Queen Beatrix and Prime Minister Ruud Lubbers of the Netherlands, Gorbachev as President of Green Cross International and Strong as Chair of the Earth Council agreed to join together to organise and lead a new civil society effort to draft the Earth Charter.

Gorbachev and Strong established a Secretariat for an Earth Charter Initiative at the University for Peace in Costa Rica and formed an Earth Charter Commission of 23 eminent persons from all regions of the world. The Commission, which they co-chaired with Kamla Chowdhry (India), Mercedes Sosa (Argentina) and Amadou Toumani Touré (Mali), oversaw the consultation and drafting process. The leadership of the Commission gave the Earth Charter Initiative credibility and made possible the most inclusive and participatory process ever associated with the drafting of an international declaration. The first meeting of the Earth Charter Commission took place at the Rio+5 Forum in Rio de Janeiro in March 1997. Over 500 NGOs gathered for this week-long conference, designed to assess progress towards sustainable development since the Rio Earth Summit. Gorbachev attended the Rio+5 Forum as President of Green Cross International and co-Chair of the Earth Charter Commission.

After working closely with the Earth Charter Secretariat for two years, I had been invited by the Commission to chair and form an international drafting committee. It was at his headquarters at the Rio+5 Forum that I first met and was warmly received by Gorbachev. Ruud Lubbers introduced us. After Gorbachev shared some reflections on the major issues before the international community, the three of us spent almost two hours discussing the Earth Charter process and the early drafts of the Charter that were taking form in the light of the open consultations on the document being conducted daily at the Forum. During his four days in Rio de Janeiro, Gorbachev was deeply engaged in the work of the Commission and delivered an inspiring address on the state of the world and the need for the Earth Charter during one of the final sessions of the Forum. At the conclusion of the Forum, Gorbachev and Strong held a news conference and released the first official draft of the Earth Charter, which was labelled the Benchmark Draft.

Over the next year Gorbachev continued to give the drafting of the Earth Charter his close attention. He hosted and presided over two Moscow Earth Charter Round Tables, one in September 1997 and another in March 1998. These Round Tables focused on the scientific basis for the principles of the Earth Charter, considered contributions from religious leaders, and explored ways to improve the Benchmark Draft. Gorbachev emphasised that the Earth Charter should be a 'people's document' and speak to the heart as well as the mind. It should stir 'people's souls', he commented (*quotations taken from personal notes on the First Moscow Round Table, 1997*). He wanted a preamble that clearly communicates the unsustainable nature of current patterns of development, explaining that natural law establishes limits as to what is safe and possible regarding the growth of industrialised societies. The Chernobyl catastrophe, he pointed out, 'showed in the most harsh form that nature does not forgive human mistakes' (*The Earth Charter in Action*). New attitudes and values, and a radical change in how people think and live are essential, explained Gorbachev. This concern was central to the mission of Green Cross International.

It was a special honour and privilege to be invited to chair the international Earth Charter drafting committee and to be given the opportunity to work on this visionary project with Gorbachev, Strong and the other members of the Commission. Chairing the drafting committee was a complex and demanding assignment. It was also a deeply rewarding experience. In this regard, I am especially grateful for and appreciative of the leadership and support that Gorbachev provided as a co-Chair of the Commission. The power of his mind, the passion that animated his engagement, and the depth of his understanding of the urgent need for a new, widely shared global ethic energised and inspired all of us involved in the project. In addition, his strong support of the drafting committee and the international consultation process was extraordinarily helpful at a number of critical points in the evolution of the draft text.

Gorbachev initially had wanted the Earth Charter to be a short and concise document with ten fundamental principles for sustainable development. However, as the consultation process progressed, it became clear that many leaders on the front lines of the battle for environmental conservation and sustainable development were looking for a more substantial document. They were concerned that an Earth Charter with only ten principles would be too general and would not provide them with the guidance and support needed. In response to this concern, Gorbachev came to support the creation of a more complex document with 16 main principles and additional supporting principles. However, recognising that many people would find a simpler Earth Charter helpful and inspiring, the drafting committee designed the Earth Charter so that the preamble and 16 main principles may be presented as an official abbreviated version. In addition, the first four principles, which are contained in a section entitled 'Respect and Care for the Community of Life' and involve only 39 words, are constructed so as to provide a concise overview of the Earth Charter's ethical vision.

The Earth Charter Commission brought the Earth Charter drafting and consultation process to a conclusion at a meeting at the UNESCO headquarters in Paris in March of 2000. A final version of the Earth Charter was launched at an international meeting at the Peace Palace in The Hague three months later. Queen Beatrix, Gorbachev, Strong, Lubbers and many other international leaders were there to celebrate the occasion. Since then Gorbachev has promoted the Earth Charter actively through Green Cross International initiatives such as 'The Earth Dialogue Forums' and in addresses and interviews that he has given throughout the world. In 2001, he presented the Earth Charter to Pope John Paul II, who congratulated him on 'a work well done in defending our environmental heritage' and who gave him his blessing and encouraged him to continue his 'meritorious effort to bring forth greater respect for the planet's resources'.

Gorbachev has also worked to implement specific Earth Charter principles and to have them incorporated into international law. For example, he has been an outspoken advocate in support of a United Nations General Assembly resolution that recognises 'the right of every human being to safe drinking water and safe sanitation'. The United Nations estimates that 884 million people live without potable water and 2.6 billion people are without basic sanitation. In July 2010 the General Assembly adopted a resolution recognising access to clean water and basic sanitation as a human right.

Over the past decade the Earth Charter Initiative has developed into a worldwide network of organisations and individuals that support and promote its ethical vision for a better world. Over 5000 organisations have endorsed the Earth Charter, including UNESCO, the World Conservation Union (IUCN), and hundreds of cities and universities. It is being widely used as an educational instrument in schools and universities and the Earth Charter International Secretariat has formed a partnership with UNESCO in support of the UN Decade of Education for Sustainable Development. The Earth Charter has become a respected reference document among international law experts, and a growing number of corporations and governments use it as a guide in defining their social and ecological responsibilities and in their sustainability planning.

Gorbachev's understanding of the deeper significance of the Earth Charter reflects his vision of the ultimate purpose of the initiative. Reflecting on the major challenges that must be addressed to achieve the goal of sustainable development, he argues that the Earth Charter is 'the third pillar of sustainable development'. His thinking in this regard is explained in the following statement.

> The first pillar is the Charter of the United Nations, which regulates the relations among states and thus sets the rules for their behaviour in order to secure peace and stability. The second pillar is the Universal Declaration of Human Rights, which regulates the relations between states and individuals, and guarantees to all citizens a set of rights which their respective governments should provide. The importance of these two documents cannot be overestimated. But it has become obvious that another document is missing, one which would regulate the relations among states, individuals and nature by defining the human duties towards the environment. In my opinion, the Earth Charter should fill this void, acquire equal status, and become the third pillar supporting the peaceful development of the modern world ... we founders and supporters should consider our mission accomplished only when the Earth Charter is universally adopted by the international community.

> (Mikhail Gorbachev, in *The Earth Charter in Action*)

On Mikhail Gorbachev's 80th birthday many of us will pay special tribute to him to celebrate his exceptional, far-sighted leadership in support of Earth's ecological integrity, sustainable development, and the creation of a third pillar that complements the United Nations Charter and the Universal Declaration of Human Rights.

Steven Rockefeller is a trustee of the Asian Cultural Council and an advisory trustee of the Rockefeller Brothers Fund. He was involved in the Earth Charter from its beginning, serving as Chairman of the Earth Charter International drafting committee from 1996 to 2000, then as a member of the Earth Charter Commission and, from 2006 to 2010, as co-Chair of the Earth Charter International Council. In 2005, he moderated the international launch of the United Nations Decade of Education for Sustainable Development.

Martin Lees

Article to Celebrate the 80th Birthday of President M.S. Gorbachev

Even for those of us who lived through the period, it is hard to remember how profoundly our lives and hopes were influenced by the deep polarisation of the world during the cold war between the United States and the Soviet Union and their respective allies. It is even more difficult for those who have grown up after this period to understand that this worldwide confrontation was the defining factor in international relations and that the threat of nuclear annihilation was a fact of life. As students at Cambridge University in the early sixties we were deeply concerned by one overriding issue: whether and how the world might be able to extricate itself from the mad policies of Mutually Assured Destruction – which were considered at the time to be both essential and rational.

Our concerns were intensified in October 1962 when, during the Cuban missile crisis, the world came to the brink of nuclear war. In the words of Soviet General and Army Chief of Staff Anatoly Gribkov: 'Nuclear catastrophe was hanging by a thread ... and we were not counting days or hours but minutes.' As the Soviet Union and the United States had sufficient nuclear warheads to destroy the world many times over, the very real risk of nuclear war was the existential issue of the day. The United Nations system, our hope for peace, was polarised and often paralysed and we could not see a way out, a way of assuring a safe and cooperative future for humanity.

It was in this intensely dangerous and conflictual situation that a new leader of the United States, President Ronald Reagan, decided in 1980 to escalate the economic and political confrontation with the Soviet Union, with the explicit goal of bringing about its collapse and the freedom of the states of Central and Eastern Europe. Fortunately for the future of humanity, a new leader of the Soviet Union emerged at this critical time, Mikhail Sergeyevich Gorbachev, who was elected General Secretary of the Communist Party in 1985 and Head of State of the Soviet Union in 1988 and who was dedicated to the peaceful solution of international confrontations across the world.

It has been my great privilege to meet and to collaborate with President Gorbachev in several different functions and contexts over almost 20 years. I have come to appreciate not only his deep insight into human affairs and his moral integrity but also his human warmth, his humour and his commitment to improving the lives and prospects of men and women across the world.

Mikhail Gorbachev came to power at an intensely difficult, confused and dangerous time in the internal politics of the Soviet Union. The pressures for radical political, economic and social change had reached boiling point and the international situation was unstable and intensely polarised.

Faced with almost overwhelming domestic and international challenges, Mikhail Gorbachev was able to preserve a steady course through what was, for the citizens of the Soviet Union, a period of devastating political, economic and institutional turmoil leading to the collapse of an empire and of a whole belief system and world view. And he remained calm and irrevocably committed to the preservation of peace, even under intense provocations and threats.

His memoirs make clear that his unswerving commitment to peace derives from his own personal experience and that of his close family who experienced the human costs, the devastation and the destruction of the internal conflicts within the Soviet Union and during the Second World War. As he wrote: 'I was 14 when the war ended. Our generation is the generation of wartime children. It has burned us, leaving its mark both on our characters and in our view of the world.'

Historians may say that the collapse of the Soviet Union was inevitable due to its internal economic and political contradictions. But it is important to remember that almost no political leaders or expert analysts, including for example the CIA, anticipated the depth and speed of the transformations which occurred. The mighty superpower of the Soviet Union disappeared together with its empire within less than a decade. The polarisation of the world community between the two contending blocs, which had been seen as an immutable fact of international relations for decades, simply evaporated.

History has repeatedly demonstrated that such massive transformations and convulsions rarely occur peacefully. As is made clear by Barbara Tuchman in *The Guns of August*, a detailed step-by-step analysis of the origins of the First World War, human error, miscalculation, emotional responses, false assumptions and the release of long-accumulated tensions can trigger explosive conflict. The world owes a historic debt of gratitude to Mikhail Gorbachev that he guided the processes of massive change towards a peaceful outcome on which the modern world is based.

With the benefit of hindsight, we can identify some of the key decisions and initiatives taken by President Gorbachev, which led to the peaceful resolution of the issues which threatened the world.

Perhaps the decision with the most far-reaching consequences was his decision not to use military force to prevent the dissolution of the Soviet Bloc as the countries of Eastern and Central Europe determined to overthrow communism and to achieve their independence. In 1988, in a radical reorientation of Soviet strategy, President Gorbachev had abandoned the Brezhnev doctrine, declaring, 'Interference in the internal affairs of another state ... is inadmissible.' This led to his introduction in 1989 in a speech at the Council of Europe of the concept of 'a common European home' for East and West.

These decisions created the conditions which allowed the collapse of the Eastern Bloc in 1989 to occur without violence and conflict. They constituted an unprecedented choice by a Soviet leader, proud of the power, prestige and influence of the Soviet Union, its historic achievements and its central role in the defeat of fascism for which it paid an enormous human and material price.

Another crucial element in Mikhail Gorbachev's strategy to defuse a dangerous international situation and to create a propitious framework for the modernisation of the Soviet Union was his total commitment to advancing disarmament. His unilateral decision in 1985 to propose arms reductions and subsequently to engage the United States in a process to eliminate nuclear weapons laid the foundations for the reduction in nuclear warheads and the critical shift from intense confrontation to the implementation of arms control agreements through negotiation. In spite of intense difficulties, this crucial process of disarmament that he initiated continues today.

The policies with which Mikhail Gorbachev is most directly associated are those of perestroika, or economic reform, launched in 1986, and glasnost, political reform, launched in 1988. These policies together led ultimately to the personal freedoms, independence and new economic conditions of the newly independent states of the former Soviet Union.

It is important to remember that the twin policies of perestroika and glasnost were seen initially as means to reform and modernise the centrally planned economies of the Eastern Bloc, with one overriding purpose, to preserve the communist system by making it more politically efficient and economically competitive. It was clear to the President that the heavy hand of planning and the vast bureaucracy built up over

70 years across the Soviet Union were not adapted to encouraging the new innovation-based economies and societies of the future.

These policies of domestic reform, of increased international cooperation and of disarmament that were initiated by President Gorbachev offered the promise of a safer and better future for the world. This was well understood by Western leaders at the time, including Mrs Thatcher, who famously declared at an early stage, 'I like Mr Gorbachev: we can do business together.'

These developments had echoes around the world, particularly in China. In the Western media, the leaders of China were portrayed as old and lethargic compared to the energetic young leader of the Soviet Union who would rapidly achieve the modernisation of his country. I had the privilege of organising private meetings between the three top leaders of China and an invited group of Western personalities and experts in June 1988, focused on an agenda of Chinese economic reform in a global context. The Chinese leaders were intensely interested to hear the judgement of the diverse international participants as to whether the new dynamic leader of the Soviet Union would be able to modernise the Soviet system through the planned economic and political reforms.

However, the lessons learned from the processes of economic and political reform in the Soviet Union were clear to the leaders of China: political stability remains an essential condition for steady economic progress. The Chinese leaders remained committed to their long-term programme of 'reform and opening-up to the outside world'. They explicitly focused on a considered sequence of carefully framed economic reforms while maintaining tight political control to avoid precisely the turbulence and confusion which they saw emerging from the political liberalisation of glasnost. As Supreme Leader Deng Xiaoping frankly told the international group: 'To compare the Chinese and Soviet processes of modernisation, you only need to compare the shelves in the stores of Moscow and Beijing.'

The intersection of these two historic processes of change was seen most vividly in the consequences of the visit of President Gorbachev to Beijing in May 1989. After decades of distrust and confrontation, this visit by the President of the Soviet Union was seen by the leadership of China to be of crucial strategic importance in establishing a new relationship between the two major countries of the communist world. But the visit became the focus of international media attention that provided new stimulus to the student demonstrations in Tiananmen

Square, leading to the repression of the demonstrations by the Chinese Government, and also to major internal political changes in China and to a new era in the relations of China and the West.

At a meeting with a small international group in December 1989, newly appointed General Secretary Jiang Zemin made clear how unacceptable and embarrassing it had been for the leadership of China that, at the time of the first state visit of the President of the Soviet Union since the founding of New China in 1949, it had not been possible for him to be escorted correctly across Tiananmen Square to the Great Hall of the People.

Another historic decision taken by President Gorbachev which had immense repercussions, most immediately for Europe, was his decision not to oppose the reunification of Germany. Working closely with his friend German Chancellor Helmut Kohl, they were able to seize a brief period of opportunity when the political constellations were favourable on both sides to create the conditions for reunification in a very short time.

From the perspective of European history and two devastating world wars, it was remarkable that the leader of the Soviet Union should not strenuously oppose this outcome, which would lead to a strengthened Germany in the heart of Europe with all the implications for the balance of power that this implies. Indeed, it was the leaders of some Western countries who were strongly opposed.

What is perhaps most remarkable about this period is that Mikhail Gorbachev, first as General Secretary and then as President, was able to guide and respond to these historic changes while the domestic political situation surrounding him in Moscow was in a state of turmoil and confusion and his policies were under vicious attack not only by the reactionary forces who wished absolutely to preserve the Soviet Union but also by the forces pressing for rapid transformation to democracy. The intensity of the internal pressures was demonstrated to the world by the failed coup attempt of August 1991. During this intensely complicated and difficult period, Mikhail Gorbachev remained calm, with the resolute support of his wife Raisa, consistently rejecting the use of force and committed to achieving negotiated solutions to intractable problems. If he had reacted hastily or violently, the world would not be as we know it today.

During the turbulent and confused period of transition from the monolithic Soviet Union to a diverse group of newly independent states, I had a number of further opportunities to meet with Mikhail Gorbachev at the Gorbachev Foundation in Moscow, after he had left the post of President of the Soviet Union on 25 December 1995. At the time, I was Director-General of the International Committee for Economic Reform and Cooperation, which aimed to mitigate the human and economic consequences of the breakup of the Soviet Union. I was able to form some impressions of the complexities and tensions across the states of the former Soviet Union, which President Gorbachev describes so clearly in his memoirs. At this time, he was deeply concerned about the devastating social and economic impacts of the collapse of the Soviet Union on the peoples of Russia and preoccupied by the continuing and damaging polarization in world affairs. He hoped that his efforts would lead to a reduction in East-West tensions, to substantial disarmament and to a 'peace dividend' of resources which could be redirected from military expenditures to building peace and world development. But this was not to be.

Most statesmen, having achieved so much in reducing the existential nuclear threats to the future of humanity, would have been content to retire from the pressures of public affairs, feeling that they had done their part. But Mikhail Gorbachev has embarked on a second life. While marginalised and excluded from the turbulent politics of the Russian Federation, he remains heavily engaged in international affairs. He continues to press for nuclear disarmament and more openness and cooperation between East and West. And he is now engaged in another vital cause, the fight to preserve a stable and healthy world environment.

Here again, Mikhail Gorbachev has taken up the challenge to press for real change. Public anger and frustration in response to the destruction and pollution of the environment, aggravated greatly by the nuclear disaster of Chernobyl in 1986, was a significant factor in discrediting the centrally managed and non-responsive communist system. Drawing the lessons from this experience, he recognised the fundamental importance to human life of a safe and stable environment and became a strong advocate of the need to achieve sustainable development.

At a conference in the Kremlin on 20 January 1990, where he had convened a Global Forum of Spiritual Leaders, Parliamentarians and Scientists, he publicly called for the establishment of a new organisation, the International Green Cross. Just as the International Red Cross can act effectively in the face of humanitarian disasters, the Green Cross should be ready to act where environmental disasters would have damaging impacts on human lives and the natural world. Under the leadership and guidance of President Gorbachev, this initiative has now resulted in the establishment of a respected and effective organisation with activities across the world dedicated to averting and mitigating the impacts of environmental degradation and disaster.

It is now becoming increasingly clear that human activities across the globe have reached such a scale as to affect the natural systems of the planet. While the nuclear threat remains, the risks of catastrophic climate change and of the degradation, overuse and breakdown of the ecosystems on which human life depends are the new existential challenges to the future of humanity. Just as young people in the past were preoccupied by the threats of nuclear war, they are today increasingly worried that their futures depend on averting the impacts of climate change and environmental breakdown, which would increase poverty and human deprivation, aggravate inequality and international polarisation and provoke conflict in many regions of the world.

Recognising these existential threats to the future of our civilisation arising from the impacts of humanity on the environment of the planet, President Gorbachev has now convened a high level Climate Change Task Force, supported by the Green Cross. I have the privilege of working with this Task Force, which will systematically consolidate the scientific facts and evidence of climate change and will convey conclusions and proposals directly to world leaders and decision-makers and to the general public so as to make clear the case for urgent action.

Mikhail Gorbachev is a rare world statesman who fully appreciates the scale and the urgency of risks and threats arising from the destabilisation of the climate and the degradation of the global environment. And he recognises the emerging potentials for conflict arising from the migration of environmental refugees and the intensifying competition for vital resources such as water, productive land and energy. He strongly insists that the current path of consumption-driven growth is unsustainable and that a new path of sustainable development will be essential to human survival. In this perspective, he has for many years been an Honorary Member of the Club of Rome, contributing his insight and experience in our efforts to press for action on the critical issues which now threaten the future of humanity.

From his unique and vast experience of international affairs, President Gorbachev remains intensely concerned by the failure of leaders across the world to recognise and to anticipate the scale and urgency of the emerging threats to the future and their inability to reach agreement on concerted action at a time in history which demands vision, leadership and concerted international action.

In another path-breaking initiative, he has therefore established the World Political Forum which brings together leading personalities from across the world, to propose how political leaders, public opinion and the media can be convinced of the reality of emerging global problems and persuaded to act.

Thus, as he approaches the age of 80, Mikhail Gorbachev remains passionately committed to the causes of disarmament and environmental responsibility, and to the securing of world peace based on the fundamental principle that critical issues can and must be resolved through reason and collaboration in human affairs to build a better world.

At the World Congress of the Club of Rome in Amsterdam in October 2009, he drew the lessons of his remarkable life across time and space and the diverse issues and cultures of world affairs. Reiterating his confidence in the capacities of human beings to resolve their problems, he called for a renewed commitment to international cooperation, for a new vision of a peaceful future in harmony with nature and for full recognition of the rights and opportunities of future generations.

The many historic contributions of Mikhail Sergeyevich Gorbachev to assuring world peace and to preserving a decent future for humanity deserve our admiration and gratitude.

Martin Lees *is a member of the Climate Change Task Force, along with President Gorbachev. He is also the former Secretary-General of the Club of Rome, where he still serves as a Senior Advisor to the Secretary-General, and is a Rector Emeritus at the University for Peace. After working in industry, Martin Lees' international career began at the OECD, where he was responsible for launching the 'InterFutures' Project on the Future of the Advanced Industrial Societies in Harmony with that of the Developing Countries. In 1982, he was appointed UN Assistant Secretary-General for Sciences and Technology for Development. During his tenure with the UN, he was responsible for establishing international cooperation with China, through the 'China Council for International Cooperation on Environment and Development' and 'China and the World in the Nineties' programmes. As Director-General of the International Committee for Economic Reform and Cooperation, he implemented many programmes in the newly independent states of the former Soviet Union between 1991 and 1996.*

Ted Turner

Our Debt of Gratitude

My good friend Mikhail Gorbachev will reach another milestone in March 2011. When we reflect on the impact he has had on the world, it is hard to believe that this humble figure grew up poor, on a state-owned farm in the south of Russia. When he was just a boy, like so many others, he suffered under Stalin's repression and Hitler's invasion. Yet the boy who grew up with oppression and violence became a man of freedom and peace.

When he became the Soviet leader, he was determined to make a difference. So, in his first year in office, he called for the elimination of nuclear weapons. In the following years, he brought reform, he befriended his enemies, changed the life of Russia, and he gave new hope to a world that wanted peace.

I came to know Mikhail Gorbachev when we were working to launch the Goodwill Games. In 1986, it had been ten years and two Olympic boycotts since athletes from the US and USSR had met in friendly competition. Mikhail agreed to host the Games in Moscow. He opened the games with a talk about peace and a call for disarmament. For me, he was a hero from that moment onward, and his greatest accomplishments were still to come.

There are some leaders in history who would have started a nuclear holocaust rather than let the cold war end. But this man came to power in the right place at the right time to help save the planet.

There is a lot of news in the world, but only one story — are we going to save humanity? Our fate hangs on one thin thread — how people use their power. Some people in the world use their power to gain more power; but a few use their power to advance peace.

That is what Mikhail has done — and what he is still doing today.

We owe a debt of gratitude to the long life and life work of our great friend and leader Mikhail Gorbachev.

Happy 80th Birthday!

Ted Turner is the founder of the cable television network CNN, the first 24-hour cable news channel, as well as WTBS, a pioneer super-station in cable television. Currently he serves as Chairman of the Turner Foundation, Inc., which he founded in 1990 to prevent damage to the natural systems, namely water, air and land. He is the Chairman of the Board of the United Nations Foundation, which was created in 1998 as a result of his $1 billion gift to support UN causes. He is also co-Chairman of the Nuclear Threat Initiative, a foundation he launched in 2001 together with former US Senator Sam Nunn to reduce the risk of and prevent the use of nuclear, chemical and biological weapons and the global response. He is also Chairman of Turner Enterprises, Inc., serves on Green Cross International's Honorary Board and is a member of GCI Circle of Friends.

Jan Kulczyk

Dear Mikhail Sergeyevich, my friend:

This, your 80th birthday, is a day for celebration, of course. We celebrate a hero of our times. Past heroes have won their fame mostly by their victories in war, but your courage is of a different kind. To the ills and follies of mankind you have applied the virtues of patience and hard work, of reason and of that good sense which sees into the future and seeks to make it better.

Others will praise the great changes you brought about for your own nation, which in your wake transformed the course of world history, bringing peace, security and the promise of a better life for future generations.

Here I speak instead of what you set out to do when you founded Green Cross International in 1993, and how your experience of life in the Soviet Union and your heroic efforts in ending the cold war led on to the radical drive to look at environmental problems in a new way. You set out to change the way we use the world of which we used to think ourselves the masters.

Your genius was in compelling and convincing the rest of us to see and treat the environment in a way we had never imagined. Instead of regarding conservation as a penalty and an economic burden, you saw it as an investment from which we, and the generations that will follow us, are sure to benefit, while in the shorter term improving international security and reducing poverty. To see the world in that perspective requires a vision of the long term for which your whole experience of life has prepared you.

So you decided to do something about it, and to recruit others to the cause. Your own network of top-level contacts is unrivalled, of course. In more than 30 countries they have inspired or founded GCI's national affiliates, which include academics, business people, activists and other leaders, who in turn spread the word to their colleagues and take action themselves. So your message is translated into action, around the world.

As the Chairman of Green Cross International who follows you, I think I see what qualified me to be your choice. The vision was yours; to bring it to reality you wanted someone to tackle the hard organising, delegating and accounting without which nothing gets done. For that, perhaps, my life in business has been the best school – provided always that the original vision is kept firmly in sight.

Gorbachev with Dr Jan Kulczyk

It has taken a long, long time to do the damage we have done to the Earth. In the massive civilisational shift, we have chopped the trees and dammed the rivers and burned the fuel. We have failed to look after the most precious resource of all, the water without which nothing can grow. All the time we were using up those resources without thought of their replacement.

In the past 50 years mankind has made great strides towards a better future – reached the moon, invented new ways of communicating with each other, even started to cut back on the weapons of mass destruction that threaten all of us. Mankind has so much to be proud of. But if we go on as we are, we will become as you understood so clearly slaves once again rather than masters of our fate. The big problem, you saw, is not that we spend too little on conserving our natural endowment, but that we spend it wrongly.

So we have made a good start on trying to do it right. The targets are clear, set out in the United Nations Millennium Goals ten years ago. That movement has to begin with small steps, practical actions that are in themselves reasonable and attainable. That is the path upon which you directed GCI.

The rewards can be far greater than at first appears. GCI has helped to arrange for the safe disposal of nuclear and chemical left-overs from the bad days of the cold war; it has brought together engineers from Palestinian and Israeli water authorities in the Jordan valley; it has helped poor villagers in Chad and Bolivia to make full use of precious water that would otherwise be wasted. Such initiatives, undertaken in close collaboration with local affiliates of GCI, conserve irreplaceable resources and reduce the risk of the greatest waste of all, which is armed conflict.

If we were simply an association of governments the predictable habits and cynicism of politics would stop us. If we were merely an association of idealists the task would not get done either. You saw when you founded CGI that private persons and private firms must engage in the effort, with efficiency as well as with enthusiasm, and for that, as you know so well, we need people of passion, persuasion and perseverance. Let that be my birthday tribute to you these 80 years on.

We have made a promising start. You showed us the way. For that we thank you, and seek to follow you. Long may that continue.

Jan Kulczyk *is a forward-looking business leader both in Poland and internationally. Since October 2006, Dr Kulczyk has been a member of the Board of Directors of Green Cross International. On 6 October 2007 he was elected the Chairman of the Board of Directors, succeeding President Gorbachev in this position.*

Pat Mitchell and Scott Seydel

Shared Memories with our Beloved Mikhail Gorbachev

There are very few people more recognised, more respected, more honoured than Mikhail Gorbachev. My husband, Scott Seydel, and I are privileged to work with him in the global environmental and sustainability movement he founded, and that Alexander Likhotal leads Green Cross International. We have so many reasons to celebrate President Gorbachev and his immense contributions to making the world a more secure and sustainable place, and in this tribute we are honoured to share some of our many memories of times with him.

My acquaintance began when Ted Turner asked me, 'How would you like to fly to Moscow and meet President Gorbachev?' Of course, I quickly answered, 'Yes!'

President Gorbachev was convening a meeting to initiate a new global environmental effort and knew Ted as a deeply committed environmentalist and media visionary. They had met when Ted launched CNN and wanted a Moscow outpost for the channel, and again when Ted launched the Goodwill Games following political boycotts of the Olympics.

How fortunate for me that Ted had schedule conflicts with the Moscow meeting, and that he chose me as his ambassador to this important gathering. Since we were already in production on the Cold War series for CNN, we both recognised a unique opportunity to speak directly with President Gorbachev about his participation in the series ... an idea that had come, ironically enough, when Ted and I were together in Russia for the Goodwill Games in 1994.

Happily, I learned that my long-time colleague in Democratic politics, Diane Meyer Simon, had also been invited to the meeting, and we would be travelling together to Moscow. This was clearly going to be an auspicious visit. And so it was. But it almost didn't happen. When we landed at the VIP airport outside Moscow, the officials who had come on board to check our passports, visas, and purpose of visit discovered that my visa had the wrong date on it ... dated not for the day of my arrival but for the following day. Even without a complete translation, we soon got the message that I was not going to be to able to leave the airport until this matter was cleared up. Diane and I began frantically dialling the numbers we had for President Gorbachev's office, and finally, an hour or so into our 'detention', a friendly English speaking voice returned our call.

'Welcome to Moscow,' the voice on the phone said in non-accented English, 'this is Pavel Palazhchenko.' I knew the name, as Pavel was President Gorbachev's ever-present interpreter, advisor and friend.

'Don't worry,' Pavel said in a calm voice and instructed us to give the phone to the government official standing near by. We did that, and a very animated conversation took place over the next 15 minutes or so. Without understanding a word of what was being said by our attending guard, we could deduct that whatever Pavel was saying was not being at all well received, and I began to have images of being returned to Atlanta and to Ted Turner with a big red 'DENIED ENTRY' stamp.

The conversation ended, the official went into a closed office where another very animated conversation with two other officials took place behind a glass window, and from time to time we would catch the name 'Gorbachev'. But when they spoke the name, it was not in the respectful, admiring way that we had become accustomed to saying and hearing it. Something beyond a wrong date on my visa seemed to be behind our detention.

Two more hours passed with no food or drink offered. Finally, one of the officials returned, looking less than happy, to tell us we are free to go to Moscow. We got in the car and sped off.

I'm not sure what I expected, but it's fair to say that nothing on that visit was what I expected ... except the man himself. When we arrived at a nondescript government building, far away from Red Square and the Kremlin, there was no one to greet us outside, so we made our way in and asked the person behind the desk to direct us to President Gorbachev's office. Another clue that something was not quite right as we followed directions to his office, down one long hallway of doors to another, realising that we were not going to be meeting the former leader of Russia in the kind of circumstances that we had envisioned or imagined.

Finally we had walked to the end of the last narrow hallway to come to a set of small corner offices. Standing outside to greet us was Alexander Likhotal, another long-time advisor of Gorbachev's who was being tapped to lead his new environmental work, and the ever loyal and present Pavel. They greeted us warmly with apologies for our delay at the airport and with no explanation of where we were or why the former head of a superpower, a world leader who had just the year before had been awarded the Nobel Peace Prize, was now working in a small corner office with no sign and no secretary and no visible recognition of who he was and what he had accomplished.

I was full of questions about all this, but before I could begin to ask them (my journalist background kicking in), Diane and I were led to a small conference room where several men were drinking coffee from paper cups and waiting to meet President Gorbachev. I could not contain my curiosity and began to ask the people around the table for an explanation of where we were and why President Gorbachev wasn't working in one of the Parliament buildings. 'Yeltsin' was the answer. The current President, Boris Yeltsin, in his zeal to distance himself from all the policies that Gorbachev had put into place had taken away Gorbachev's government office, his Moscow apartment, and had even removed all of his papers and books and placed them under the state's protective custody. The current circumstances for a man the world had embraced for his courage and charm, a man affectionately referred to by millions as 'Gorby', was more and more surprising, and I was feeling the anger that I still feel any time someone speaks of him or his work without the proper understanding or appreciation of the enormous contributions he made to world peace and prosperity.

I was also feeling, at that particular moment, very hungry and reached for one of the pieces of bread left on the table. I took a big bite just as the door flung open and in walked a smiling President Gorbachev. He extended his hand to me and to Diane. With a mouthful of bread, I could not speak as I shook his hand, turning red with embarrassment.

He laughed out loud and said, '*Bon Appétit* and welcome to Russia.'

It was not the most auspicious beginning for our relationship from my perspective, but we have often laughed together at the sight I must have presented to him with my mouth too full to speak.

He took his seat at the head of the table and began to talk about the urgency of the mission to shape a strategic global response to the threats to the planet, which he had identified as the environmental ravages from years of the military build-up and the arms race, leaving stockpiles of chemical and nuclear weapons. He went on to explain further his idea for a kind of environmental Red Cross, modelled as a global rescue effort that would be called Green Cross. He spoke eloquently and passionately about his plan for creating a global movement that would be made up of local chapters in various countries, united by a mission to clean up the environmental residue of the cold war and create a value shift between all humankind and the earth we inhabit so that different kinds of policies could be put in place to ensure clean air and water, proper use of natural resources and new and renewable forms of energy. It was an ambitious agenda but there was no question in my mind as he spoke that he had already committed himself, his global stature and recognition to making this his life's work going forward.

A few people at the table that day had heard the germ of this big idea in a speech he had given a few months before in Kyoto, and the Japanese delegation there on this day were already poised to launch the first Green Cross organisation in Japan. There was also an Italian delegation, a Swiss one, and a few others, like Diane and myself, who had come to listen but were not sure of what we would be expected to do or how to respond.

What was so clear to us in those first few hours was the power of his presence and his ability to persuade, influence, charm and cajole. Clearly, this was a man at the height of his personal powers. He had already brought down a wall or two of distrust, had united people and countries that had long seen each other as enemies and stood up to criticism and cynicism and, before he had even turned 60, he had convinced other global leaders to join him in finding ways to a new multilateral peace among nations.

I knew that I was in the presence of a great man and it didn't matter how big the room was, this was a man who once again had identified a mission and he was committed to bringing all of his personal power, all his global respect and adulation, to bear to reverse another cold war of sorts, the one that had led the planet to the brink of a global environmental disaster.

That first afternoon in that small nondescript, unnamed Moscow office building, President Gorbachev had articulated a plan to build a global environmental movement. And as we said our goodbyes, I promised to repeat everything I had heard to Ted Turner and enlist him in the movement.

Diane and I returned to the United States, determined to be part of this new and important movement. Ted agreed immediately that there must be a US chapter of Green Cross International. However, when we searched the name, it was taken by an insurance company, so we settled on Global Green USA.

Ted Turner and Diane contributed the start-up funds, and Diane convinced Matt Petersen, a young California environmental conservationist, to become its first (and current) Executive Director. She became the founding Chair and Ted Turner was our founding President. As he had promised, President Gorbachev travelled to Washington to lead our first big fund-raiser in the nation's capital.

It wasn't difficult to attract an audience of Washington's movers and shakers to hear Mikhail Gorbachev talk about his new mission. There were some who questioned why a leader who had already ended a global conflict, was a Nobel Peace laureate, had written several best sellers, was *Time*'s Man of the Year, and already had a guaranteed place in history, needed to do something else … especially something as ambitious and challenging as launching and leading a global environmental movement. He would always smile when this question would arise and remind everyone that he was still young, with many years ahead to do good work. There was also the dynamic, charismatic woman who shared his life and this new commitment, Raisa, and getting to know her during those first years of Green Cross was an unexpected and deeply felt pleasure and privilege.

She and President Gorbachev travelled the world on behalf of Green Cross International, raising funds to support the growing number of chapters around the world, and raising the environmental consciousness everywhere they went. Because the situation in Russia had further deteriorated, he and Raisa often seemed more at home … and certainly they felt more appreciated and honoured … outside their own country. Many countries offered them homes and stipends to take up residence, but they remained loyal to the place of their birth, and their support came largely from the lectures he was invited to give all over the world and the books they both wrote.

Because of his global stature and record of accomplishments, President Gorbachev could shape the message of sustainability in a way that appealed to those outside the environmentally concerned. And because of what he had done before in his life he could make the connections between sustainable, renewable resources and peace and prosperity for all, and this was evidenced time and time again as he engaged more and more supporters. He made the environment, the restoration of a better balance between the planet and how we 'use' it, a trumpet call to action that many hundreds of thousands of people in every country heard and responded to.

Over those years of his visits to the United States, often to speak at a Global Green USA event, we had some really good times together on a personal level and many profoundly important times together for the Green Cross movement. He and his beloved Raisa became a big part of my life, and of the life that I came to share in 1995 with my life partner, Scott Seydel.

After many shared encounters, President Gorbachev had become my friend so it felt important that he meet Scott and join in approving our pending marriage. Soon we found ourselves seated together after a Global Green Awards Gala in California, and Scott was getting a lot of questions to make certain he passed muster. Following this impromptu interview, Mikhail turned to me and said, 'I approve of this fellow so marry him quickly and let's put him to work!'

Having served on several boards of environmental organisations dedicated to resource conservation, Scott was happy to join Global Green USA. Following Diane Meyer Simons, me, and Senator Gary Hart as Global Green's Board Chairs, Scott accepted the post in 2004, and remains the Board's leader.

Scott and I agree that our marriage having been blessed by Mikhail Gorbachev has added a special flavour to our union, and we have both supported his initiative and continuing efforts since that eventful Global Green Awards banquet.

It was at a similar occasion, in the green room preceding a Global Green Gala, in the company of Ted and Jane Fonda, where we were talking with President Gorbachev and Raisa about their lives in Moscow since the dissolution of the USSR and fall of the Berlin Wall, that we learned that there had been no provision for the Gorbachevs' livelihood or protection of and public access to his legacy. Some funds had recently been raised to initiate the design and construction of a Gorbachev Library in Moscow to provide for careful preservation and accessibility to these historic documents. There was still a shortfall, however, and so there would be significant delays that threatened to endanger documents that were being steadily removed from public archives. Within minutes of hearing of this problem, and in his usual generous and spontaneous way, Ted wrote the check for the millions of dollars still needed, and once again served both the Gorbachev's needs and humanity's access to the personal papers of a man who altered world history.

This was a very emotional moment for all of us, made even more so by our recent knowledge that Raisa was suffering from an incurable illness. The Library was a shared dream that Ted's foresight and love of Mikhail made a reality for her, her daughter and granddaughters.

Even before the Library could be completed, we received news that Raisa was critically ill and being treated in the final stages of her bout with leukaemia. When she later passed away, I travelled to Moscow for the state funeral. As Raisa's admirer and close Americanski friend, I felt deep emotion and sadness as she was laid to rest. She was an amazing woman that I admired so greatly, and the impact of her lifelong support and guidance on President Gorbachev and everything in his life has been well documented. As I've continued my friendship with the family and have seen Irina and her family grow together, I'm always reminded of Raisa and her courage, forthrightness and commitment to doing what's right and important. Irina and her beautiful daughters will carry this great family's legacy forward. There is no doubt.

There are so many memories, but I will share only two more because they say so much about the man and his work.

On one occasion, he was invited to speak at the University of Georgia, my alma mater. It's a large school and when we were making our way to the coliseum for his speech to a sell-out crowd of 18,000 plus, there was a huge traffic jam. In typical humility, Gorbachev enquired about whether there was a football game that night, oblivious to the fact that the traffic jam was his talk. And when he spoke that night about the need for global action on the part of young people to organise, to protest when needed, to create change, to take the future into their hands, the crowd rose to its feet for a 15-minute ovation. There has never been a more memorable moment and to this day I meet students who were there and they tell me how it changed their lives.

And then there was the visit Scott and I made with Gorbachev, Alexander, Pavel, Matt and his wife, Leila, to upstate New York to visit David Rockefeller. What a night that was as these two great men talked about the negotiations that had led the world from the brink of war, the inside story of how he dealt with Reagan who was so sceptical during the arms negotiations. He told funny stories about everyone! He and David also talked about farming because those are Gorbachev's roots. He is within his heart a farmer who has witnessed the ways that the earth protects and feeds us.

Every time I heard him speak I was more awed by the depth of his knowledge, the scope of his interests and the strength of his convictions. He never hesitated to speak his mind, and every time I was moved even more to admiration and respect for his kindness, his open-mindedness, his big heart and his ready laugh and smile.

He had seen the worst of men, had endured harsh and unfair treatment at the hands of a country that he literally moved from isolation to being on its way to the world power it is again today ... and slowly I have watched him return to favour in Russia and increase in stature everywhere. He could have retired to a dacha, written books and waited for the world to see his accomplishments in the proper perspective, but instead he took up another fight; he went to front lines all over the world with the message that just as the cold war had ended without the conflagration that was feared so the world can move back from the brink of environmental disaster if we act now act both locally and globally.

That was his mission in the founding of Green Cross and it has been conveyed to all who've joined its movement. Scott and I feel it a privilege to be a part of this movement and to follow this great man's vision.

The importance of his presence within the Green Cross movement was never so keenly felt as when Global Green hosted the biannual GCI Congress in New Orleans following the disastrous ruin of the city by hurricane Katrina in 2007. Our Global Green USA chapter had teamed with foundations, federal and state agencies, and local charitable institutions to begin rebuilding affordable homes in the 9th Ward that had been totally wiped out by the storm.

Matt Petersen and his staff of green residential home builders, headed by Walker Wells, had enlisted actor Brad Pitt to assist in initiating the reconstruction, including refurbishing local schools with green materials and air/water systems.

President Gorbachev opened the GCI Congress by admonishing federal officials to attend to the certain ravages to be inflicted by continuing changes in climate and weather systems, and to prepare for similar tragedies if Mother Nature's signals are not heeded. The headlines were timely as Americans were beginning to grasp the relationship between carefree consumption and the impact of wasted energy and resources on climate.

At the end of the Congress, President Gorbachev expressed hope that the Green Cross initiative would extend to all corners of the Earth. It was then that he also announced his relinquishment of the active post of President of Green Cross and his ascendancy to its Board leadership as Founder and President Emeritus. This was a moment we will always remember, but it was also a moment of great sadness that we've since learned was premature in that even from his semi-retired status we can depend on Mikhail Gorbachev's leadership and guiding hand in the work of Green Cross around the world.

One last moment of memory: when we all travelled to Moscow for the opening of the beautiful Gorbachev Foundation and Library building, Ted, Scott and I stood by the small tree planted in front of the building that had a small plaque on the ground saying, 'This building was funded by US philanthropist and entrepreneur Ted Turner.

That was the only recognition Ted would allow. Today that tree is strong and tall and people from all over the world see the connection between these two men who have always stood tall and, like that tree, provided the roots from which many important movements have grown and spread and changed the world.

Pat Mitchell is a founder and board member of Global Green USA, the US affiliate of Green Cross International, and an honorary board member of GCI. Currently she is the President and CEO of the Paley Center for Media. Before this, she was the President and CEO of the Public Broadcasting Service (PBS) from 2000 to 2006, which made her the first woman and first producer and journalist to hold the position. As President of Turner Broadcasting's Original Productions from 1992 to 2000, Pat Mitchell produced numerous award-winning documentaries and series. She is a member of the Council on Foreign Relations and the US Afghan Women's Council, and an adviser to the Center for Public Leadership at the Kennedy School of Harvard University.

Scott Seydel is a member of the Green Cross International Board and Chairman of the Board of Global Green USA. He is also the chief executive of several chemical processing companies, where sustainability and environmental stewardship are the cornerstone through an emphasis on energy and waste minimisation, and recycling.

Diane and Charlie Gallagher

My wife Diane and I have had the privilege of knowing and supporting President Gorbachev over the past decade, and have enjoyed many wonderful social experiences with both the President and his daughter Irina. His important contributions to global environmental issues, as well as his leadership in ending the cold war, clearly have established his place in world history. Although we do not have the opportunity to be with him as often as we would like, we will always consider him a close friend. So on this milestone event of his 80th birthday, we offer a toast, and celebrate his incredible life.

Diane and Charlie Gallagher
Denver, Colorado

Diane and Charles Gallagher *are founders of the Diane and Charles Gallagher Family Foundation that seeks to provide educational opportunities and college scholarships for inner city youth. Mr Gallagher is also the Chairman and Chief Executive Officer of Gallagher Enterprises LLC. The Gallaghers are also members of the Green Cross International Circle of Friends.*

Diane and Charlie Gallagher in conversation with Gorbachev

Rabbi Awraham Soetendorp

Keeping the Door Open

In the early autumn of 1985, I travelled to Paris on a bus chartered by the Dutch Solidarity Committee for Soviet Jewry to participate in a European demonstration which would coincide with the visit of the newly elected General Secretary of the Communist Party of the Soviet Union, Mikhail Gorbachev. Having been in the forefront of the struggle for the freedom of movement and religious and cultural identity of Soviet Jewry for over 15 years, this was the most natural act of solidarity, though I felt some hesitation. As early as 1970, on the day after a demonstration of thousands, I was allowed to enter the Soviet Embassy. I had told the secretary that the actions of the recently founded Solidarity committee were not directed against the Soviet people but were only undertaken to appeal to the authorities to alleviate oppressive measures and grant freedom according to the principles of the Universal Declaration of Human Rights. From the outset, the efforts initiated by the small Jewish community that had been decimated by the Nazis in the Second World War were supported by very large sections of Dutch society. To give just one example, in 1982 during a period of only two months one million signatures were collected to appeal for the freedom of all prisoners and refuseniks, prominent amongst them Anatoly Sharansky. For me, a child survivor saved by a Catholic German, Ria van der Kemp, and her husband, it was a natural lifelong duty. But now, a new leader had arisen who had already shown a remarkable sensitivity and readiness to listen. I thought that if I could only have the opportunity to speak to him and share our concerns, but alas, the chance of that ever happening was so remote.

We might have merely glimpsed each other across the different sides of the barricades, and history resumed its course. It was only five years later that an appointment to meet was made by Evgeny Velichov, then the Vice President of the Soviet Academy of Sciences and a governing member of the Global Forum of Spiritual and Parliamentary Leaders for Human Survival. The world had changed dramatically and was filled with new hope, and it all started with the one man who had chosen to withhold weapons and responded to the demand for freedom by opening the doors, Mikhail Gorbachev.

In January 1990, the Global Forum was invited by the Soviet Government and its President to hold a major conference on ecological integrity in Moscow. This breakthrough gathering saw many political and religious leaders joined by scientists and business representatives, amongst them Al Gore, Sheikh Ahmed Kuftaro, Grand Mufti of Syria, Elie Wiesel, Carl Sagan and Chief Oren Lyons. For the first time, a Jewish Shabbat service was held at the Kremlin after dusk on Friday, and later in the evening prayers were given by representatives of other faiths. It was then that President Gorbachev made his prophetic appeal to establish a Green Cross for the environment. A new global vision was born, and it was carried by the news media all over the world.

The extraordinary meeting of minds and souls ended in a true spirit of sisterhood and brotherhood. Our appointment had not materialised because I had fallen ill. It was a sobering experience not even being capable of watching the proceedings on the television in my hotel room in Russia. Later that year, the opening of the Anne Frank exhibition marked the revolutionary change. Thousands upon thousands of Jews had been allowed to leave, freedom to practise Judaism had been granted, and Sakharov was freed from exile.

In the autumn of 1991, my wife and I spent some time in Moscow helping to build new liberal Jewish communities during the last few months of Gorbachev's presidency. It was during the Rio conference in 1992 that Akio Matsumura, the visionary founder of the Global Forum, issued our invitation to Gorbachev to assume the leadership of the proposed Green Cross International, the implementation of his own vision. He answered in the affirmative and became an active partner in the following formative months. The idea was welcomed by the then Prime Minister Ruud Lubbers, and the Dutch Government gave their support.

A new conference of the Global Forum, convened in Kyoto in April 1993 on the theme of value change, was dedicated to the establishment of Green Cross. Just before the inaugural session a serious problem occurred concerning doubts that had arisen about whether the foundation for the establishment of the new ecological movement was solid enough. Deliberations had taken place all through the night, and in the tense room, just before the planned proceedings, Mikhail Gorbachev appeared. We saw each other for the first time and shook hands. He smiled and pulled me down to sit next to him on the sofa. I felt his empathy, a captive cooperative power. He turned to me and asked through an interpreter whether I believed we should proceed to form Green Cross now. I answered emphatically in the positive. He held my hand and asked whether I could say that with my whole heart. Moved to tears I said loudly, 'Yes.' He smiled again and said, 'Let us do it.' He pulled me up and we walked together to the hall where Green Cross was officially established.

When I reflect on this moment of spontaneous friendship and trust I am moved. Of course, Gorbachev had already made up his mind, but it is the ability to open up to the unknown other and show an immediate trust which transcends formal barriers that marks this precious man.

His decision to devote the latter years of his life to the struggle for a healthy planet from a holistic concept was momentous. When he said yes to an emerging, fragile, idealistic alliance of different cultural backgrounds he took a risk, but he did it on the basis of humility and the willingness to listen to the whisper of truth that I believe has always guided him. When the newly formed Green Cross was faced with the challenge to join forces with the Earth Council to attempt to bring about an Earth Charter, he became the inspiring champion. The envisioned holistic and ethical framework within which ecological integrity, reverence for the community of life, social and economic rights, democracy, non-violence and peace were intertwined concurred with his deepest convictions.

In April 1993, when he visited the Netherlands for the first time, I was privileged to meet the real source of inspiration that allowed him to grow to moral leadership, his companion in life, Raisa. An indelible memory was her impromptu speech at an official luncheon with representatives of the environmental movements of the Netherlands where she expounded upon the basic principles of the Ethics of Spinoza. Later, at the reception given by the Solidarity Committee for Jews in the former Soviet Union, she turned to her husband and said, 'Mikhail Sergeyevich, you remember that after being greeted by banners with the name of Sharansky I asked you who this man was and what he represented?' Mikhail smiled, 'And how we felt at home in Israel recently where we were surrounded by the Russian language everywhere?' I thanked them for everything they had done to make this historic transition possible. In later years, my wife Sira and I had the privilege to experience Raisa's wisdom and heart. May her memory be a blessing forever and ever.

When the Earth Charter reached its final form and was presented to Queen Beatrix of the Netherlands, after an unprecedented participatory process, we were urged by Gorbachev to embody the consciousness of being one human family, one Earth community with one common destiny. He has shown what the philosopher Bergson called the prophetic *élan vital* (vital force), to plant the future into the present, to speak to power as no one else was able to do, and demand to take measures that in the short run may interfere with national self-interest but are necessary to safeguard the community of life.

At the last general assembly of Green Cross International it was so gratifying to behold the growth of the family of conscience and concern. Alexander Likhotal has worked miracles in the footsteps of the life president. Gorbachev asked me what my main occupations were these days. I answered that I, for whom courageous foster parents had held open the door, increasingly felt that it was I who was now trying to hold the door open for the babies of today, who are desperate for life and look to us for safety. Mikhail placed his shoulder against mine and said 'We have broad shoulders, we all of us together can keep the door wide open.'

Mikhail Sergeyevich, I know you are right. In the words of the Earth Charter, the choice is ours: form a global partnership to care for Earth and one another or risk the destruction of ourselves and the diversity of life.

You have reached your 80th birthday, called by the psalmist the age of great strength. We all still desperately need your voice of truth nourished by ethical imperative and spiritual awareness. May your example inspire us to move from the brink of moral bankruptcy, and in the year 2015 fulfil the Millennium Development Goals.

I had the privilege to sing in your presence the song of Shabbat inviting the angels of peace. May these angels of peace protect you, the ultimate peacemaker, on your road into the future.

Rabbi Soetendorp has been involved with Green Cross International since the beginning, as a co-founder and member of GCI's Honorary Board as well as Chairman of the Board of Green Cross Netherlands and an Earth Charter Commissioner. He is Rabbi of the Liberal Jewish Community in The Hague, presides over the European region of the World Union for Progressive Judaism, and is co-Chair of the Global Forum of Spiritual and Parliamentary Leaders. He is also a member of the International Advisory Committee of the World Peace Summit and of the Steering Committee of the World Council of Religious Leaders, launched in Bangkok in June 2002.

Diane Meyer Simon

If we are fortunate, in each of our lives there are some people who have the ability to remind us of who we truly are and why it is we came to be. Through their example, they help us see more clearly what can be, and they give us the inspiration to stand a little taller, think a little deeper and act a little quicker on the things that truly matter most. For me, no one has done this with more grace, courage or conviction than Mikhail Sergeyevich Gorbachev.

I first saw the Gorbachevs about a year or so before Mikhail Sergeyevich became the leader of the USSR. He and his beautiful, delicate wife, Raisa Maximovna, were on CNN stepping out of a car. It was then I found myself almost frozen in time, experiencing an inexplicable connection with two people I had never met. I left the family room with the forethought that our paths would one day cross, that I would one day know them, that I would work with them. I then returned to my role as a wife and a mother of three small children and two stepchildren with that profound moment etched for ever within my memory. I embraced that thought with gentle contentment.

As the years passed, I held onto the secret of that foresight. I secretly knew that the Gorbachevs would change the world from inside out, so as communism faded in the USSR, the East divided into separate pieces and the Wall fell I smiled with a confident smile, knowing that this was only the beginning of what Gorbachev would do for our world.

Many years later, in 1993, shortly after Gorbachev founded Green Cross International, I sent him a congratulatory letter, sharing my deep appreciation for his efforts and never expecting a reply. A few months later, to my great surprise, I received a phone call from the then Executive Director of Green Cross International, Roland Wiederkehr, asking if he could meet with me to discuss the mission of GCI in greater detail, and I jumped at the chance to hear more about it. When I met with Roland, I never suspected he would be inviting me to Moscow to personally meet with Gorbachev, especially since I denied during the meeting that I was of the calibre to play a significant role. Though I had many years of employment in political public service in Washington, DC, and had a great deal of experience in environmental non-profits, I certainly didn't consider myself an environmental maven by any means.

Needless to say, I found myself on a plane for Russia with my family and two close friends, Pat Mitchell and Marianne Williamson, by my side, and together we all stepped into the magical and miraculous world of that elegant couple I had seen many years before on the news.

By the time we left our meeting in Moscow, I had not only been invited to join their GCI Honorary Board, but I was asked to found the American affiliate of GCI, Global Green USA. This was indeed a profound honour for me, and now I could do more for an issue that had always been very close to my heart. It was a dream coming true.

It has been 18 years since that fateful meeting. Both individually and collectively, we have seen our share of life's ups and downs and experienced the many highs and lows that build one's character. We have celebrated great accomplishments, and we have never failed to honour the extraordinary vision and dignity that will forever represent both dear Raisa and Mikhail.

Mikhail Sergeyevich Gorbachev was born in a small agrarian area of Russia during a time that promised very little beyond the life of a farmer. There was little, if any, chance of attending university, but opportunity came when a young and determined Gorbachev produced the largest crops in the area from several difficult harvests. It wasn't long before this lover of the land caught the eye of some very powerful people within the communist government system. His 20-plus-hour days in the fields had paid off, and he was suddenly on his way to the meaningful life he was meant to live, changing other lives – while making history.

Since Gorbachev founded Green Cross International, so many environmental organisations have popped up all over the globe that it is impossible to read a list of the non-profits because more and more are being founded as we speak, causing the list to be never ending. For me, the most profound aspect of Mikhail Sergeyevich Gorbachev's character is his incredible intuition. He adopted our Earth when he became the Founding President of Green Cross International, the global movement to shift our values in respect to our human relationship with the Earth at a most crucial time in our lives. He is completely dedicated to reclaim a healthy Earth from our greed and carelessness. Again he is literally changing our world in order to heal it for generations to come. With his inspiration, many countries have organized GCI Affiliates and are working daily to focus our attention on this shift in values to save our environment in a wide range of efforts from greening communities, greening schools, to attacking global warming and eradicating weapons of mass destruction left over from the cold war. The man who ended the cold war is cleaning up the dangerous weapons that still remain here on our Earth. Gorbachev has followed the voice from within to again be a force on this globe when it is so needed.

As Mikhail Sergeyevich Gorbachev reaches his 80th year, we celebrate with the world his words, his brilliance, his intuition, his courage and, most of all, his love and respect for all living things and the Earth that is our home. He is both universal humanitarian and global political leader, an inspirational world figure who listened to his sharpened intuition and, in sharing that voice, gave others permission to grow.

And so it is, as I stand a little taller, think a little deeper and act a little quicker on things that matter most, I am reminded of who I am by the courage and grace of a man who became my dear friend, a man who came to remind all of us of what could be if we work to fulfil our dreams. Perhaps Rudyard Kipling too had the foresight to anticipate the man who would become Mikhail Sergeyevich Gorbachev when he wrote the famous words in his poem 'If' – words that so accurately describe a young man who went on to change the world...

> If you can talk with crowds and keep your virtue,
> Or walk with kings – nor lose the common touch,
> If neither foes nor loving friends can hurt you,
> If all men count with you, but none too much;
> If you can fill the unforgiving minute
> With sixty seconds' worth of distance run –
> Yours is the Earth and everything that's in it...

I humbly thank you, my dear friend, for all you do to raise us up, allow us to stand tall and for showing us what true greatness is. With my deepest gratitude and greatest hope, I wish to you, President Mikhail Sergeyevich Gorbachev, all the eternal riches of a life well lived.

Your presence on Earth continually changes it for the better. You are so loved.

Diane Meyer Simon is Founder, President Emerita and Past Chair of Global Green USA. She founded Global Green USA following a Moscow Board Meeting of Green Cross International in August 1993. Ever since, she has committed herself to personally spear-heading the Global Green agenda and shaping a message of international environmental responsibility for an American audience.

Shoo Iwasaki

The World's Greatest Smile

People with charming smiles have always fascinated me. From my experience, those who have a nice, attractive or impressive smile seem to be the ones who lead the world. There are many people with such smiles, but there are very few that I can really rely on from the bottom of my heart. Fortunately, I have had a chance to meet one such person, Mr Mikhail Gorbachev.

It was April 1993, when the Green Cross International inauguration convention was held in Kyoto, Japan. We were all waiting for Mr Gorbachev to arrive at the entrance of the convention centre with great anticipation.

Mr Gorbachev's car arrived and he walked towards us smiling and waving. What a wonderful smile! Struck by his smile, we all welcomed him with great applause. When he was walking in front of me, he suddenly stopped and offered his hand to me, even though we had never met before. I was so surprised and excited. I thought to myself, 'The world's greatest smile was just in front of me. Can it be real? How happy and blessed I am!' I decided right then and there that I should follow him, and devote all of my efforts to his cause.

Since then, he has sometimes scolded me, but I always feel as if I were being scolded by a brother. He is like an older brother to me, someone whom I have supported for the past 17 years. As such, I have had numerous opportunities to meet him privately as well as publicly during these years.

One of my fondest memories is when he visited my home in Japan with his wife, Mrs Raisa Gorbachev. She had an amiable smile that was as wonderful as her husband's. She spoke to my wife, Toshiko, and greeted each of my family members with a gentle smile, as if she had known us for many years. My wife adored her, as if Raisa were her elder sister.

When Mrs Gorbachev was hospitalised in Germany, my wife and I prayed to God every day for her quick recovery. Soon after Mrs Gorbachev passed away, I met Mr Gorbachev at a meeting. I had expected that he would be so depressed, but his smile was so nice that I almost forgot to extend my condolences to him. I wondered how he could smile as before when he was so shocked and depressed after the tragedy.

I thought I wanted to be a man who could have such a smile under any hardship.

I once visited Mr Gorbachev in Moscow to solve a little misunderstanding with Green Cross International. At the meeting I, as President of Green Cross Japan, insisted on 'action, not just talk'. However, our stance was not accepted favourably and we left feeling rather uncomfortable. Nevertheless Mr Gorbachev, smiling, put a break to our discussion, and invited me to have dinner with him.

One year after our meeting in Moscow, the General Assembly of Green Cross International was held in Zurich, Switzerland to commemorate the organisation's 10th anniversary. In his opening speech, Mr Gorbachev strongly stated that 'Green Cross must take actions. Each national organisation is encouraged to carry out certain implementing projects, not just talk.' As soon as he was seated, he patted me on the shoulder, smiling, and said that he expected a lot from me.

I was really touched with the fact that Mr Gorbachev, a great world leader, seriously considered the suggestion I made to him a year ago. I felt that he was really my most reliable big brother, and liked him even more. His family and mine have kept a friendly relationship ever since.

I sometimes wonder why I have such friendly feelings towards him, as he is a famous world leader. All the people around me, who express the same feeling, wish to join the celebration of Mr Gorbachev's 80th birthday.

He is loved by so many people. I believe that Mr Gorbachev might be a world saviour. I am sure that the time will come when his wonderful smile changes the world. Until then we will make each step in concert with him. It is our determination that each of us is to devote all of our efforts to the peace and environment of the world.

Mr Gorbachev, my big brother, I sincerely wish you good health and to be active as our great leader for years to come.

Shoo Iwasaki is the Founding President of Green Cross Japan as well as a member of the Green Cross International Board of Directors. He is a former Nishi Nippon Broadcasting Corp. announcer and a graduate of Chuo University in Japan. He also holds honorary degrees from Kyonggi University in South Korea and from Emerson College in the United States.

Guido Pollice

Buongiorno Senatore, bella ciao, bandiera rossa, biondo Tevere and a few other words make up President Gorbachev's Italian vocabulary, in addition to the names of his Italian friends with whom he is on good terms (Gianni, Antonio, Giulietto, Fiammetta, etc.).

It is a bare vocabulary, compensated by the certain and continued presence of Pavel Palazhchenko, the faithful interpreter of every meeting, from the most important and sensitive to the more convivial.

But these Italian words, said with love and passion to his interlocutors, give you the impression and then the certainty that you are speaking with a man that communicates to you humanity, peace of mind and persistence.

In the over 50 years of my life in politics I have met and worked with good, reputable Italians and people from overseas, like Michel Rocard, Jacques Cousteau, Yevtushenko, Pietro Nenni, Lula, Spadolini, Umberto Eco, Rita Levi Montalcini and many others, but President Gorbachev's stature is unmatched.

From the first time you meet him, he immediately makes you feel at

Gorbachev with Guido Pollice

ease. He lets you forget his strong personality and that you are speaking with a man that was for many years a person who could determine the fate of the world.

It is thanks to him that the process of change in Russia and in Europe has been painless.

In the hypothetical field, maybe we can say that he sped things up in a context of which we are not fully aware.

However, history is not determined by *ifs* and *buts*, and this is not the right circumstance to judge facts and events related to the President.

We wish a long life to Gorbachev, not only for him but also for our own selfish reasons.

In 1992, at the conference in Rio, Gorbachev already knew that the future of the planet is connected to environmental protection and that the winning idea is the commitment of men and women to that goal.

This was, for me, Mr Gorbachev's second strategic choice and in this case, too, he has been a forerunner with regards to all the others that have followed his footsteps (Al Gore, Barack Obama, etc.). The big people of the Earth are doubly indebted to him, and it's no accident that everyone in the world gives him such a warm welcome and devotion.

We wish for the President to carry on with his intense work, so that Governments around the world will adopt the Earth Charter.

It is a long and difficult task to sew up what is torn, to open dialogues between those who do not communicate, to confront oneself with different religions and beliefs, and to believe in the dialogue between populations, without considering Peace as an impregnable totem.

All these things are waiting for Mr Gorbachev now, and it will be less difficult if all of us, the members of the Green Cross family, keep up with the challenge that the President has launched.

Guido Pollice is the Founding President of Green Cross Italia. During a long political career he served as the President of the Green Party in Italy and as a Senator for the Lombardia region.

Giorgio Armani

I am delighted to take this opportunity to send my very best wishes for a Happy Birthday to President Mikhail Gorbachev. He is a truly great man whose achievements extend well beyond the political arena, a man who has indisputably changed the course of history.

I particularly admire President Gorbachev's wholehearted commitment as President of Green Cross International, and the determination with which he has worked for and promoted this project to make clean water universally accessible and affordable – a fundamental human right absolutely essential for good health.

Water is life – that is a simple truth. However, although water covers the major part of the Earth's surface, it remains inaccessible to a vast number of human beings. If we could just guarantee drinkable water to everyone who needs it we would have succeeded in transforming and sustaining the long-term health of so many vulnerable and deprived people, thereby providing them with an improved standard of living.

It is my profound wish that as a result of this appeal by President Gorbachev genuine and tangible progress will be made towards the goal of working in an environmentally sensitive way for greater social equality.

Giorgio Armani is an acclaimed Italian fashion designer with wide-ranging business interests. He has been an active supporter of GCI, in particular its campaign to make clean drinking water available to every human being on Earth.

Sam Cheow

Dear Mister President,

We would like to extend our sincere congratulations on this momentous and joyful day. The salons and stylists of Pureology are honoured to partner with Green Gross International to help fulfil your vision of a secure and sustainable future. We remain committed to raising awareness of the need for water conservation, and to helping those in need to gain access to clean water.

 **Sam Cheow** is Assistant Vice President of Pureology Worldwide.

Jean-Christophe Babin

Dear Mister President,

We are happy to join in and congratulate you on the joyous occasion of your 80th anniversary. At TAG Heuer we believe that the future is green for the watch industry and that is why we have been working for years to reduce waste and the environmental footprint of our operations. Through our partnership with Green Cross International we are proud to participate in your efforts to promote a vision of the world that is secure, fair and sustainable.

Jean-Christophe Babin is President and Chief Executive Officer of TAG Heuer.

Alexander Likhotal

The Right Side of the Kremlin Wall

December 1991, the Kremlin, Moscow, around 10 p.m. The long day is over but the press service of the President is still in the office. Down the corridor in the President's quarters Gorbachev, Boris Yeltsin and Alexander Yakovlev discuss the procedures of the power transfer. Neither the Soviet Constitution nor any law has ever envisioned the possibility of the dissolution of the USSR, and the necessary procedures – from the transfer of the nuclear codes to the way to issue the official announcements – had to be elaborated.

But the press service was in the office not only because MS (short for Mikhail Sergeyevich and used by his staff) could have needed someone. People remain human even in historic and dramatic times and we had a good reason to 'unwind' – one of our colleagues was celebrating his 50th birthday that day. Closer to midnight somebody raised a toast: 'I wish all of us to always be on the RIGHT side of the Kremlin wall!' We laughed at what seemed a witty and time-appropriate joke – knowing that in a couple of weeks we would all be out of the Kremlin. But, with the passage of time, I have started to think more and more about this toast – about why the time of perestroika really was the 'right' time to be inside the Kremlin wall.

Now, with 20 years of hindsight on these events, it is clear to me that the key to this question is Gorbachev's personality. Amongst the Soviet and post-Soviet leaders of Russia he stands apart. In contrast to all of them, who either served the 'cause' or simply serviced their own power ambitions, Gorbachev served history, which renders all the discussions about whether it was his action or his inaction that opened the way for transformation irrelevant.

When he came to power he had a choice. He could have chosen to stay on the same throne as his predecessors, which would have been the easy road to take: inertia was strong and the country was still rich in natural resources. He opted for a different fate. Why did he do it?

For the first time, a man of morals – not a purely 'political animal' for whom the goal justifies any means but a person of (unconsciously) Christian morality – was at the top of the Soviet leadership. François duc de La Rochefoucauld said that it is never more difficult to speak than when one is ashamed to be silent. Gorbachev had the courage to break this silence. As it happens in history, 'in the beginning was the

Word'. On the night of his election by the Politburo he had said to his wife: 'We cannot continue living like this!' THAT was the real start of perestroika. Courage and Conscience ruled for the first time in the Soviet period in the Kremlin!

As Joseph S. Nye points out, when Gorbachev came to power in 1985, there were only 50,000 personal computers in the Soviet Union; in the United States there were 30 million. Four years later there were about 400,000 personal computers in the Soviet Union, and 40 million in the USA. By the mid-1980s, only eight per cent of Soviet industry was globally competitive. It is difficult for a country to remain a superpower when the world doesn't want 92 per cent of what it produces. Gorbachev saw that the grey stagnation of the Soviet economy, its inability to match the vitality and inventiveness of Western capitalism, was not only due to the burden of empire and a bloated war machine. A stultifying political system inhibited imagination and enterprise. Gorbachev believed that the inventiveness of a talented nation could only be unleashed by letting ordinary people take more control of their lives through some form of democracy. He launched glasnost, freed the media, brought Andrei Sakharov back from exile, released political prisoners, and then organised the first contested elections to be held anywhere in the Warsaw Pact. In March 1989, Soviet voters threw out Party bosses from the legislative branch all over the country, and transformed the nation's politics.

Abroad, Gorbachev's reforms meant ending the 40-year cold war and the attendant arms race, which had imperilled the United States and the Soviet Union – and the rest of the world – with tens of thousands of nuclear weapons. In 1985 President Gorbachev and President Reagan stated at the Geneva Summit: 'A nuclear war cannot be won and must never be fought' – adopting, in effect, a declaration of the need to rid humankind of nuclear weapons. In December 1989, at a summit meeting in Malta, Gorbachev and President Bush announced that the cold war was over. Treaties providing for major arms reductions were signed, and even more far-reaching ones were being negotiated.

Gorbachev's advocacy of the universal values of humankind, understanding that we cannot be free unless we liberate other nations, and the renunciation of the Brezhnev Doctrine created the circumstances under which it was impossible for the Eastern European regimes to survive. By the summer of 1989, East Europeans were ready to move. Gorbachev refused to sanction the use of force to put down demonstrations. By November, the Berlin Wall had fallen. Adam Michnik, one of the leaders of the Polish anti-communist opposition, said in July 1989: 'Were it not for the "perestroika virus", our [democratic movement] could not have got where it is today.'

How did it occur to Gorbachev that people's thoughts and words were not grounds to imprison or execute them? How did the post of the Communist leader come to be held by a man who believed that people's lives and sufferings were more important than the prestige of a super-power? On 7 December 1988, Gorbachev was speaking at the United Nations in New York when the Spitak earthquake struck in Armenia. Despite the importance of his presence in New York, he rushed back to Russia, where, for the first time in Soviet history, he requested international help – breaking with the Soviet regime's tradition of not accepting help from 'imperialists'. Contrast this with Putin's refusal of foreign assistance offered to save the men on board the *Kursk* submarine in 2000 and it looks like an atavistic revival of the 'pride' complex. National 'prestige' has again become more important than human lives.

Being a politician, it was obviously not unusual for Gorbachev to be confronted with a choice between 'disastrous and unpalatable', most regrettably during the dramatic Baku, Tbilisi and Vilnius incidents that led to loss of life. But let us not forget that in these cases force was used not to keep the power or crush political opposition. In the real world, not restricted by the pure moralist's categories of good and evil, it is sometimes necessary to understand the shades of good and evil – to understand that sometimes one has to sacrifice a good for the higher good or choose a lesser evil to avoid a bigger one. This ethical compass has steered Gorbachev's political decisions.

He believed that no political goal could justify shedding human blood, that people are history's 'actors' and not instruments for reaching any goals. This is why Gorbachev stood the 'power test' – he was not just fighting for power or struggling to keep it. As John Galbraith said: 'There are times in politics when you must be on the right side and lose.' Gorbachev stood on the right side and lost . . . the power, but historically he won as a person and his perestroika has won too.

Not without serious mistakes, but his political courage, conciseness and ingenuity began the process of transforming the Soviet Union into a modern country at ease with itself and the outside world and this unleashed the world's transformation.

The end of the cold war not only made history, it saved history. Psychologically we are always inclined to disregard what could have happened but has not. Vaclav Havel is surely right when he argues that

Gorbachev's 'historical achievement is enormous: communism would have collapsed without him anyway, but it might have happened ten years later, and in God knows how wild and bloody a fashion'. Without the 'decompression' of Gorbachev's perestroika the country could have easily slipped into a Yugoslav scenario with all the nightmarish consequences of a nuclear superpower ending up in a bloody conflagration.

Unfortunately, much of Gorbachev's legacy and achievements have been squandered. But, given the impacts of perestroika, the ball is still rolling with the belated global perestroika we are going through so painfully today. The famously anti-communist Pope John Paul II warned in 1992 that 'the Western countries run the risk of seeing this collapse of communism as a one-sided victory of their own economic system, and thereby failing to make necessary corrections in that system'. Unfortunately, his prediction did come true and, after 20 wasted years lost to capitalist alleluia chanting, it took a financial crisis almost as massive as that of 1929, with a global impact on employment and growth, to realise the necessity of a new world order to replace the old one. Twenty years later, we are finally closer to this goal. But there is still much to do, and many obstacles to overcome.

And Gorbachev would not have been Gorbachev had he been content to 'rest on his laurels' and reap the benefit of his international recognition. Sticking to his credo 'If what you have done yesterday still looks big to you, you haven't done much today', Gorbachev remains a 'prophet of change'.

Like the biblical Isaiah, who warned Jews 3000 years ago that they could not continue living the way they did, Gorbachev urges the world to realise the need of change: to start thinking about the fact that half the population of the world lives on one or two dollars a day, that 60 per cent of the ecosystems have been damaged, with the atmosphere polluted, oceans and rivers poisoned, and that climate change poses an unacceptable risk of catastrophic and irreversible harm on a global scale within the next decade, threatening security and development and putting the very future of human society as we know it in jeopardy, while world leaders try to respond to the challenge with incremental managerialism instead of demonstrating bold and transformational leadership.

Back in 1990 when he saw the world heading into a perfect storm of interconnected environmental, development and security crises, this synergy was not prominent on the world agenda, and many thought it strange that a political figure such as Gorbachev would take on the role of a sustainable development leader. But he was not afraid of being ridiculed or questioned, and he has been proved right as the issues of sustainable development have today become a top political priority.

Under his leadership, Green Cross International, founded by him to deal with these issues, has become a mature organisation, with successful projects and a network now consisting of 32 national organisations. This is to a great extent thanks to the commitment, guidance and leadership of its Founder.

The world has not yet found answers to the ethical challenge Gorbachev confronted it with. The conflict between ethical vision and real politik has deepened. Ambitions and selfish interests continue to reign in politics, which has learnt to pay lip service to universal values as a PR instrument. Thus the great principles of humanity have been marginalised as rhetoric tools used to feign ethical concern. However, the great flaw in this practice is that imitating ethical policies cannot resolve actual challenges.

The need for change is more critical than ever in the face of the simultaneous crises engulfing everything from the economy to energy sources, and to the very atmosphere of our planet. We are at a crossroads, clearly signposted by scientific evidence, and must choose between collective chaos or grasping the chance to embark on a new, sustainable era.

This is also the historical perspective against which Gorbachev will eventually be judged. Therefore 'why did he do it?' is the wrong question. The right one is: for whom? He did it for his own country, which still needs time to understand this (*'There is no prophet without honour, except in his own country'*), for the world, for all of us.

And though the 80 years that Gorbachev is turning is a venerable age, we at the Green Cross all know that he still has a role to play in serving history – now from the outside of the Kremlin wall.

Alexander Likhotal, President of Green Cross International, is a member of the Club of Rome, the Climate Change Task Force, the International Council for the Earth Charter and the Board of Directors of the Universal Forum of Cultures, and is an Adviser to the Club of Madrid. In addition to an academic career as a Professor of Political Science and International Relations, he served as a European security analyst for the Soviet Union leadership, and was Deputy Spokesman and Advisor to the President of the USSR, Mikhail Gorbachev.

Picture credits

Colour plates:

1: Churchill Archives Centre, Thatcher papers, THCR 8/2/31, reproduced by kind permission of Graham Wiltshire FRPS

2: © George Bush Presidential Library Foundation; photographer, Chandler Arden

5: Gosia Wieruszewska

6: Green Cross Japan

9: World Political Forum

10: © Patrick McMullan

11: Gosia Wieruszewska

13: Cinema for Peace

14: GEG Agency

15: Global Green USA

16: UN PHOTO/Jean-Marc Ferré